VOLUME 2

BY
MIN-WOO HYUNG

Los Angeles * Tokyo

Translator - Seung-Ah Lee
English Adaptation & Lettering - Jake Forbes
Cover Artist - Raymond Swanland
Graphic Designer - Anna Kernbaum
Layout- Justin Renard
Associate Editor - Stephen Grest
Editor - Jake Forbes

Production Manager - Mario Rodriguez
Art Director - Matt Alford
VP Production - Ron Klamert
Publisher - Stuart Levy

email: editor@TOKYOPOP.com
Come visit us online at www.TOKYOPOP.com

A  MANGA

TOKYOPOP® is an imprint of Mixx Entertainment, Inc.
5900 Wilshire Blvd., Ste. 2000, Los Angeles, CA 90036

ISBN: 1-59182-009-X

First TOKYOPOP Printing: September 2002

10 9 8 7 6 5 4

Manufactured in the USA.

PRIEST

PRELUDE TO THE DECEASED
PART 2

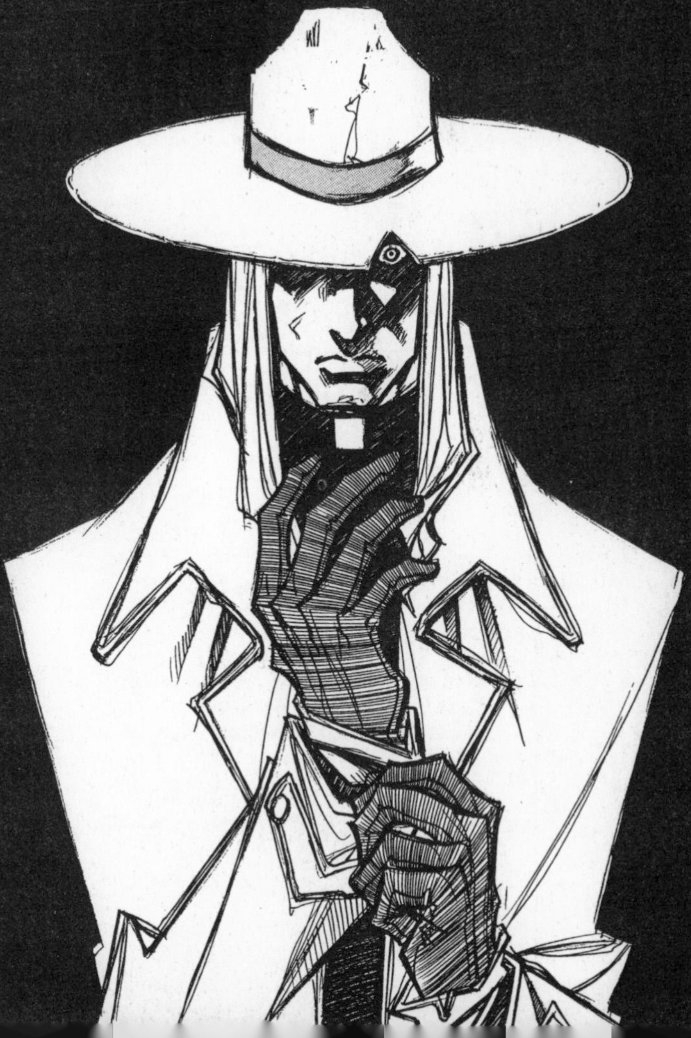

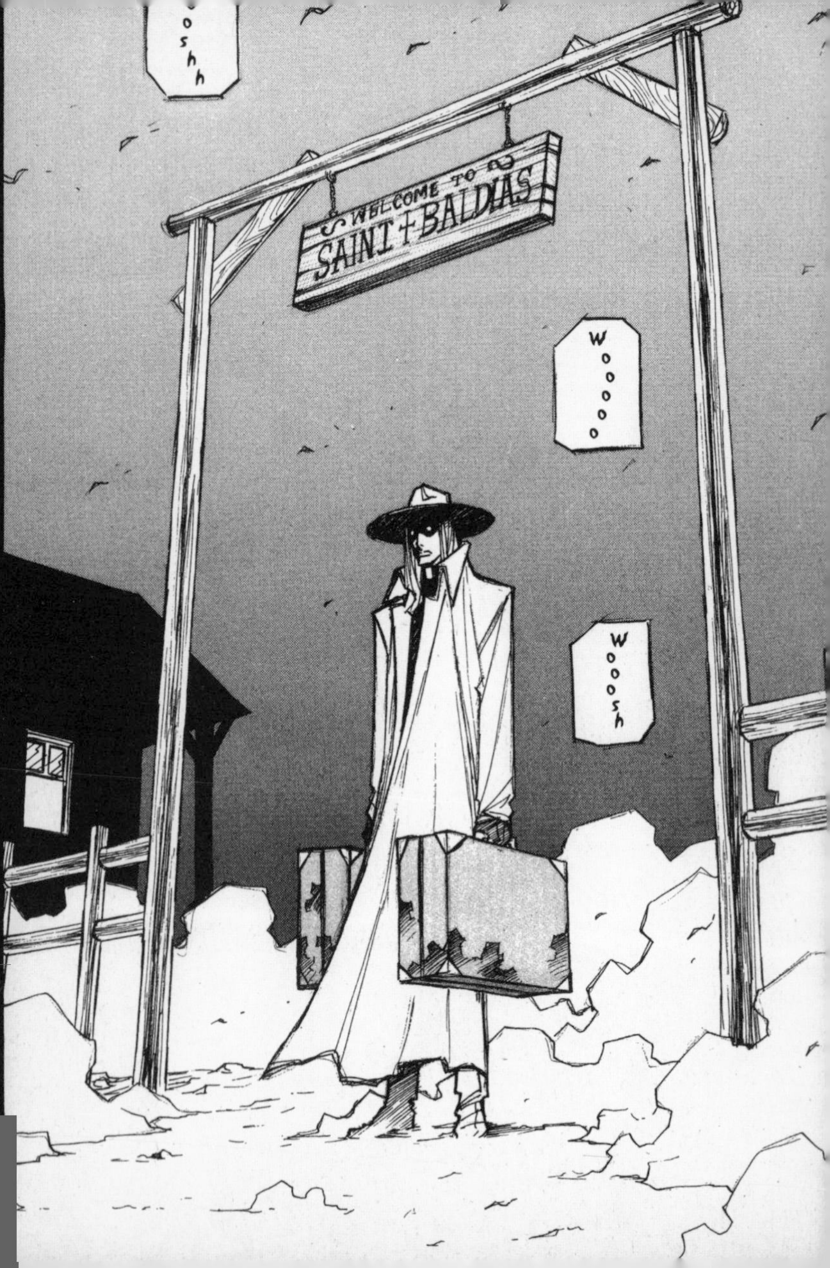
oshh
WELCOME TO
SAINT ✝ BALDIAS
Woooo
Wooosh

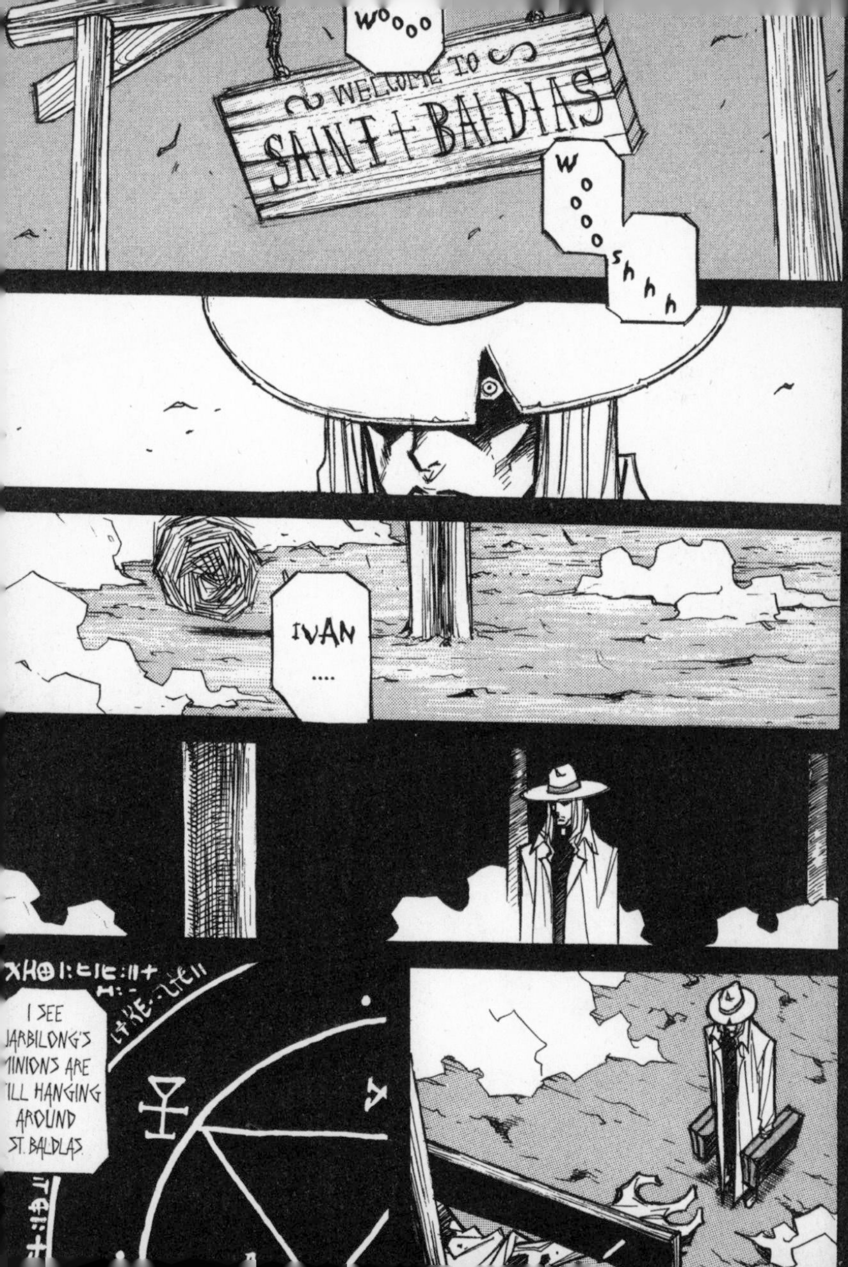
WOOOO
~ WELCOME TO ~
SAINT BALDIAS
WOOOOSHHH
IVAN ....
I SEE JARBILONG'S MINIONS ARE STILL HANGING AROUND ST. BALDLAS.

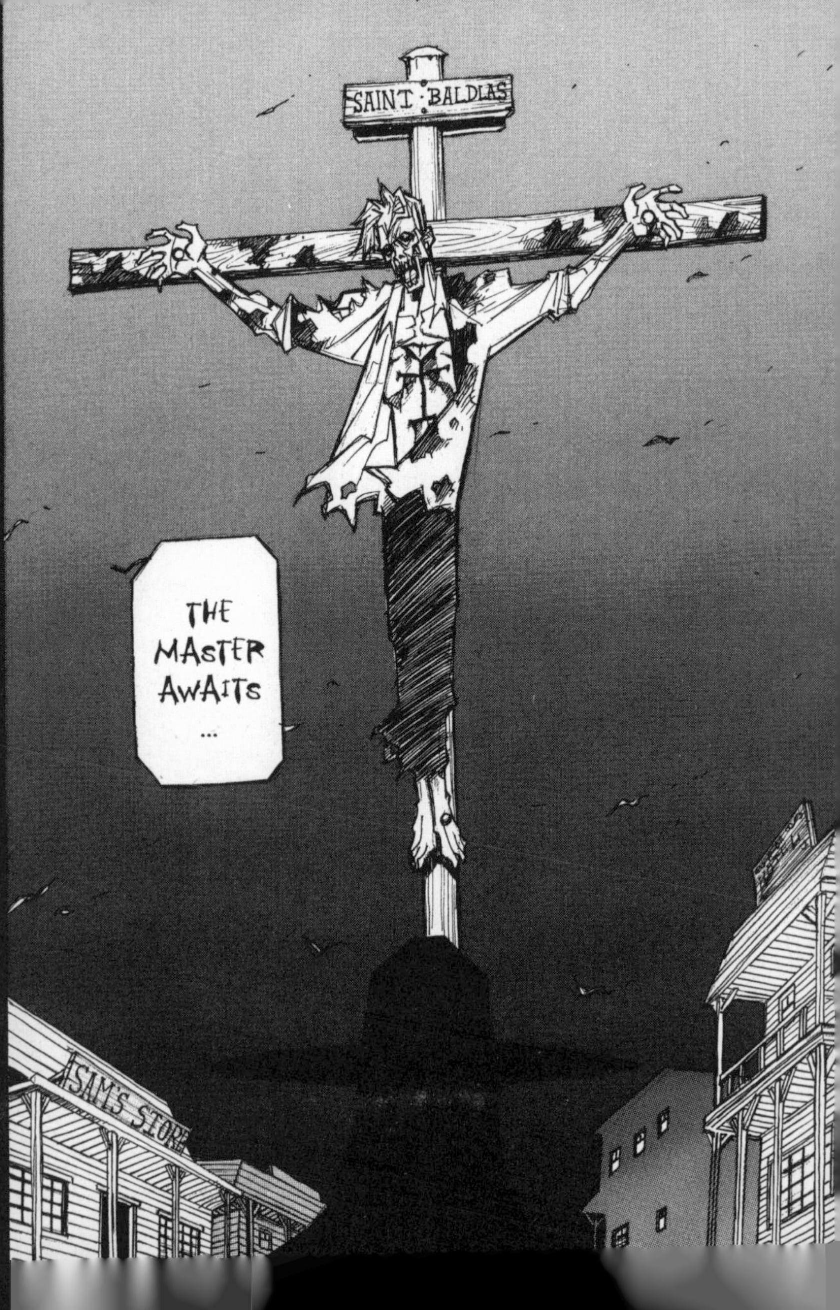
SAINT BALDLAS
THE MASTER AWAITS ...
SAM'S STORE

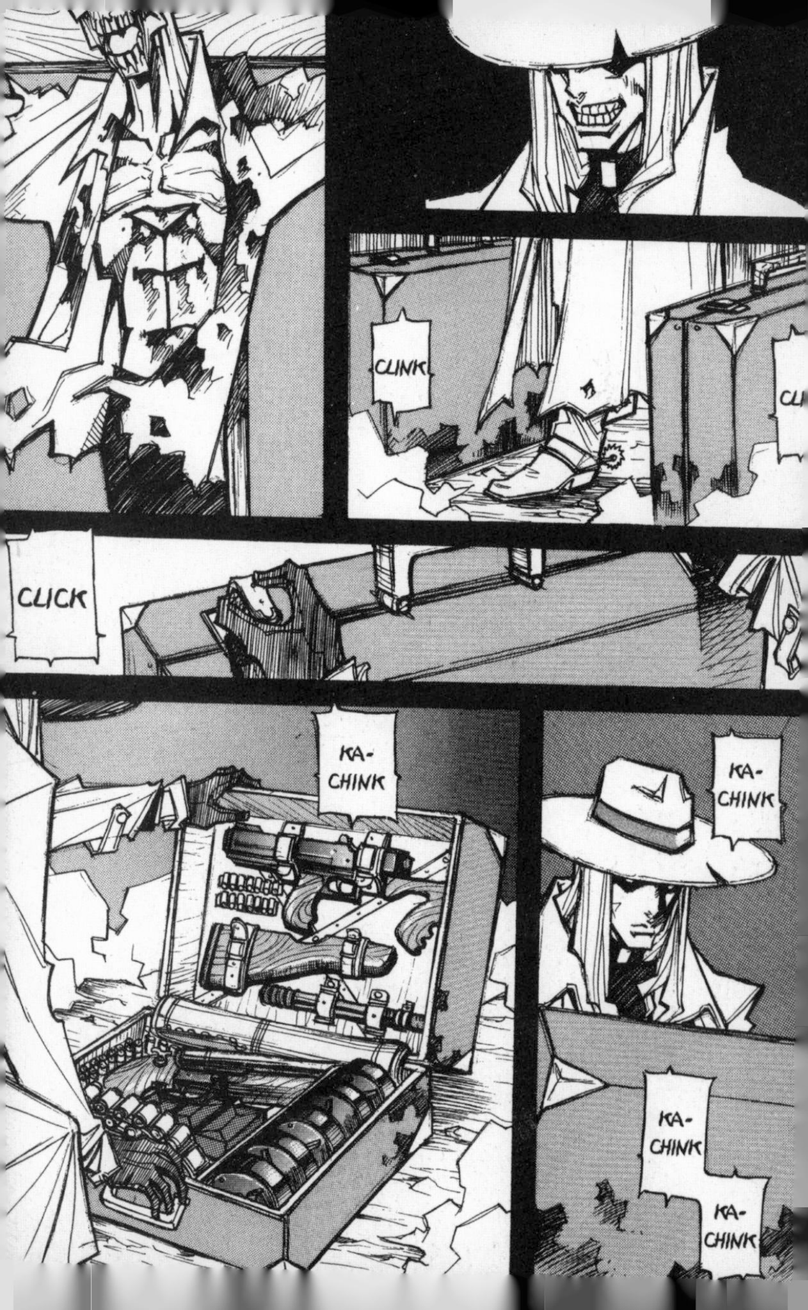
CLINK
CLICK
KA-CHINK
KA-CHINK
KA-CHINK
KA-CHINK

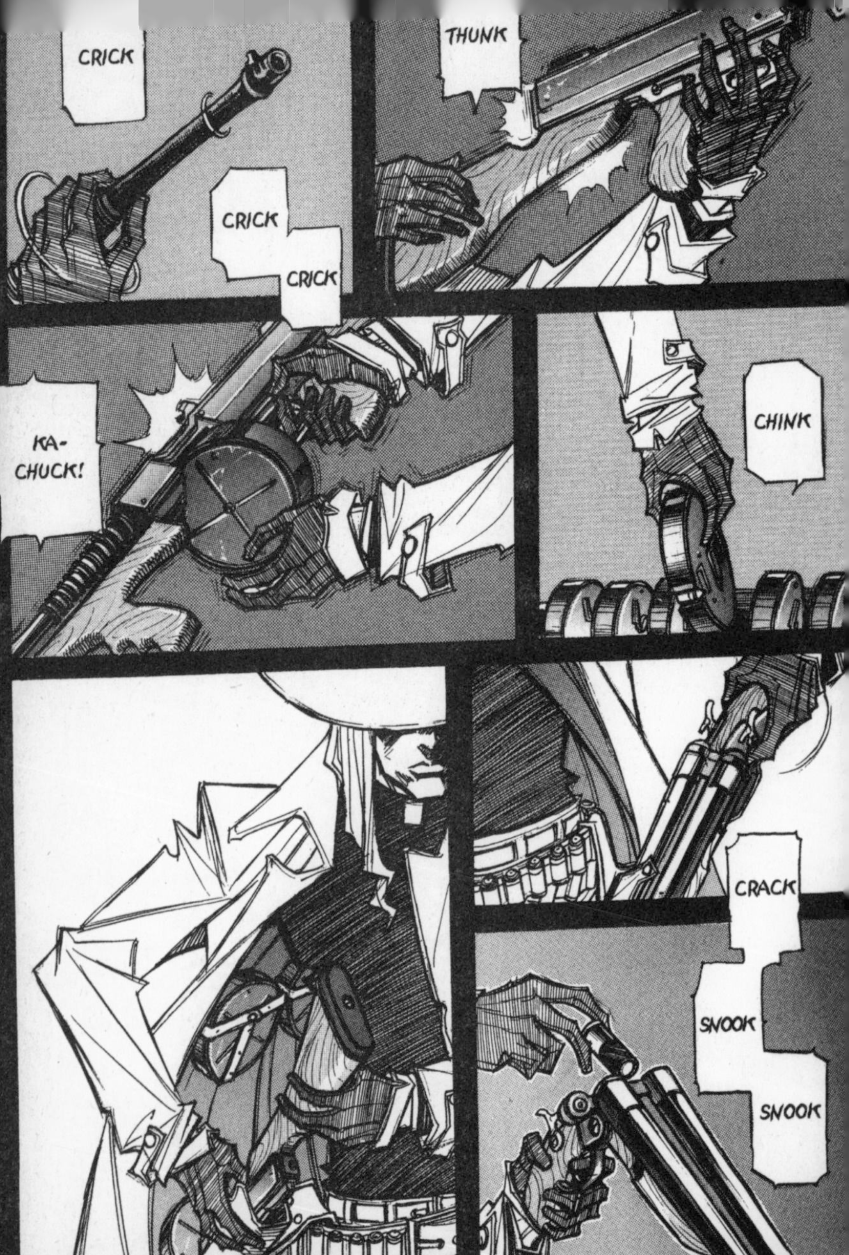
CRICK
CRICK
CRICK
THUNK
KA-CHUCK!
CHINK
CRACK
SNOOK
SNOOK

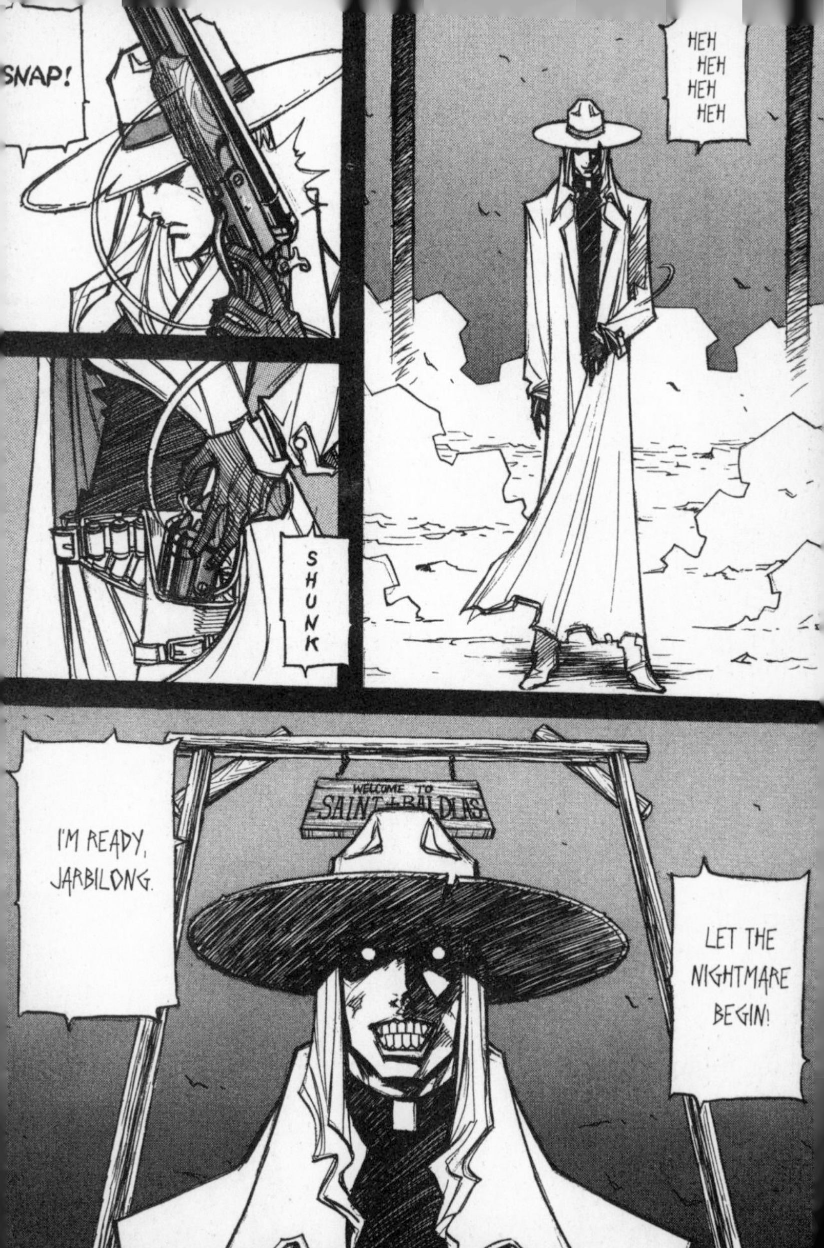
SNAP!
SHUNK
HEH HEH HEH HEH
WELCOME TO
SAINT+BALDLAS
I'M READY, JARBILONG.
LET THE NIGHTMARE BEGIN!

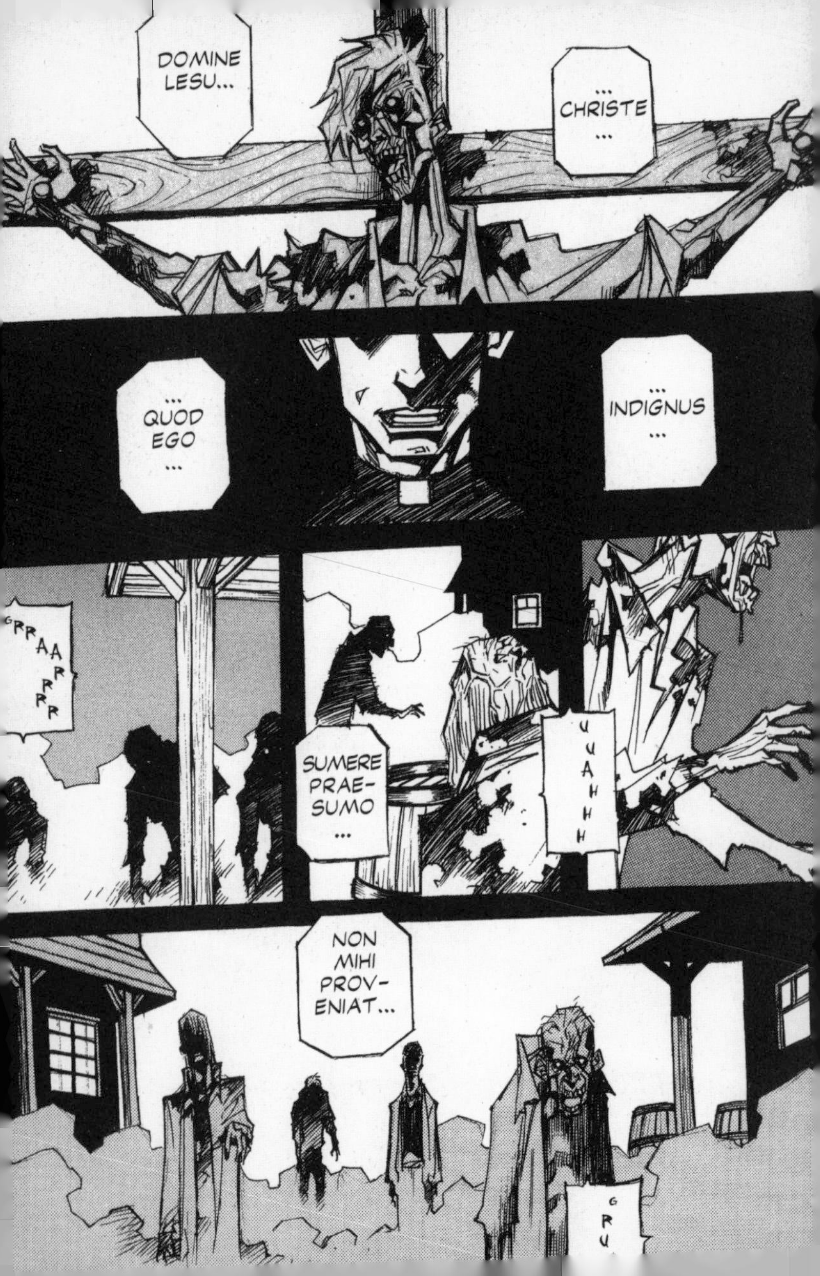
DOMINE LESU...
...CHRISTE...
...QUOD EGO...
...INDIGNUS...
GRRAARRRR
SUMERE PRAE-SUMO...
UUAHHH
NON MIHI PROV-ENIAT...
GRU

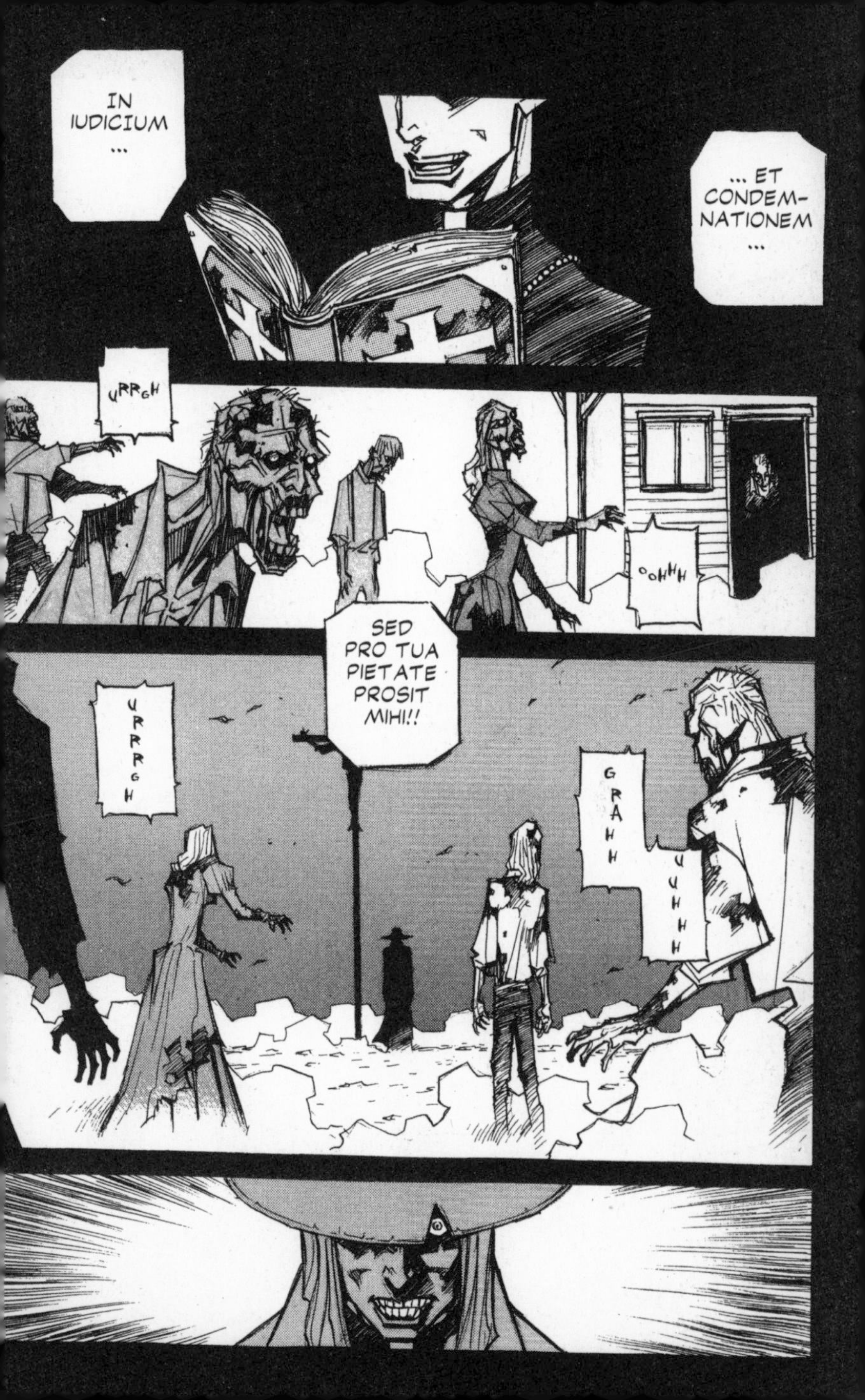

IN IUDICIUM ...
... ET CONDEMNATIONEM ...
URRGH
OOHHH
SED PRO TUA PIETATE PROSIT MIHI!!
URRRGH
GRAHH
UHHHH

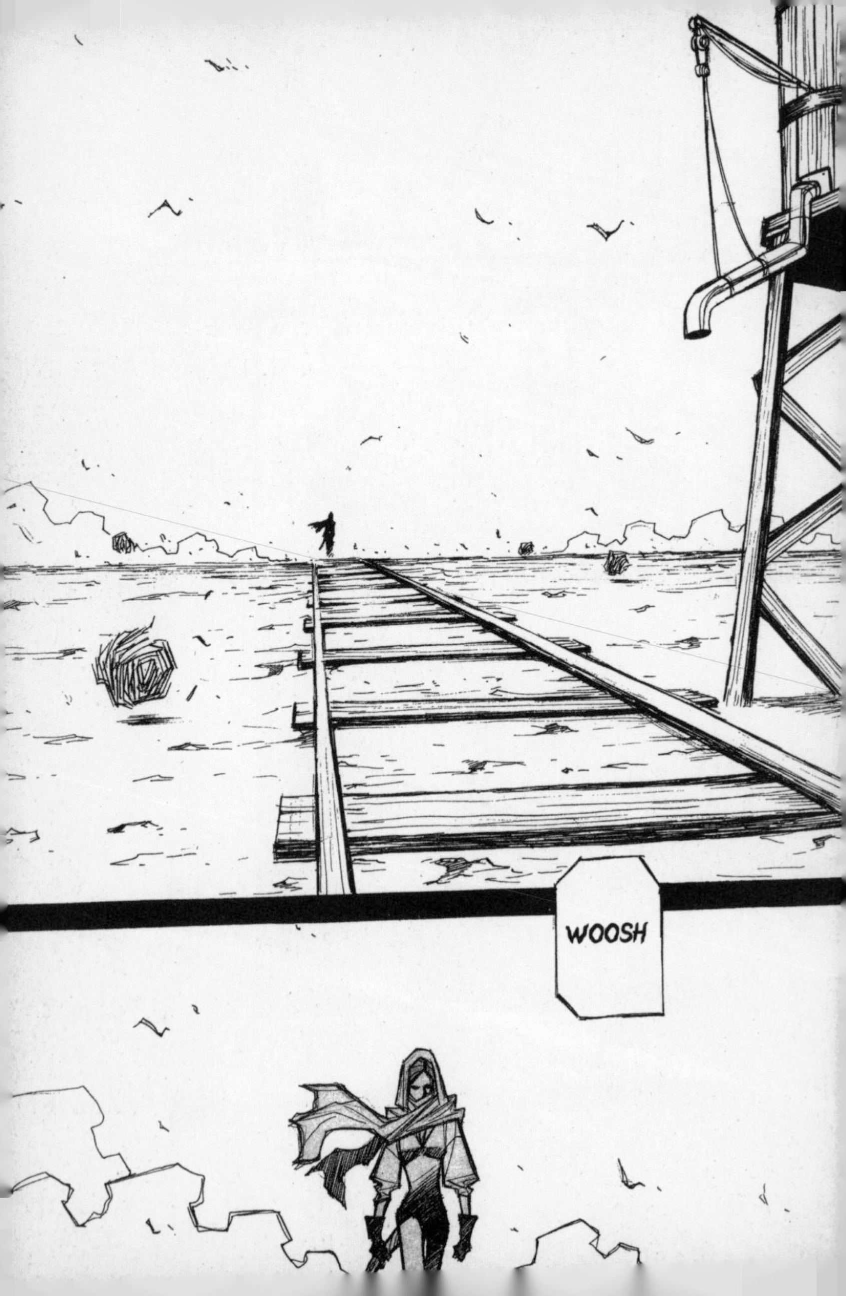
WOOSH

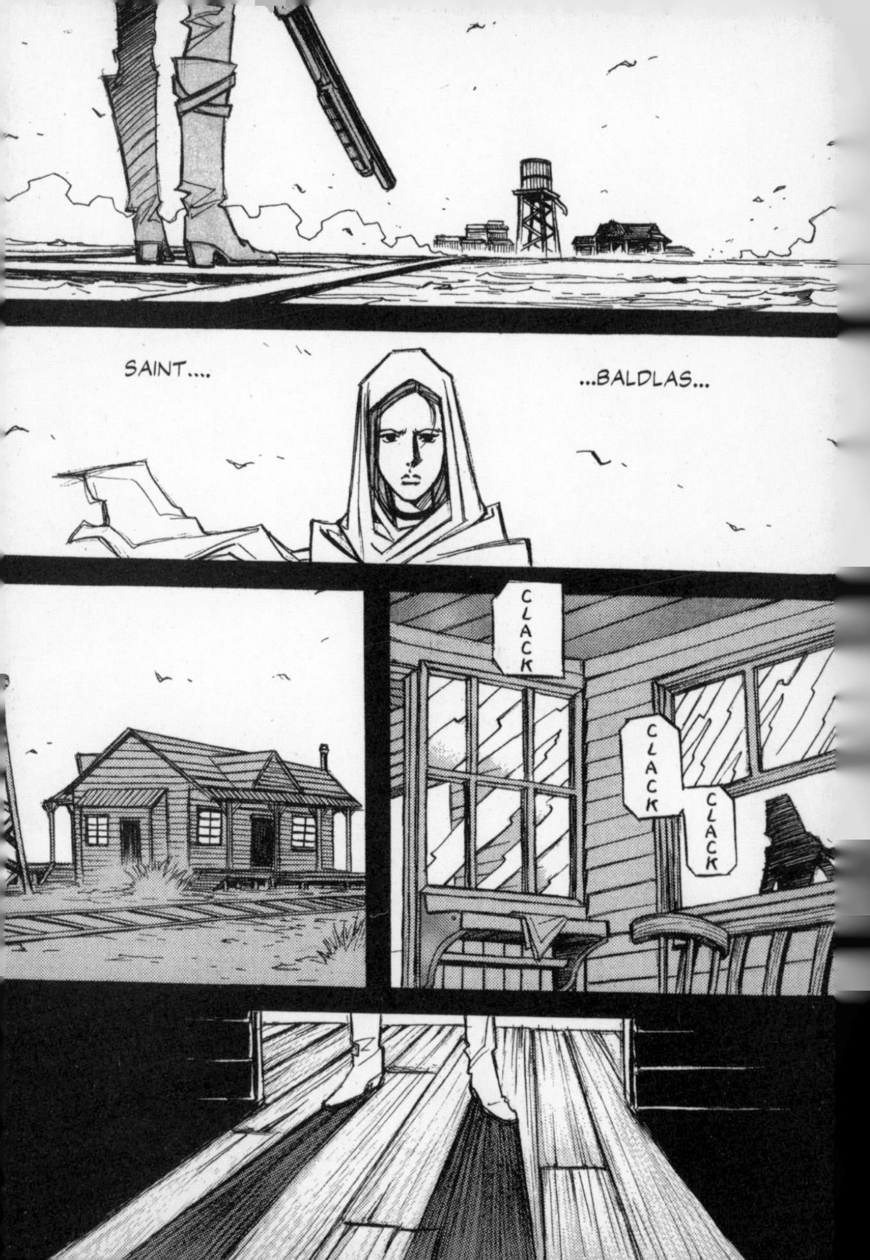
SAINT....
...BALDLAS...
CLACK
CLACK
CLACK

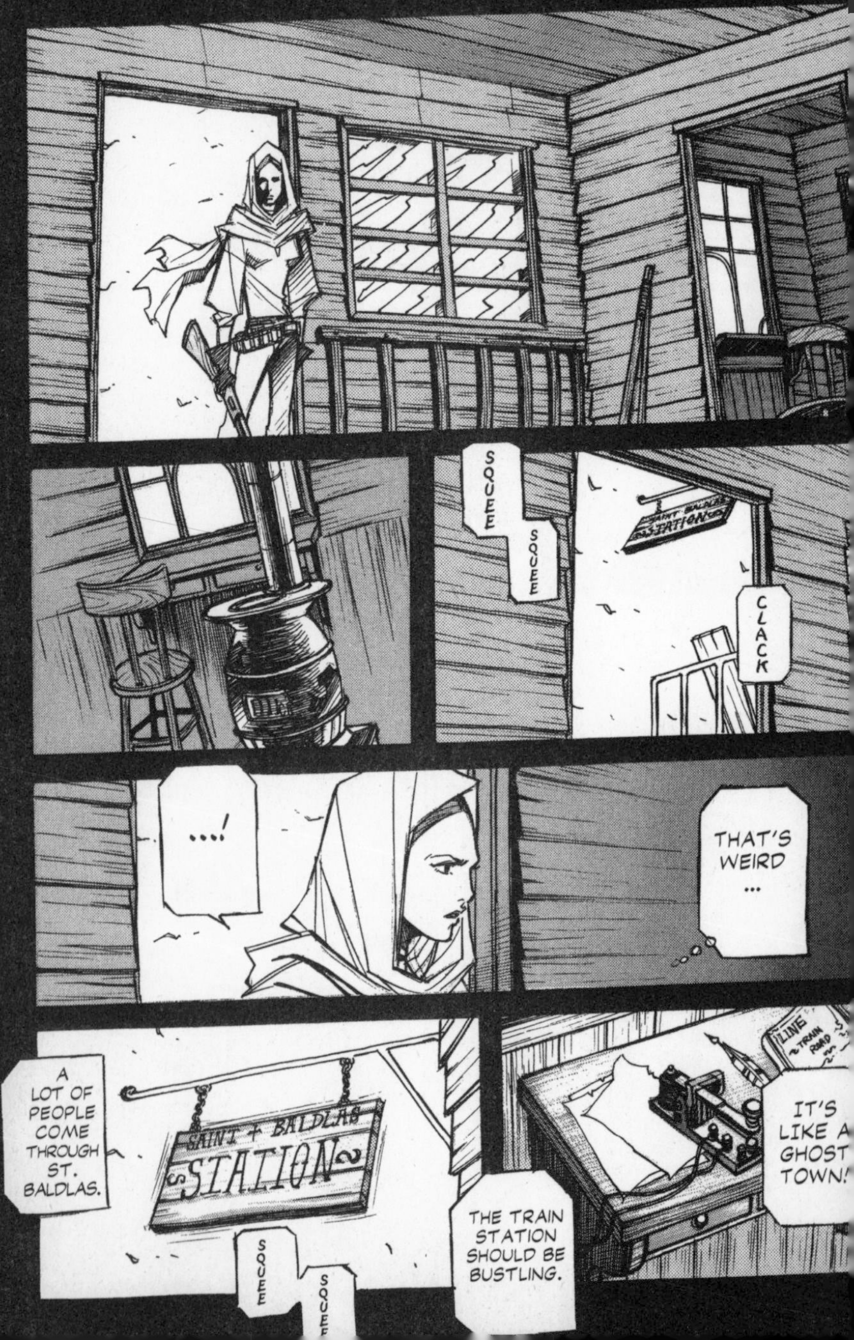
SQUEE
SQUEE
SAINT BALDLAS STATION
CLACK
...!
THAT'S WEIRD ...
A LOT OF PEOPLE COME THROUGH ST. BALDLAS.
SAINT + BALDLAS STATION
SQUEE
SQUEE
THE TRAIN STATION SHOULD BE BUSTLING.
LINE TRAIN ROAD
IT'S LIKE A GHOST TOWN!

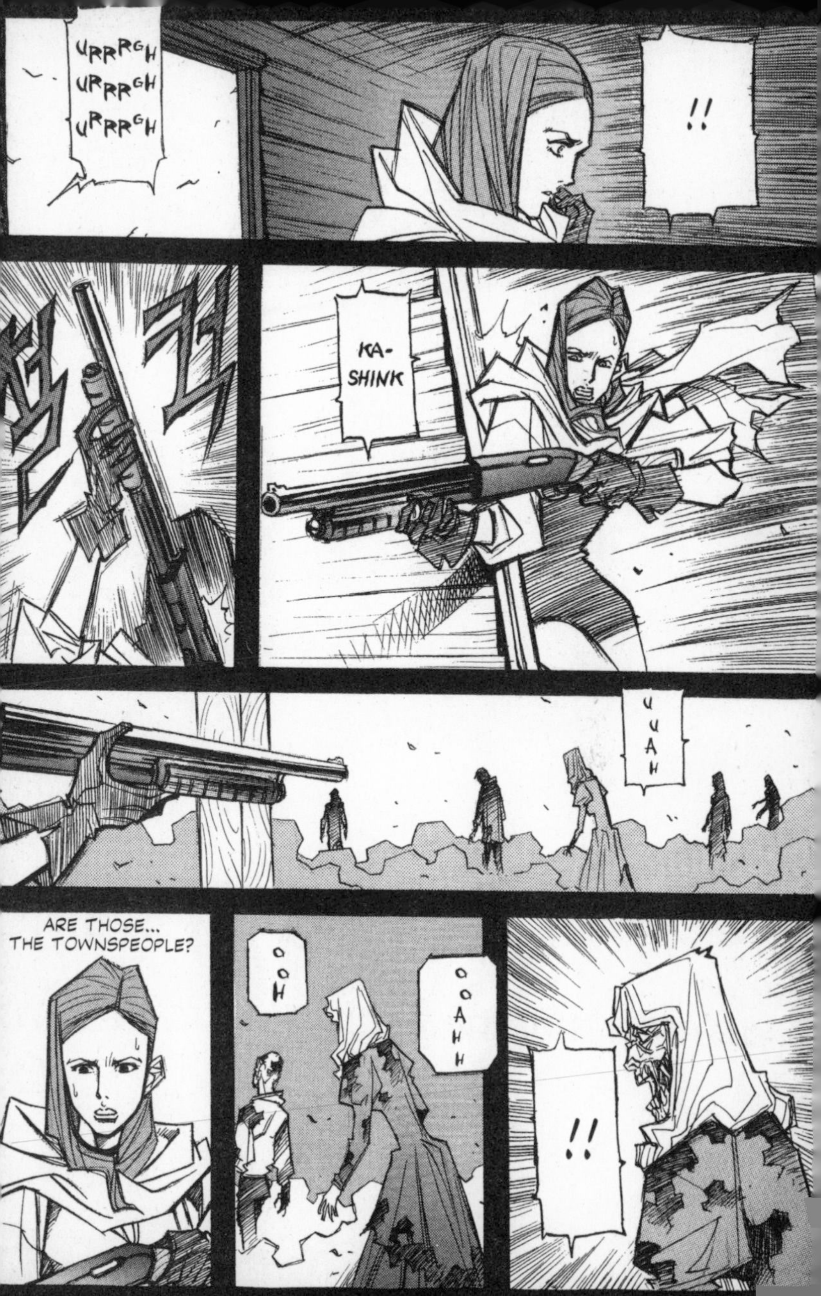
URRRGH
URRRGH
URRRGH
!!
KA-SHINK
UUAH
ARE THOSE... THE TOWNSPEOPLE?
OOH
OOAHH
!!

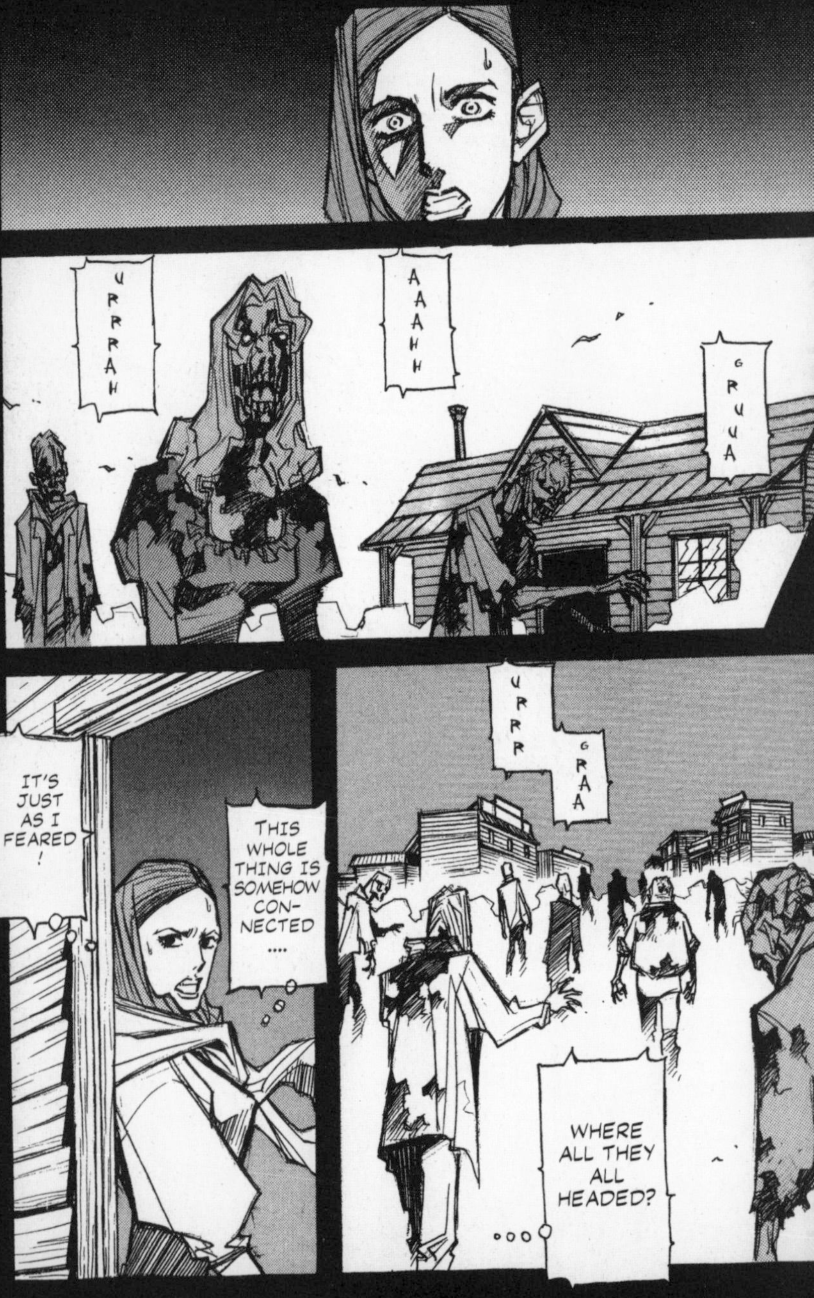
URRRAH
AAAHH
GRUUA
IT'S JUST AS I FEARED!
THIS WHOLE THING IS SOMEHOW CON-NECTED ....
URRR
GRAA
WHERE ALL THEY ALL HEADED?

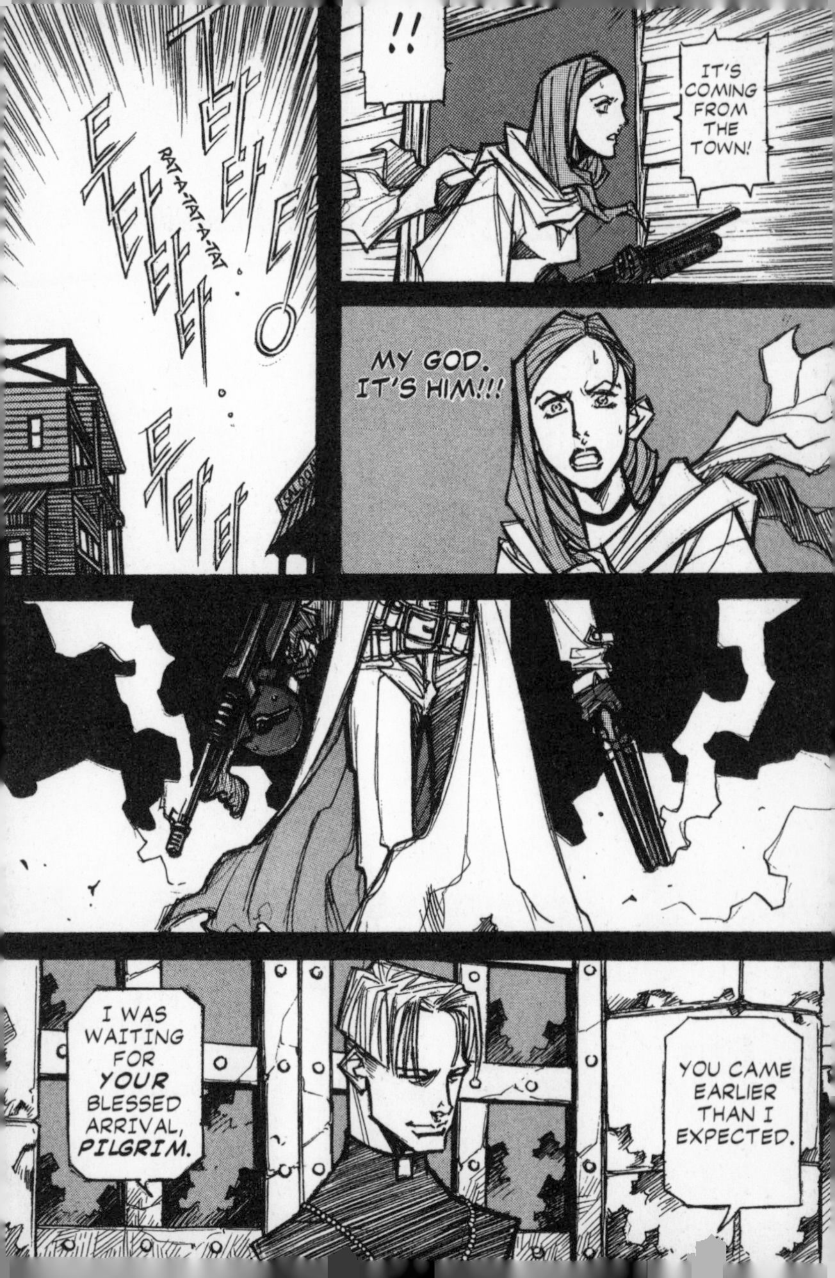
RAT-A-TAT-A-TAT
!!
IT'S COMING FROM THE TOWN!
MY GOD. IT'S HIM!!!
I WAS WAITING FOR YOUR BLESSED ARRIVAL, PILGRIM.
YOU CAME EARLIER THAN I EXPECTED.

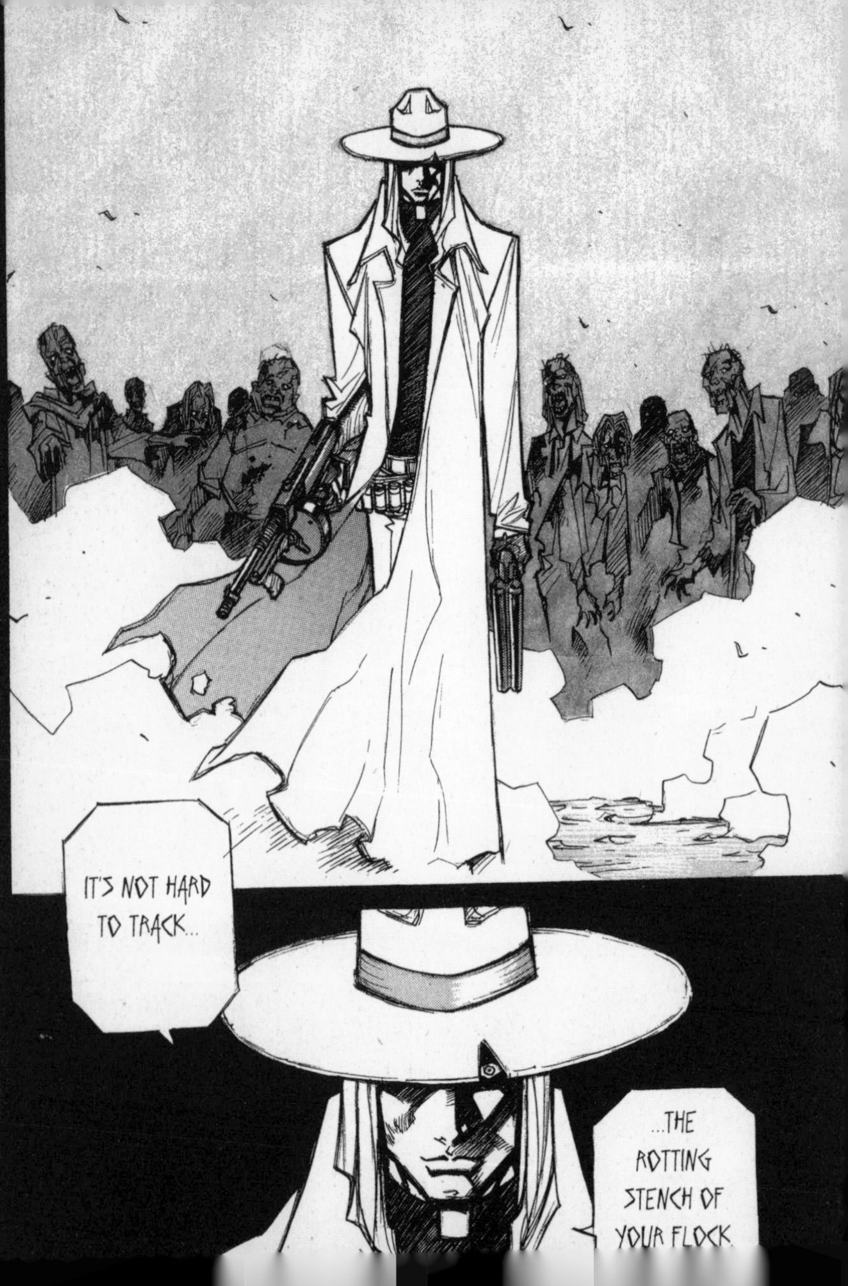
IT'S NOT HARD TO TRACK...
...THE ROTTING STENCH OF YOUR FLOCK.

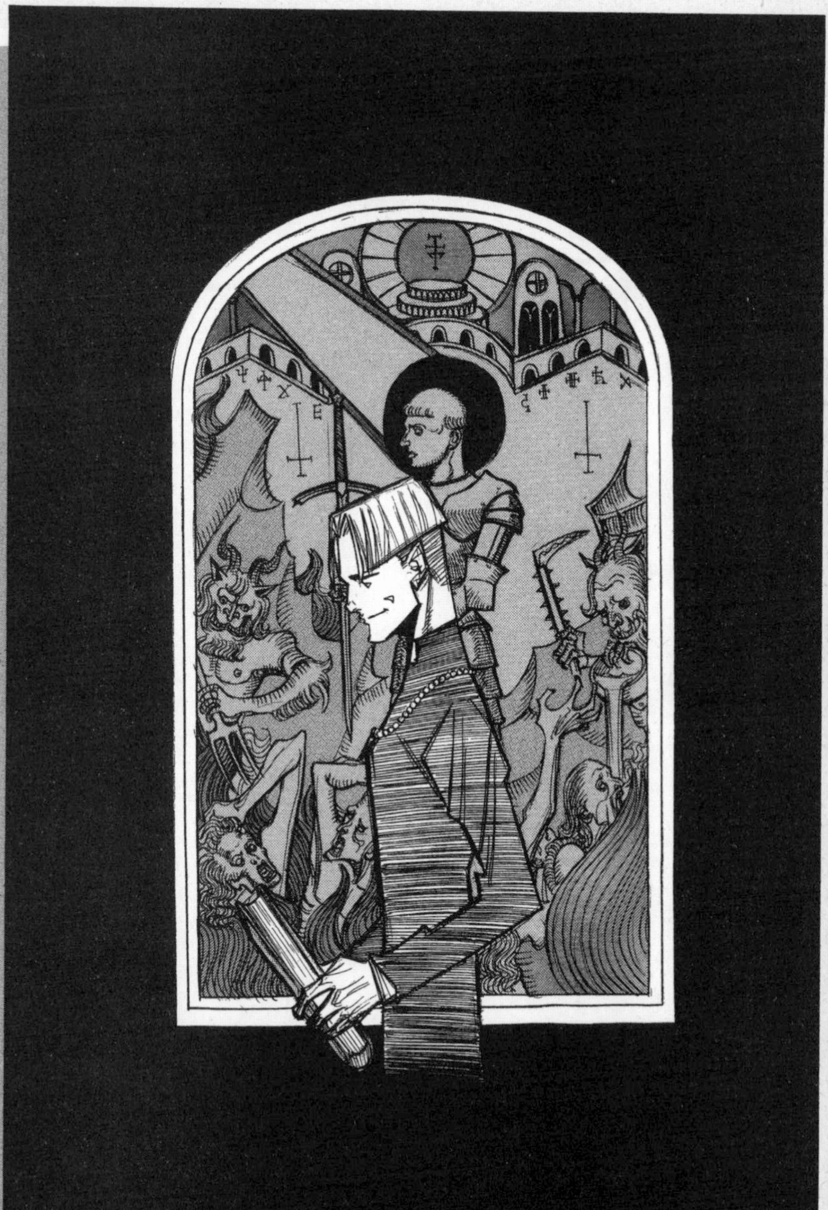

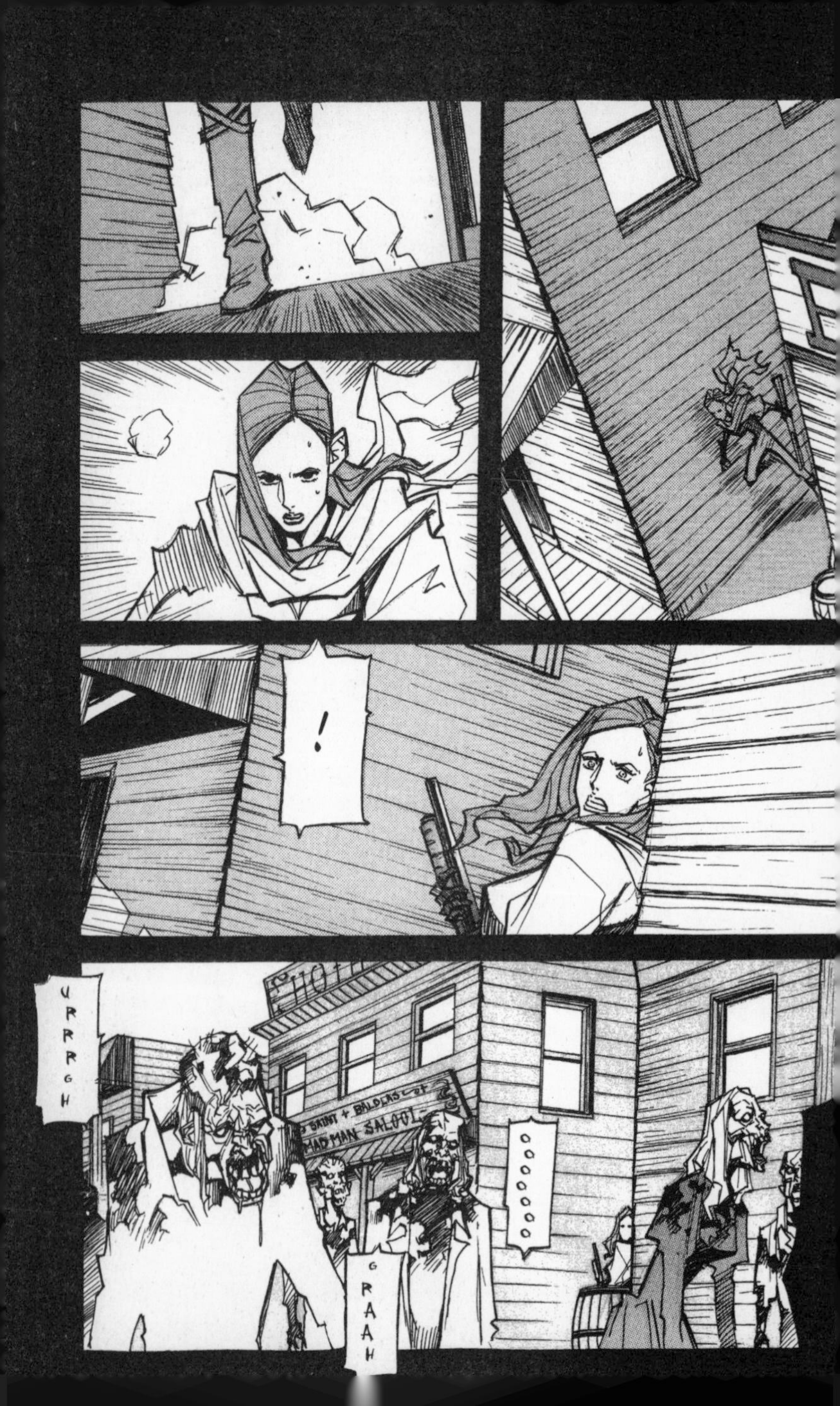
!
URRRGH
OOOOOOO
GRAAH

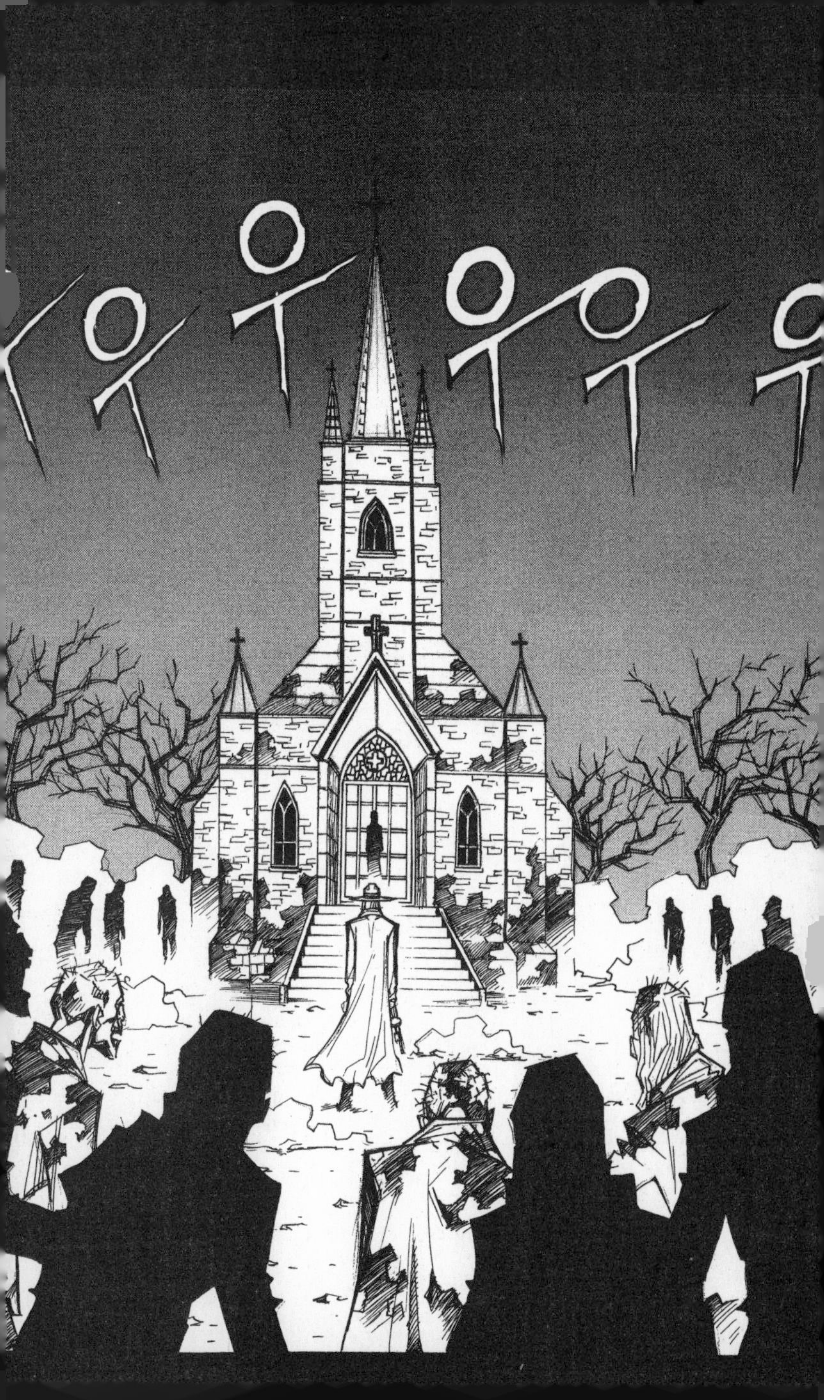
우우우우우

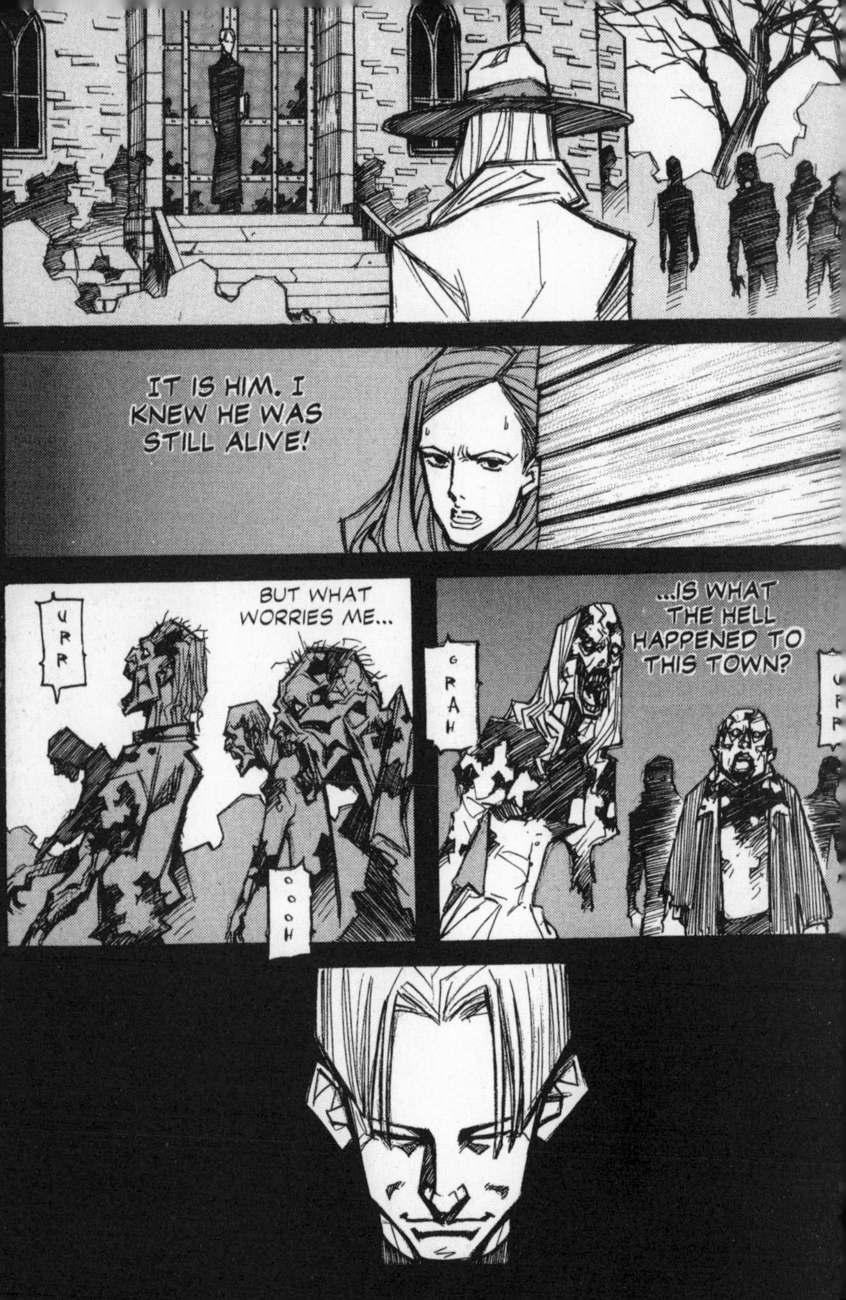
IT IS HIM. I KNEW HE WAS STILL ALIVE!
URR
BUT WHAT WORRIES ME...
OOOH
GRAH
...IS WHAT THE HELL HAPPENED TO THIS TOWN?

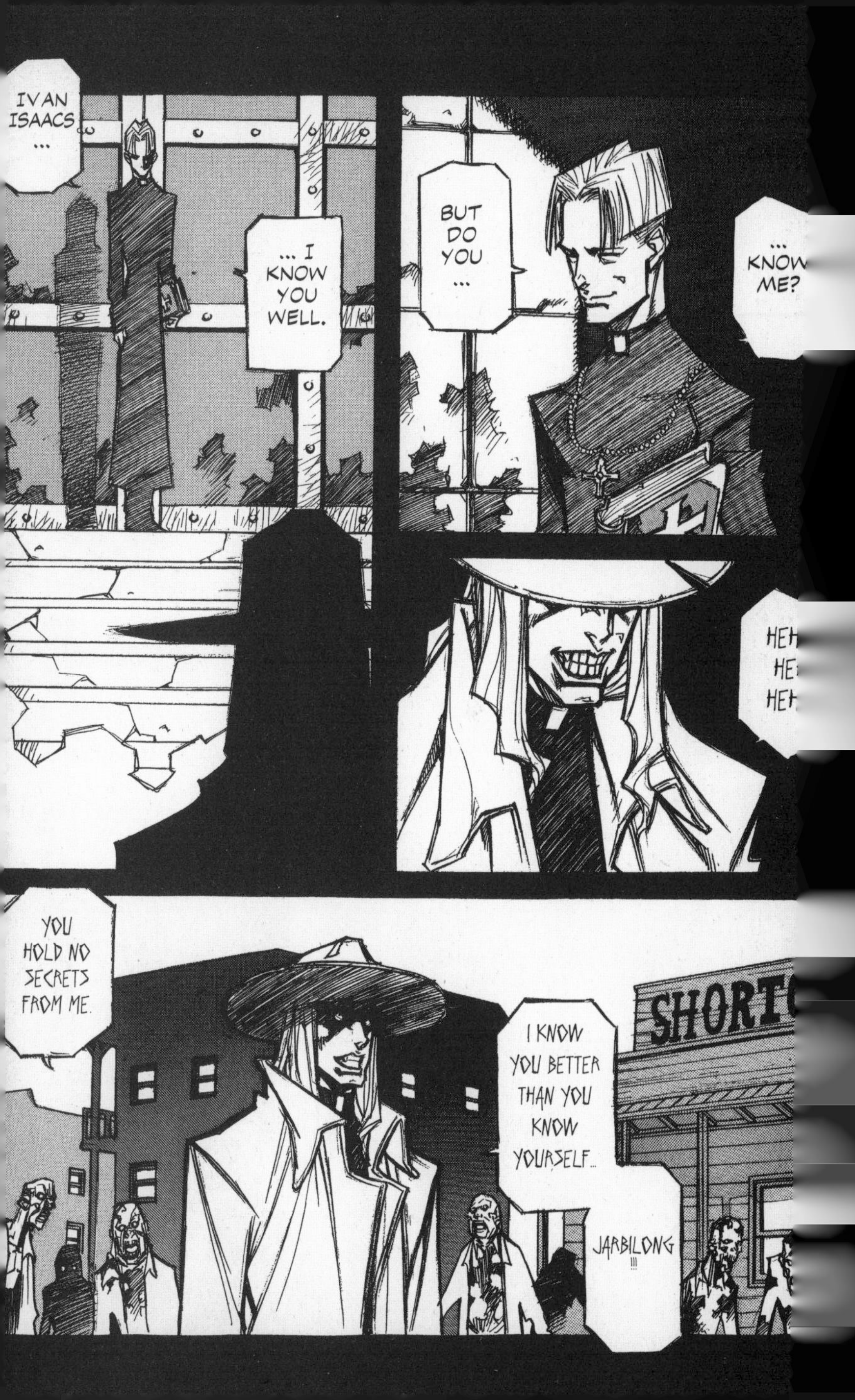
IVAN ISAACS ...
... I KNOW YOU WELL.
BUT DO YOU ...
... KNOW ME?
HEH HEH HEH
YOU HOLD NO SECRETS FROM ME.
SHORT
I KNOW YOU BETTER THAN YOU KNOW YOURSELF...
JARBILONG !!!

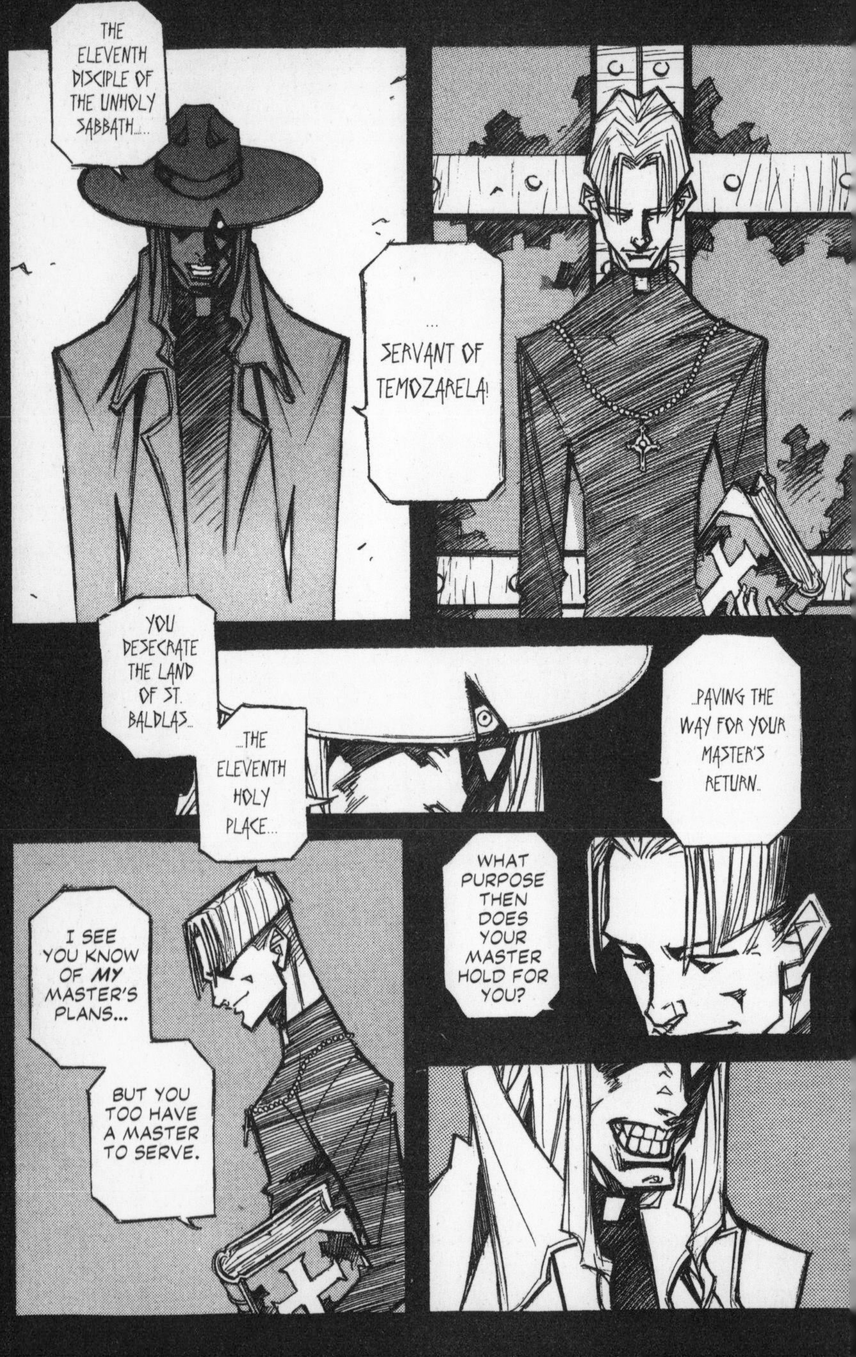
THE ELEVENTH DISCIPLE OF THE UNHOLY SABBATH......
... SERVANT OF TEMOZARELA!
YOU DESECRATE THE LAND OF ST. BALDLAS...
...THE ELEVENTH HOLY PLACE...
...PAVING THE WAY FOR YOUR MASTER'S RETURN..
I SEE YOU KNOW OF ***MY*** MASTER'S PLANS...
BUT YOU TOO HAVE A MASTER TO SERVE.
WHAT PURPOSE THEN DOES YOUR MASTER HOLD FOR YOU?

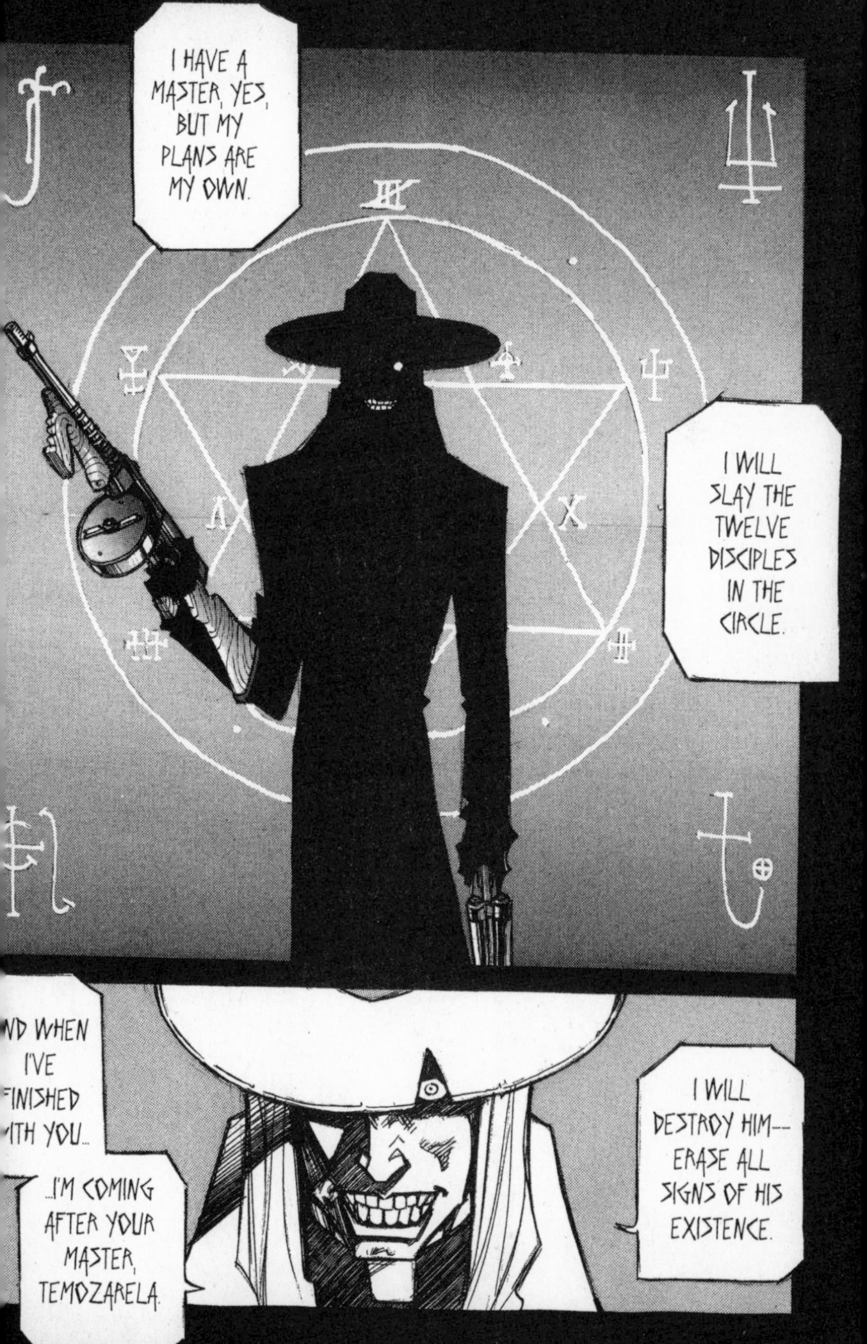
I HAVE A MASTER, YES, BUT MY PLANS ARE MY OWN.
I WILL SLAY THE TWELVE DISCIPLES IN THE CIRCLE.
ND WHEN I'VE FINISHED ITH YOU...
...I'M COMING AFTER YOUR MASTER, TEMOZARELA.
I WILL DESTROY HIM--ERASE ALL SIGNS OF HIS EXISTENCE.

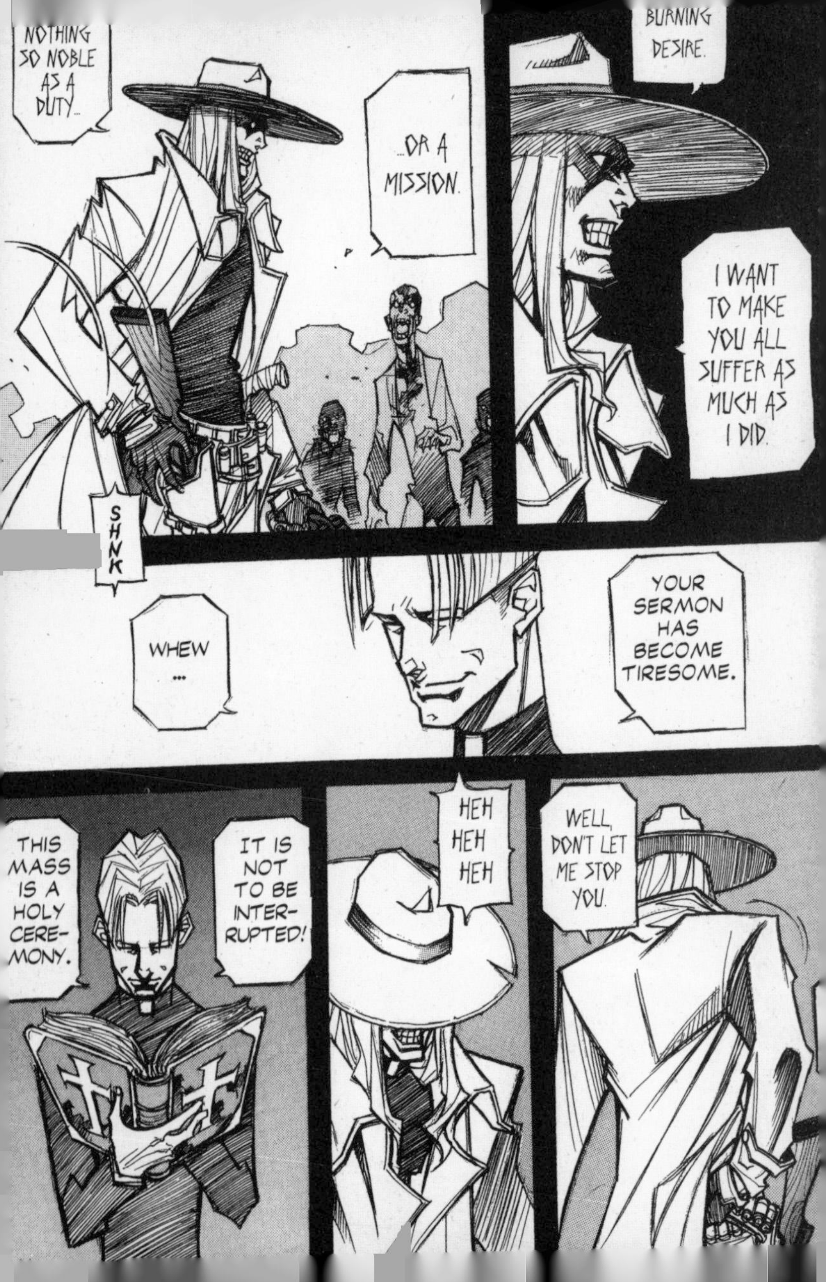
NOTHING SO NOBLE AS A DUTY...
...OR A MISSION.
BURNING DESIRE.
I WANT TO MAKE YOU ALL SUFFER AS MUCH AS I DID.
SHNK
WHEW ...
YOUR SERMON HAS BECOME TIRESOME.
THIS MASS IS A HOLY CEREMONY.
IT IS NOT TO BE INTERRUPTED!
HEH HEH HEH
WELL, DON'T LET ME STOP YOU.

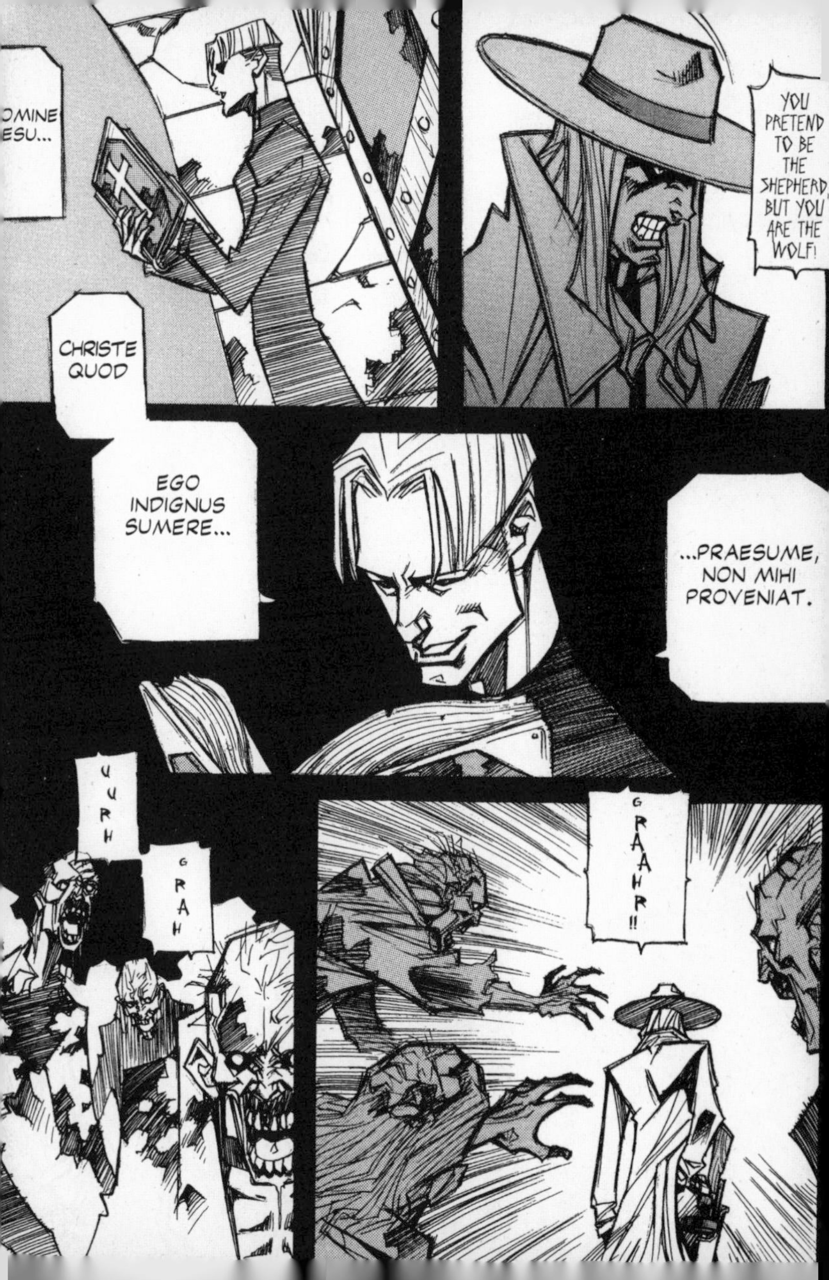

OMINE
ESU...
CHRISTE QUOD
YOU PRETEND TO BE THE SHEPHERD, BUT YOU ARE THE WOLF!
EGO INDIGNUS SUMERE...
...PRAESUME, NON MIHI PROVENIAT.
UURH
GRAH
GRAAHR!!

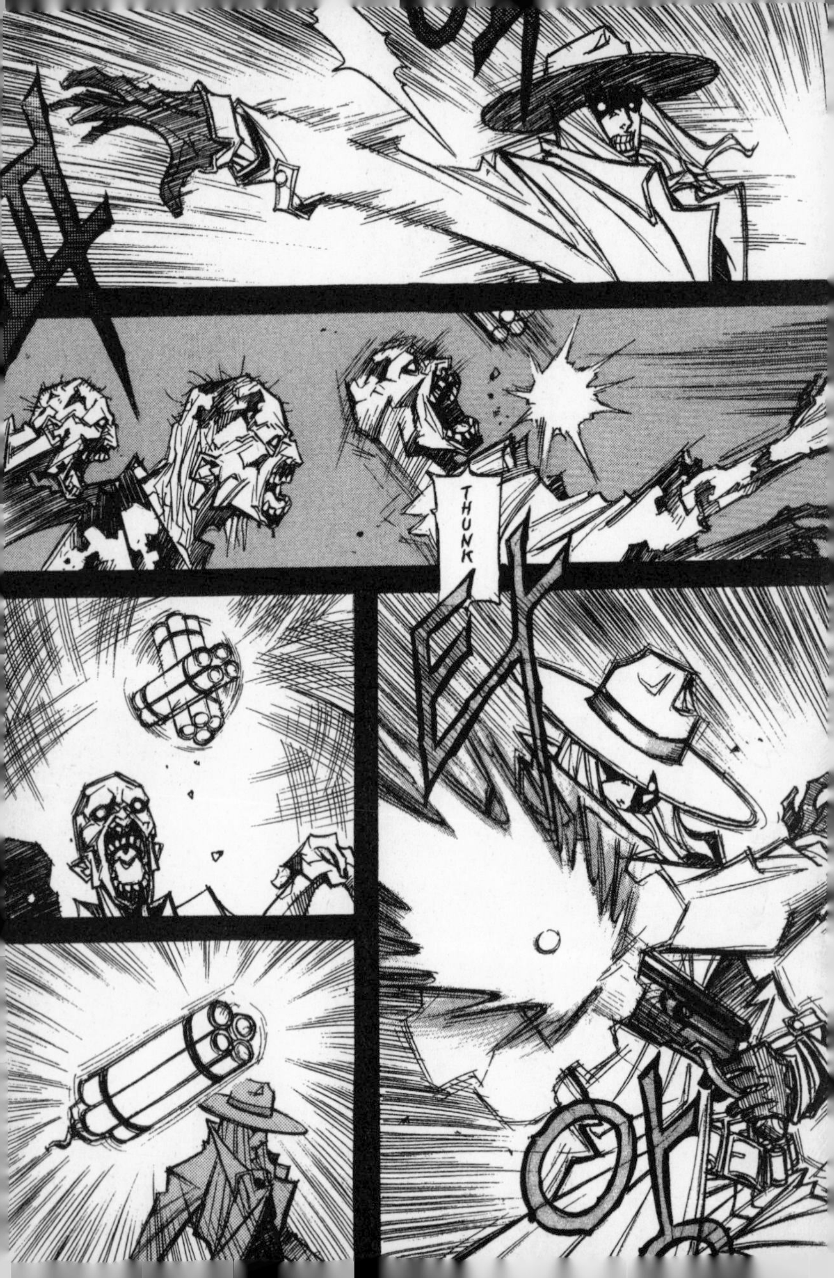
THUNK

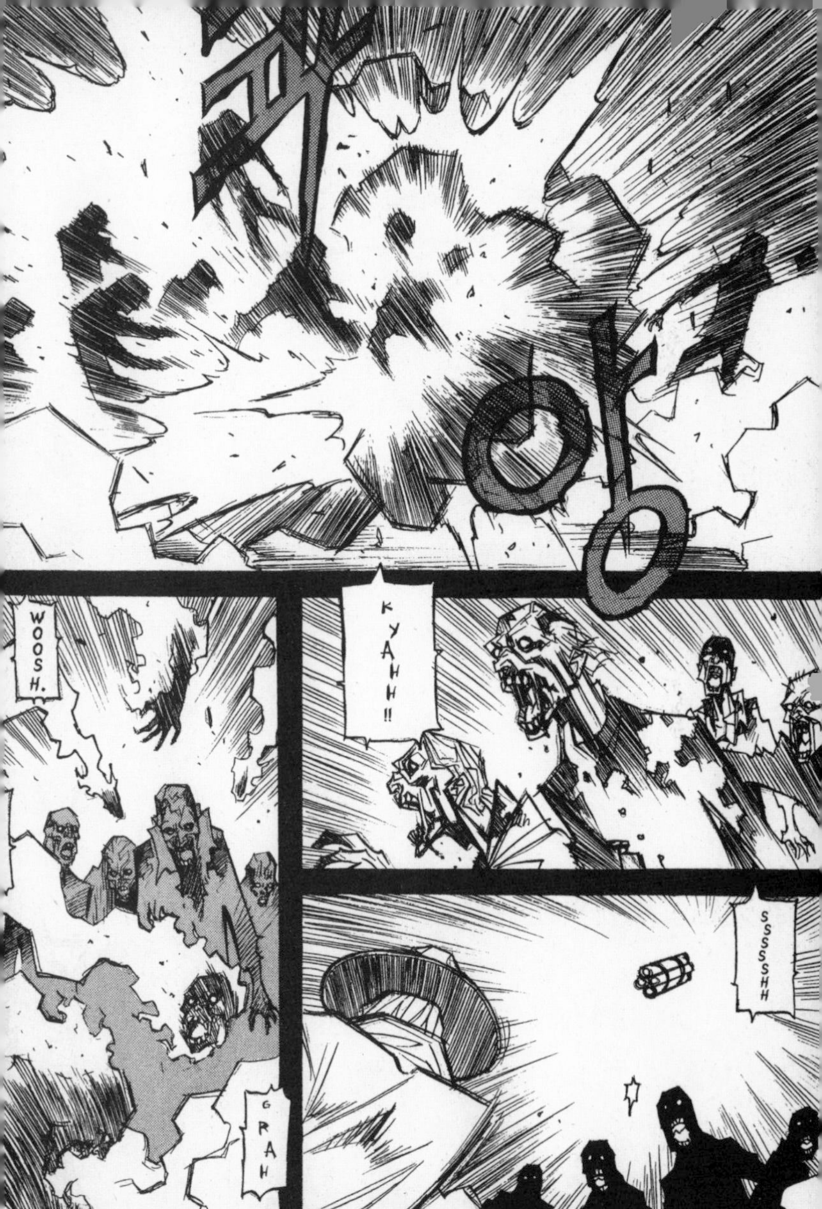
WOOSH.
GRAH
KYAHHH!!
SSSSSHH

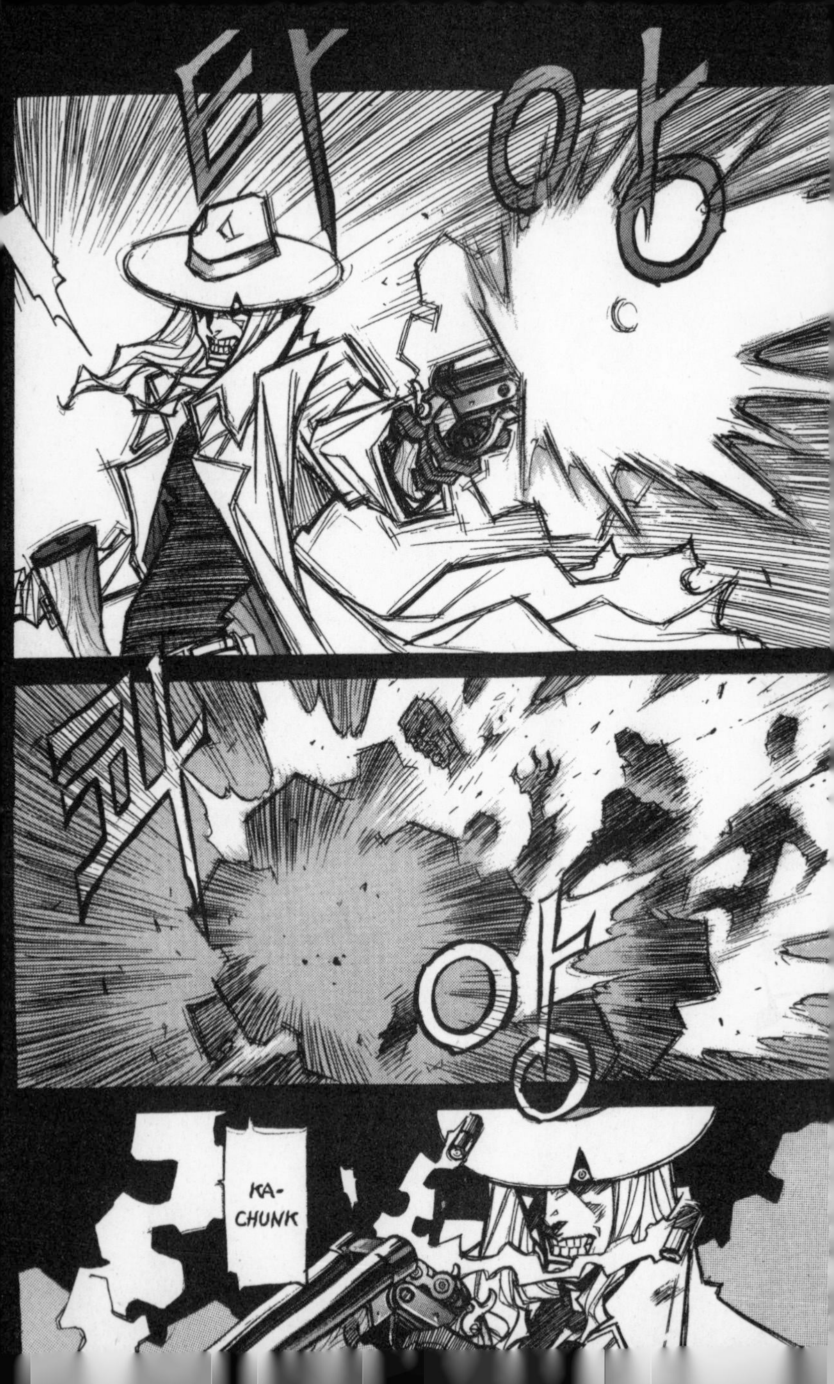
KA-CHUNK

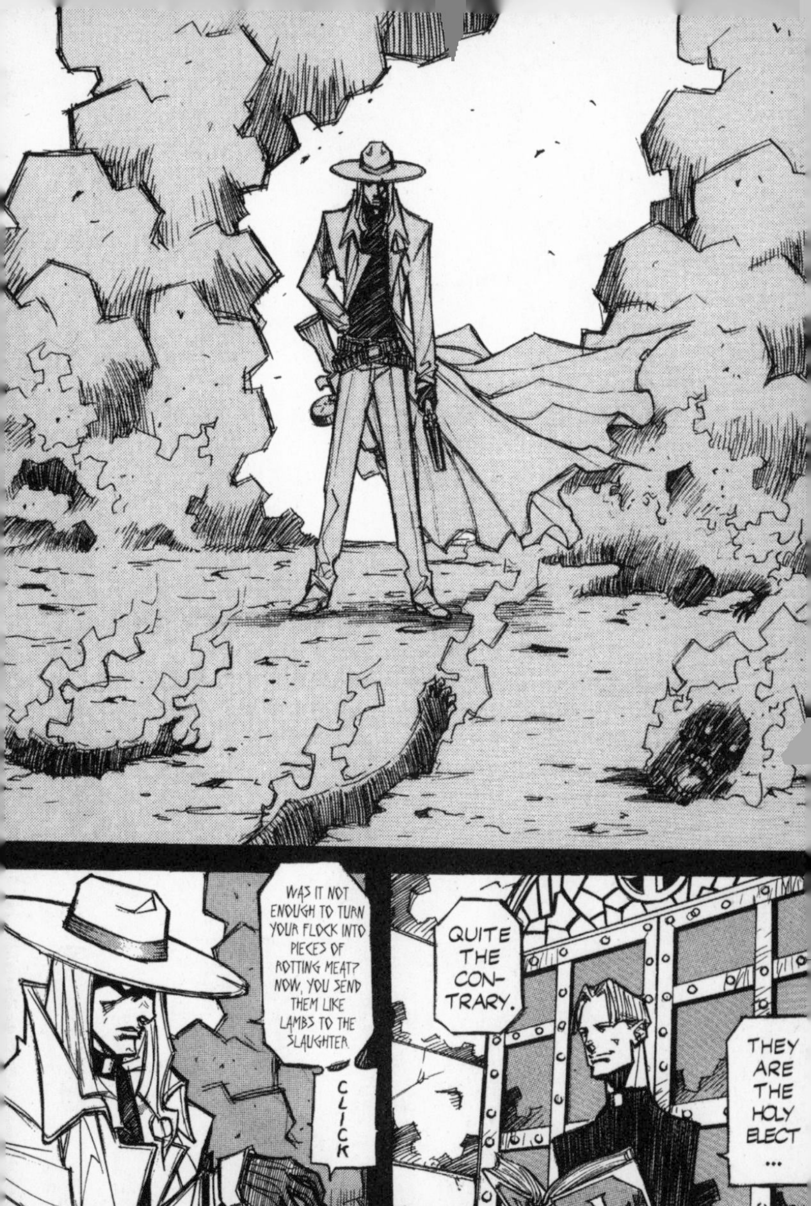
WAS IT NOT ENOUGH TO TURN YOUR FLOCK INTO PIECES OF ROTTING MEAT? NOW, YOU SEND THEM LIKE LAMBS TO THE SLAUGHTER.
CLICK
QUITE THE CON-TRARY.
THEY ARE THE HOLY ELECT ...

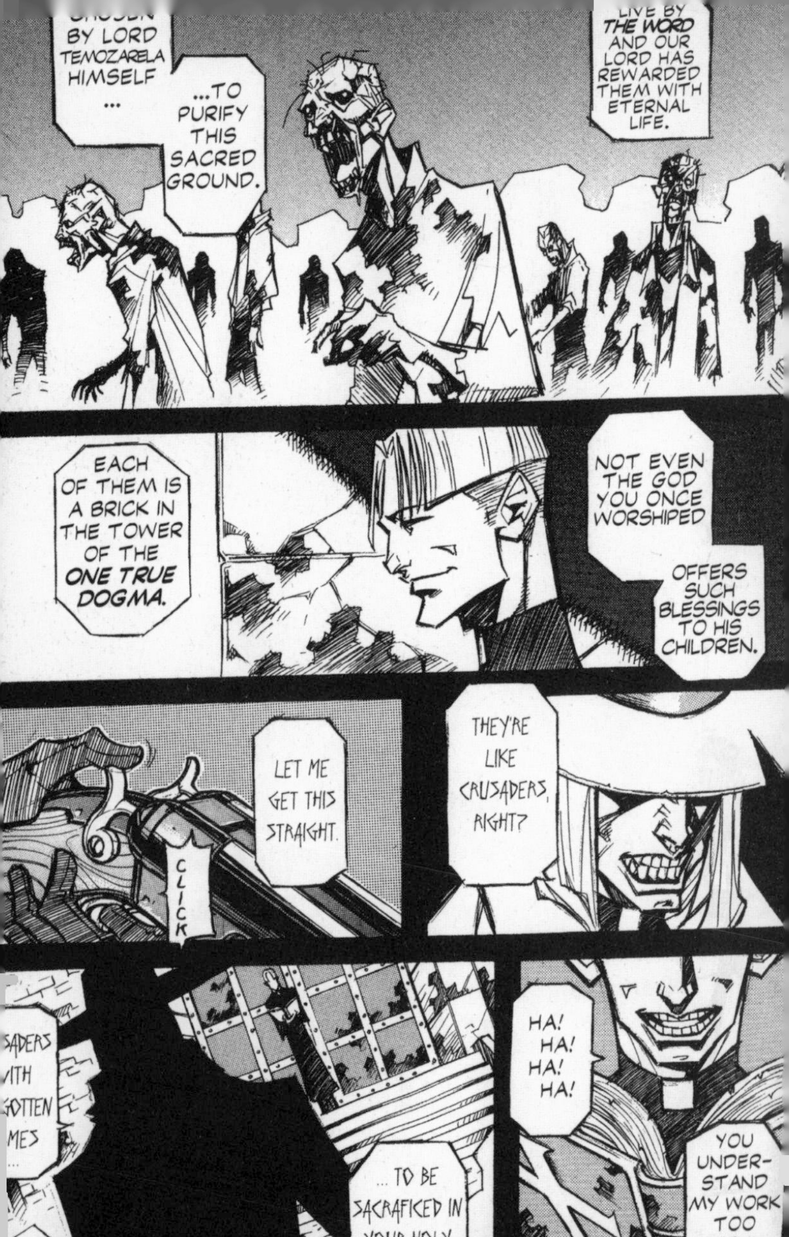
BY LORD TEMOZARELA HIMSELF ...
...TO PURIFY THIS SACRED GROUND.
LIVE BY THE WORD AND OUR LORD HAS REWARDED THEM WITH ETERNAL LIFE.
EACH OF THEM IS A BRICK IN THE TOWER OF THE ONE TRUE DOGMA.
NOT EVEN THE GOD YOU ONCE WORSHIPED
OFFERS SUCH BLESSINGS TO HIS CHILDREN.
LET ME GET THIS STRAIGHT.
CLICK
THEY'RE LIKE CRUSADERS, RIGHT?
... TO BE SACRAFICED IN YOUR HOLY
HA! HA! HA! HA!
YOU UNDER-STAND MY WORK TOO WELL,

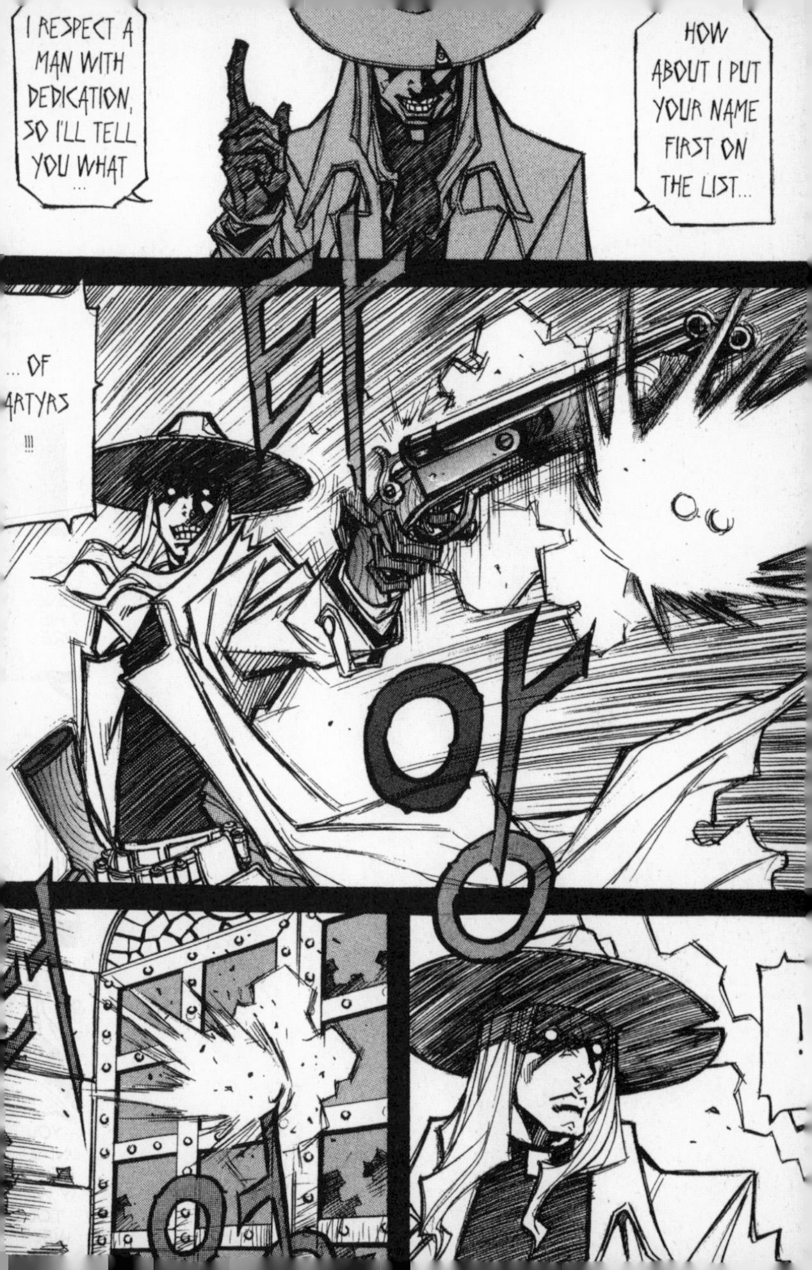
I RESPECT A MAN WITH DEDICATION, SO I'LL TELL YOU WHAT ...
HOW ABOUT I PUT YOUR NAME FIRST ON THE LIST...
... OF ARTYRS !!!
!

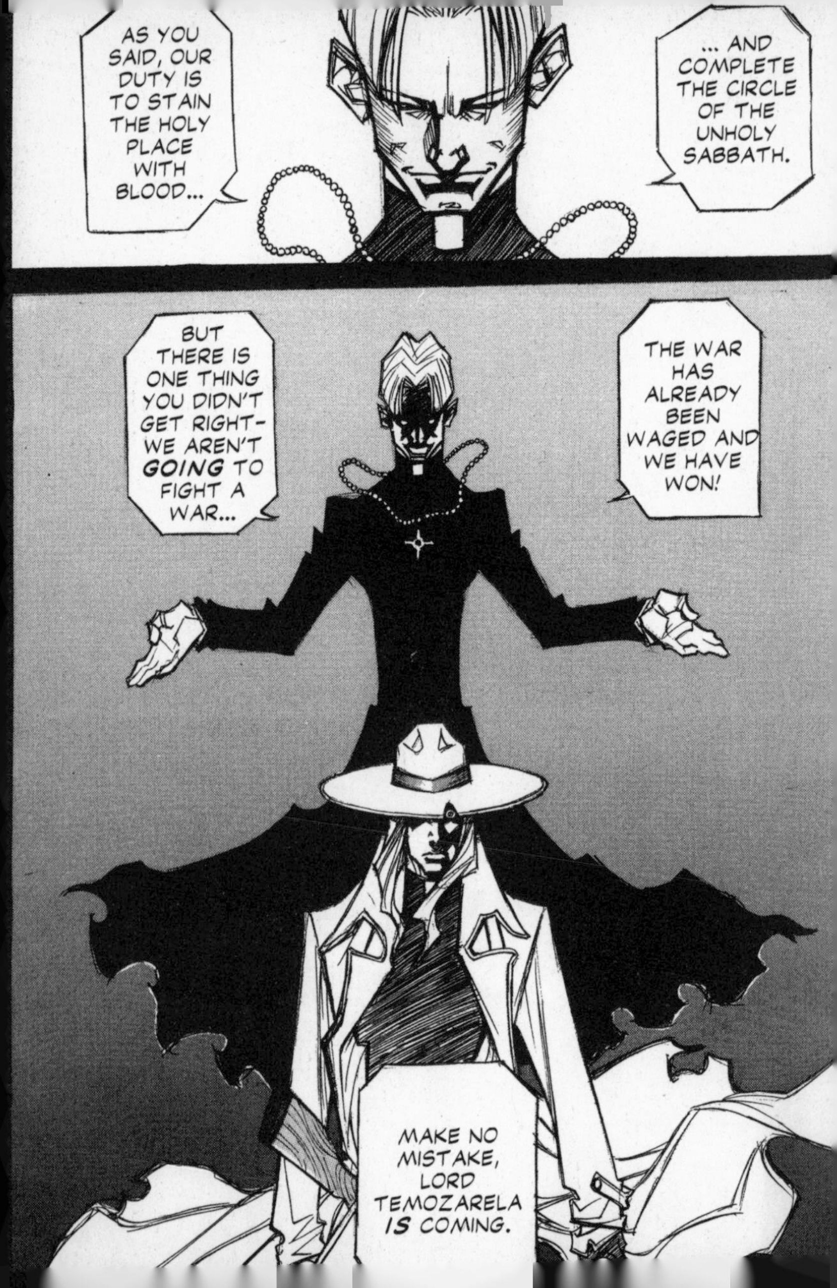
AS YOU SAID, OUR DUTY IS TO STAIN THE HOLY PLACE WITH BLOOD...
... AND COMPLETE THE CIRCLE OF THE UNHOLY SABBATH.
BUT THERE IS ONE THING YOU DIDN'T GET RIGHT- WE AREN'T **GOING** TO FIGHT A WAR...
THE WAR HAS ALREADY BEEN WAGED AND WE HAVE WON!
MAKE NO MISTAKE, LORD TEMOZARELA ***IS*** COMING.

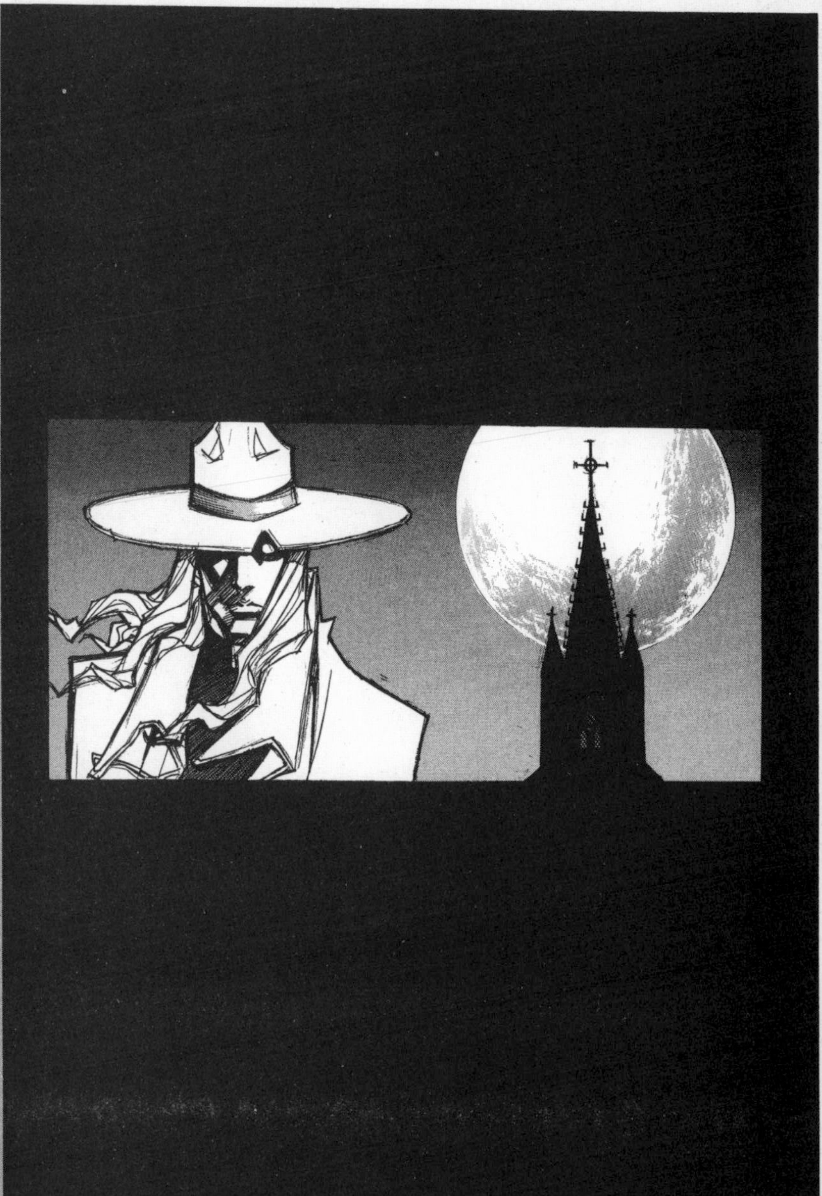

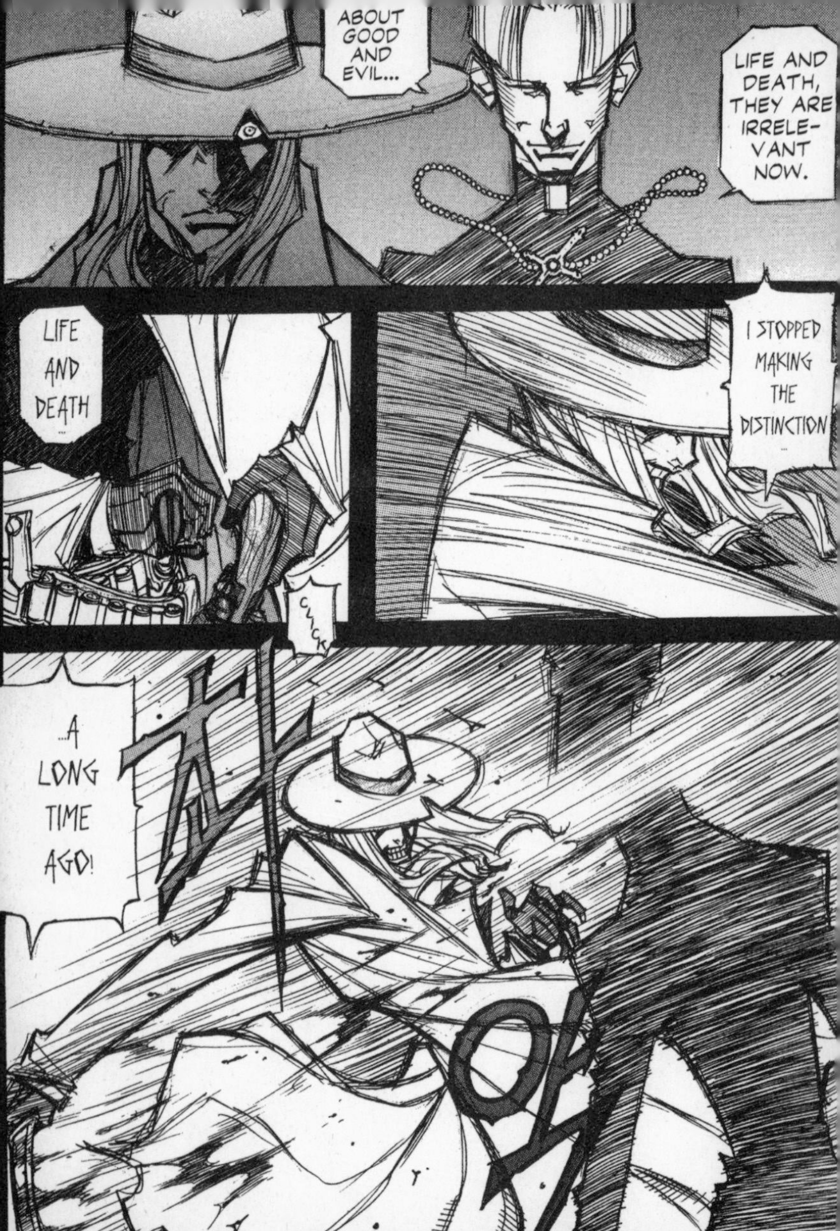
ABOUT GOOD AND EVIL...
LIFE AND DEATH, THEY ARE IRRELE-VANT NOW.
LIFE AND DEATH ...
I STOPPED MAKING THE DISTINCTION ...
CLICK
...A LONG TIME AGO!

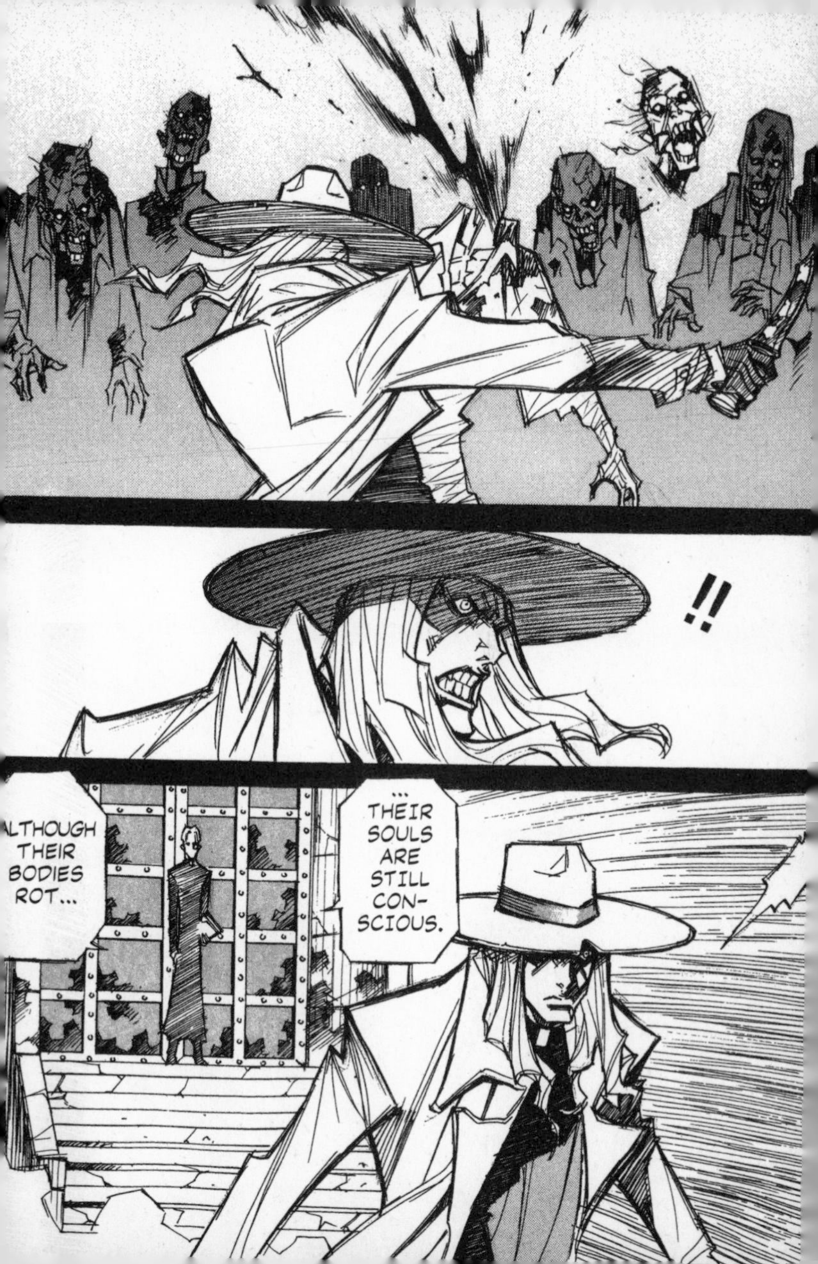
!!
ALTHOUGH THEIR BODIES ROT...
...THEIR SOULS ARE STILL CON-SCIOUS.

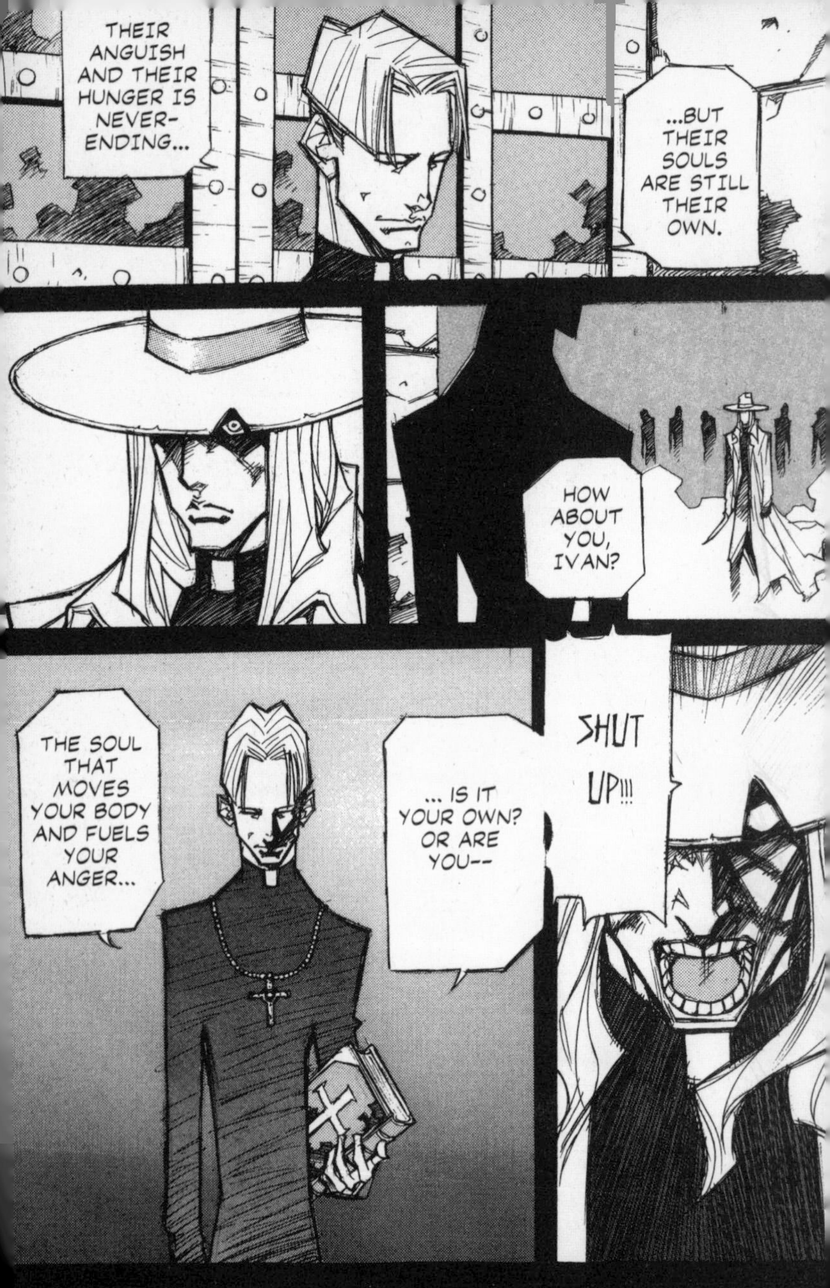
THEIR ANGUISH AND THEIR HUNGER IS NEVER-ENDING...
...BUT THEIR SOULS ARE STILL THEIR OWN.
HOW ABOUT YOU, IVAN?
THE SOUL THAT MOVES YOUR BODY AND FUELS YOUR ANGER...
... IS IT YOUR OWN? OR ARE YOU--
SHUT UP!!!

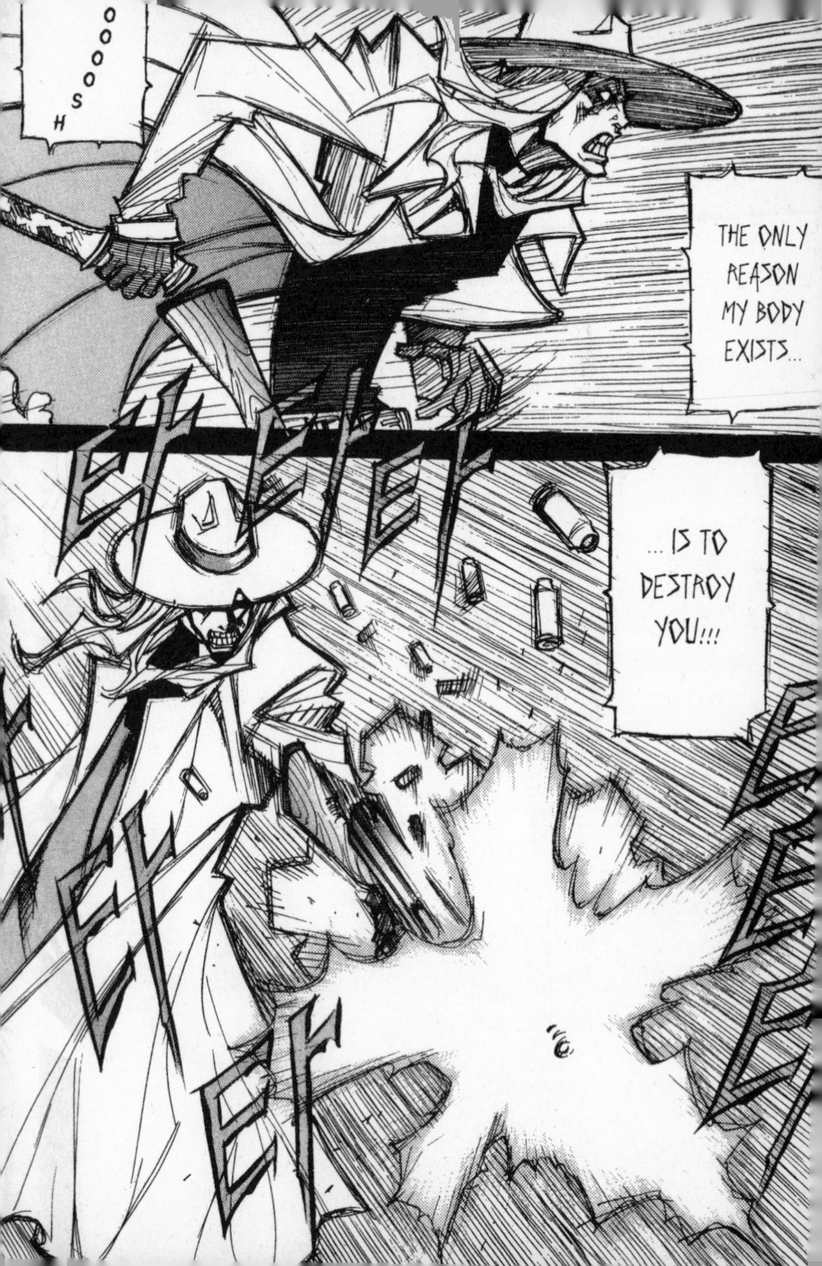
OOOOSH
THE ONLY REASON MY BODY EXISTS...
...IS TO DESTROY YOU!!!

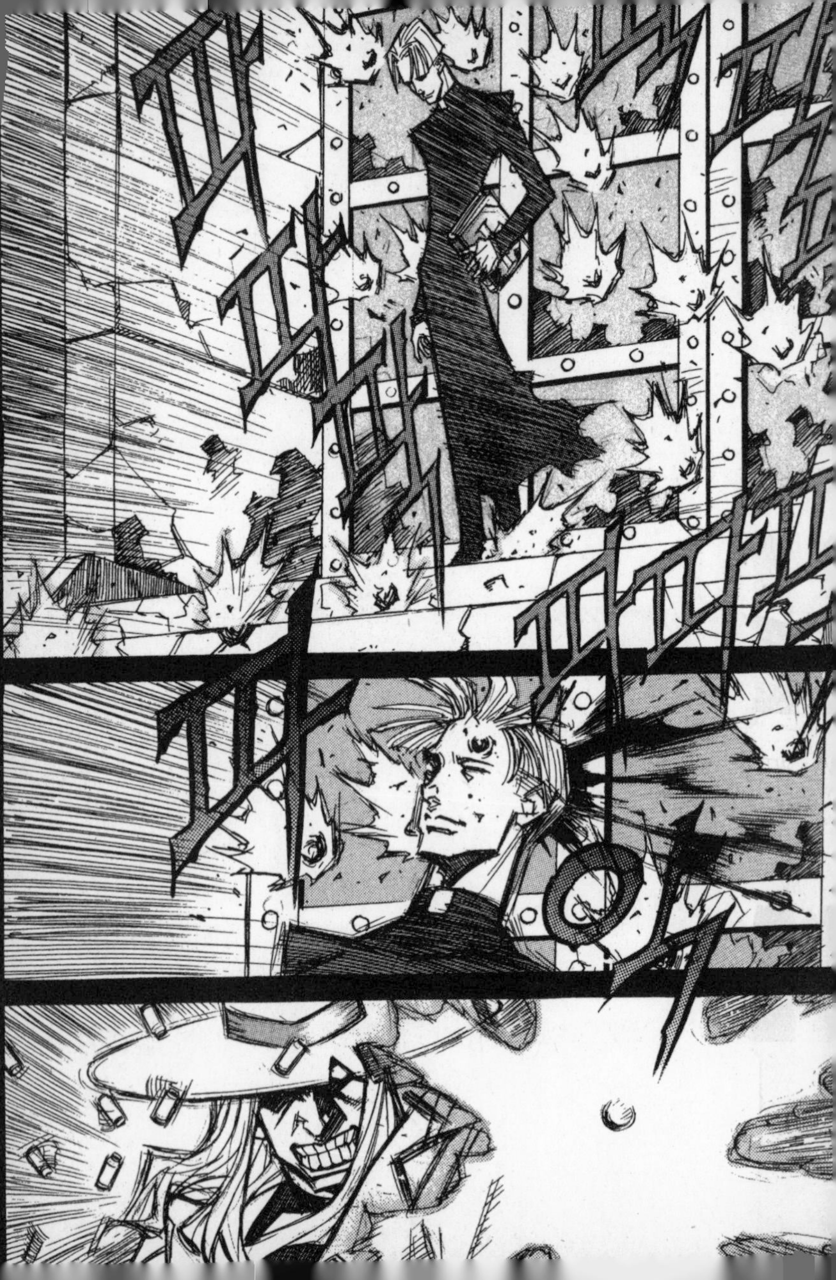

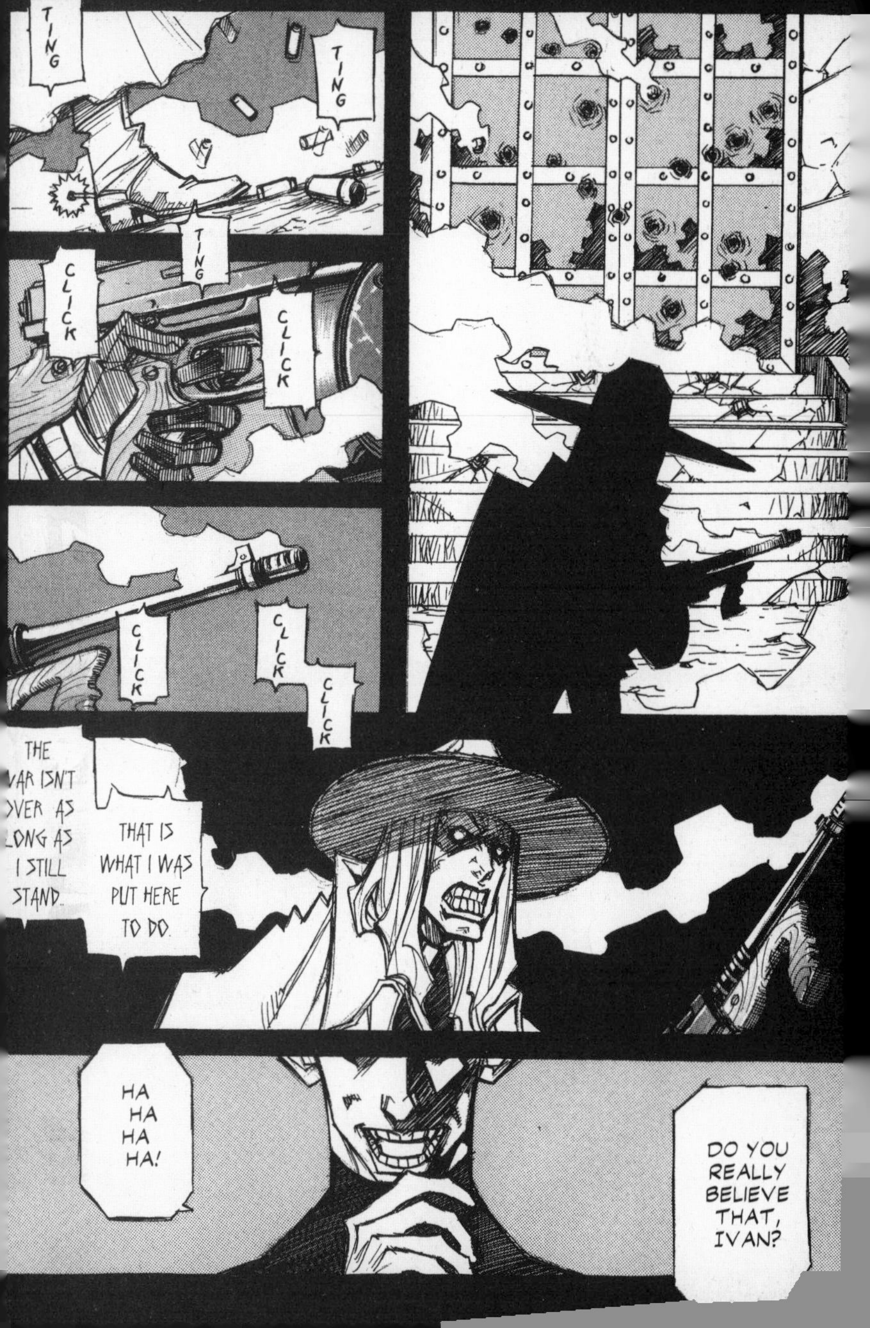

TING
TING
TING
CLICK
CLICK
CLICK
CLICK
CLICK
THE WAR ISN'T OVER AS LONG AS I STILL STAND...
THAT IS WHAT I WAS PUT HERE TO DO.
HA HA HA HA HA!
DO YOU REALLY BELIEVE THAT, IVAN?

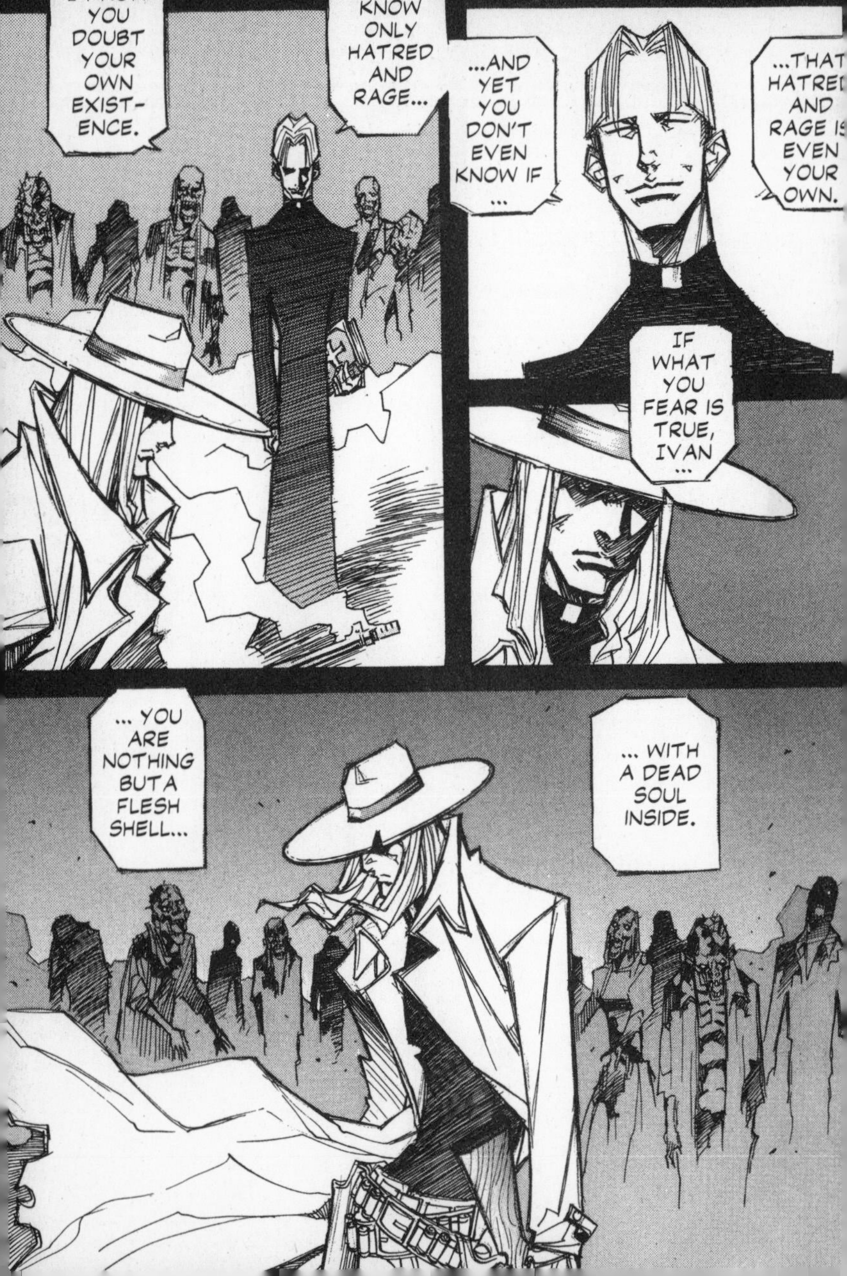
I KNOW YOU DOUBT YOUR OWN EXIST-ENCE.
YOU KNOW ONLY HATRED AND RAGE...
...AND YET YOU DON'T EVEN KNOW IF ...
...THAT HATRED AND RAGE IS EVEN YOUR OWN.
IF WHAT YOU FEAR IS TRUE, IVAN ...
... YOU ARE NOTHING BUT A FLESH SHELL...
... WITH A DEAD SOUL INSIDE.

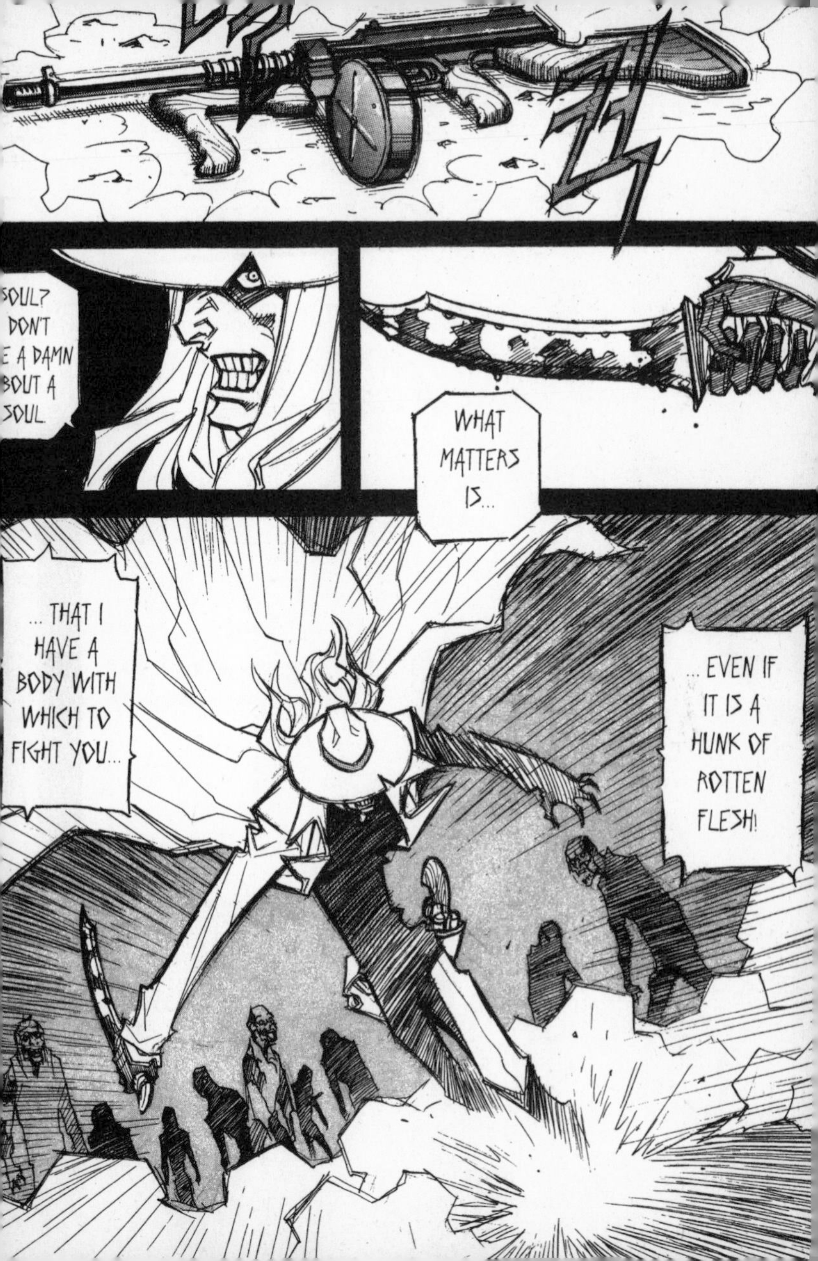
SOUL? DON'T E A DAMN BOUT A SOUL.
WHAT MATTERS IS...
... THAT I HAVE A BODY WITH WHICH TO FIGHT YOU...
... EVEN IF IT IS A HUNK OF ROTTEN FLESH!

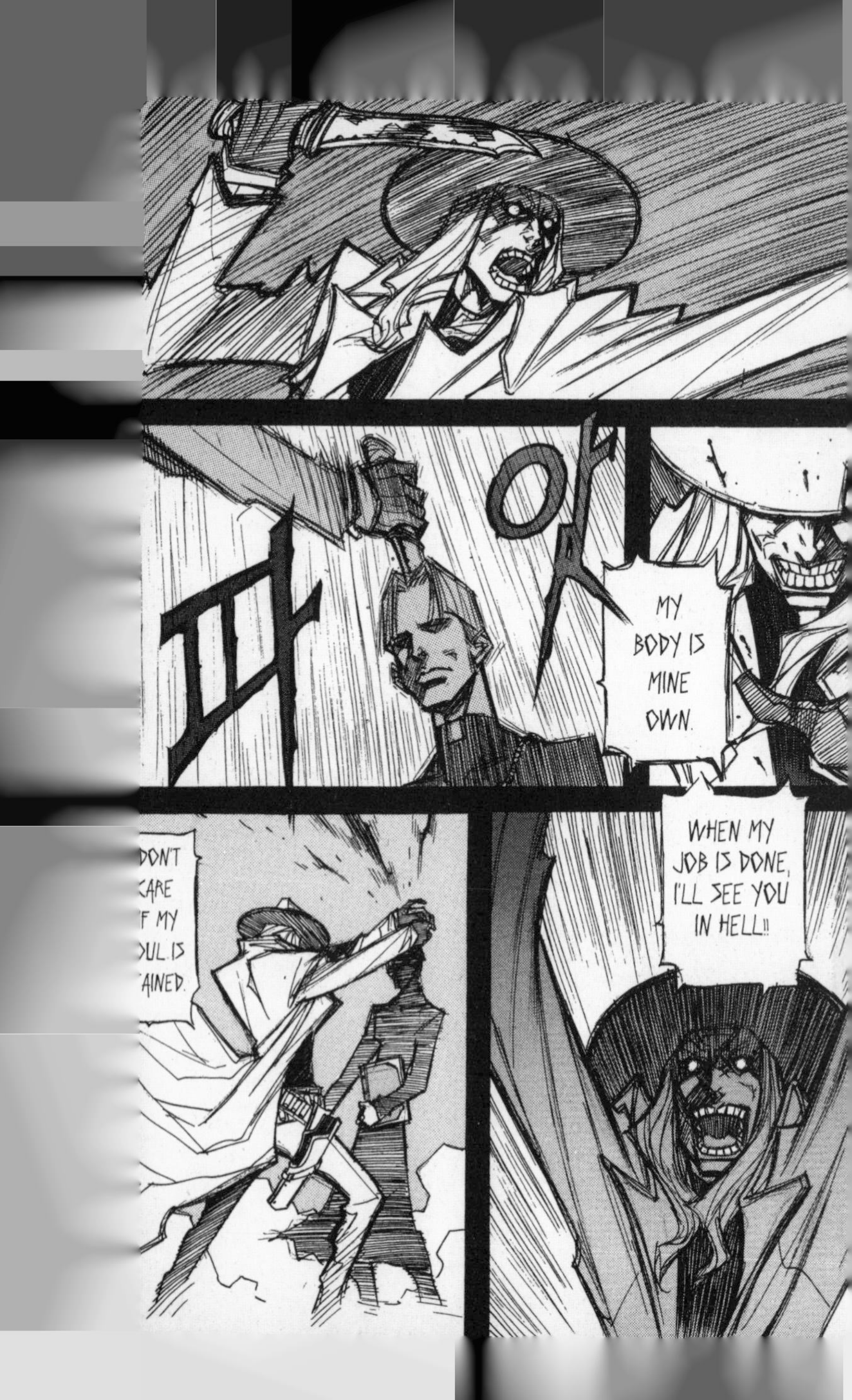
MY BODY IS MINE OWN.
DON'T CARE F MY OUL IS AINED.
WHEN MY JOB IS DONE, I'LL SEE YOU IN HELL!!

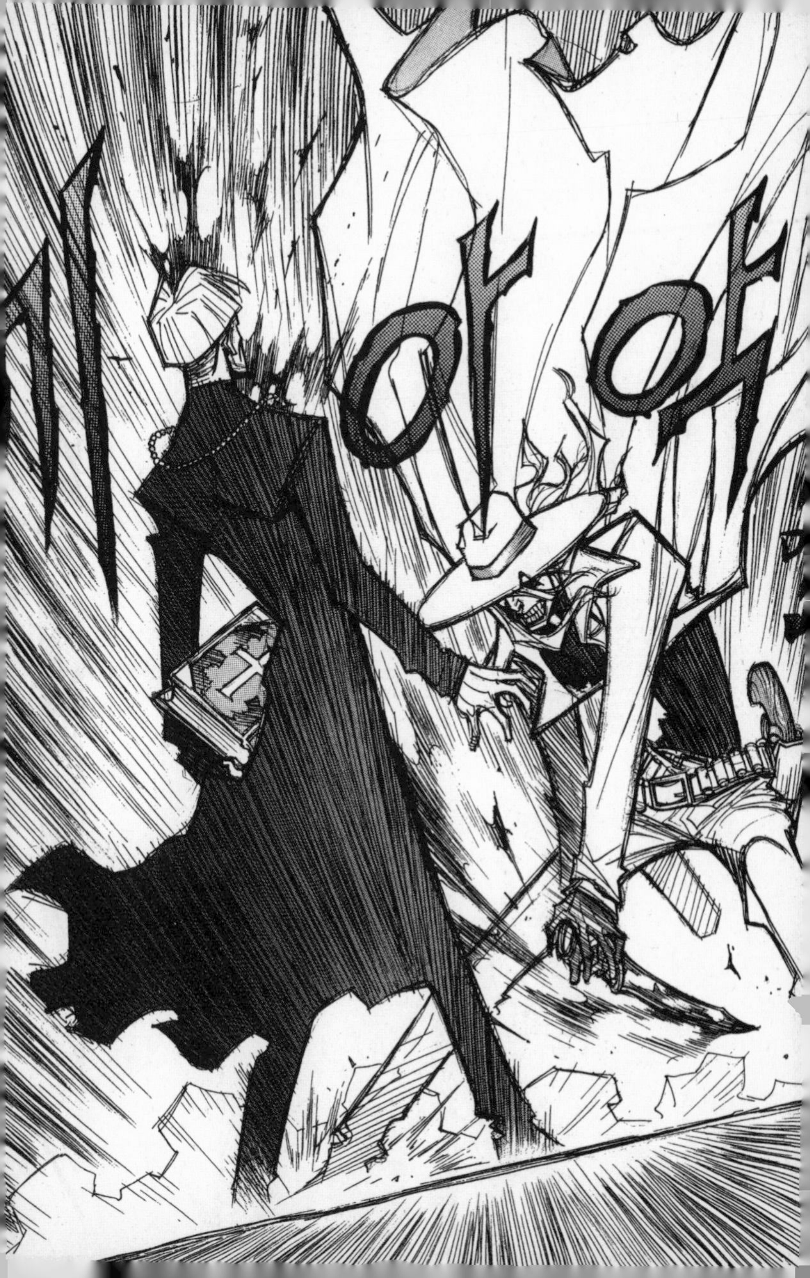

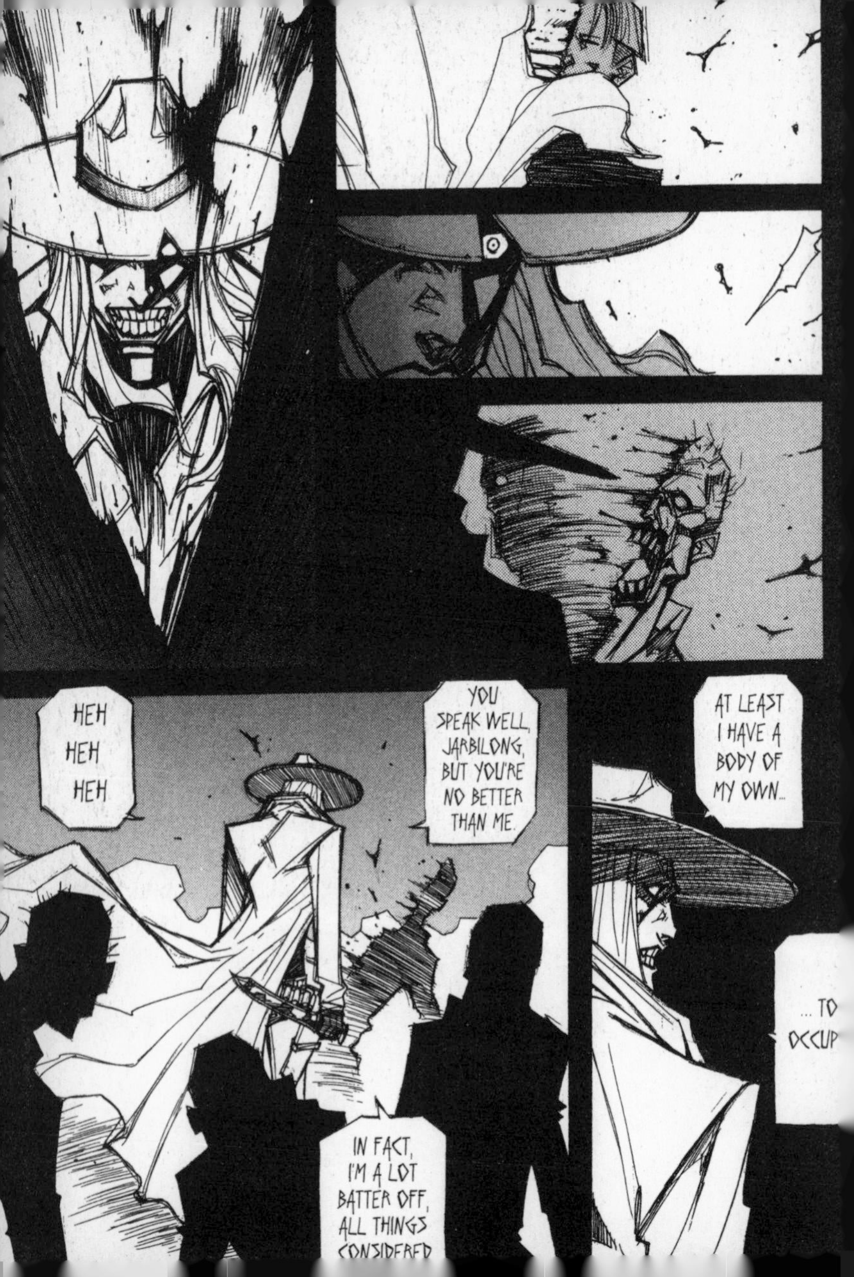
HEH HEH HEH
YOU SPEAK WELL, JARBILONG, BUT YOU'RE NO BETTER THAN ME.
IN FACT, I'M A LOT BATTER OFF, ALL THINGS CONSIDERED
AT LEAST I HAVE A BODY OF MY OWN...
...TO OCCUP

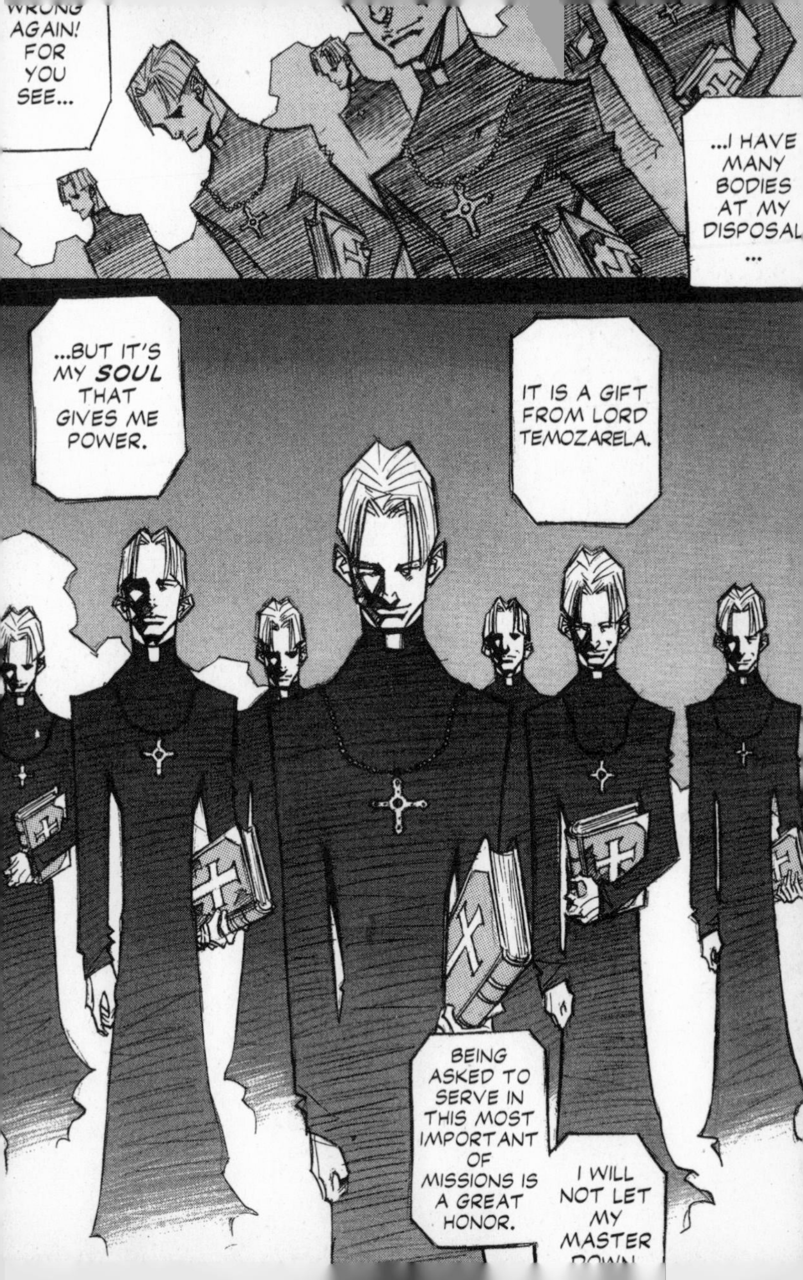
AGAIN! FOR YOU SEE...
...I HAVE MANY BODIES AT MY DISPOSAL...
...BUT IT'S MY **SOUL** THAT GIVES ME POWER.
IT IS A GIFT FROM LORD TEMOZARELA.
BEING ASKED TO SERVE IN THIS MOST IMPORTANT OF MISSIONS IS A GREAT HONOR.
I WILL NOT LET MY MASTER

HEH, HEH, HEH. FINE SENTIMENTS. I'M SURE YOUR MASTER WOULD BE PROUD.

BUT I'M NOT GOING TO LET THAT GET IN MY WAY.

IT JUST MEANS THAT I WILL HAVE TO KILL OVER AND OVER AGAIN...

...UNTIL ALL OF YOUR BODIES HAVE BEEN DESTROYED.

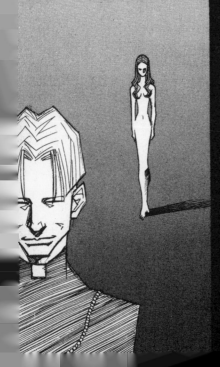

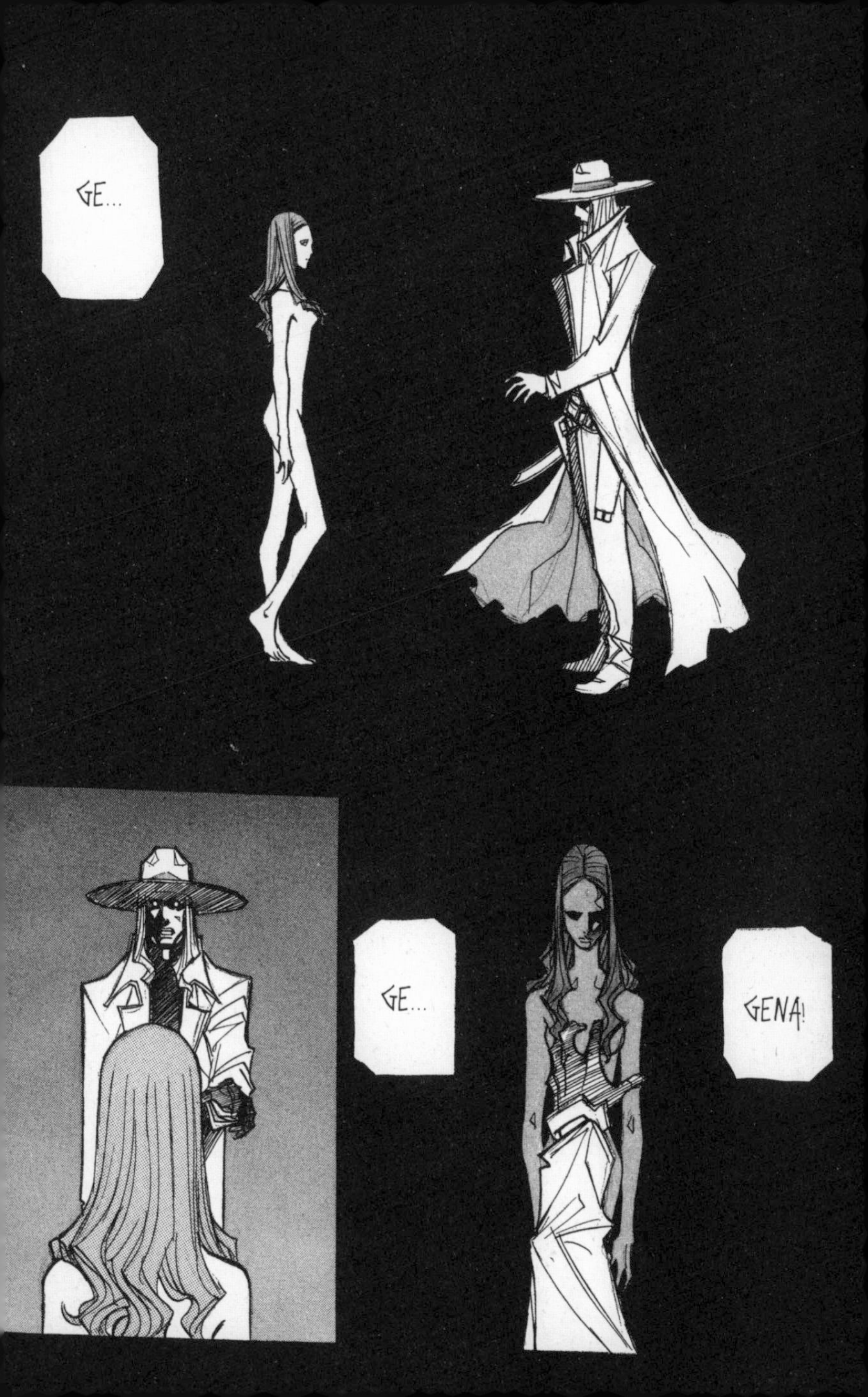
GE...
GE...
GENA!

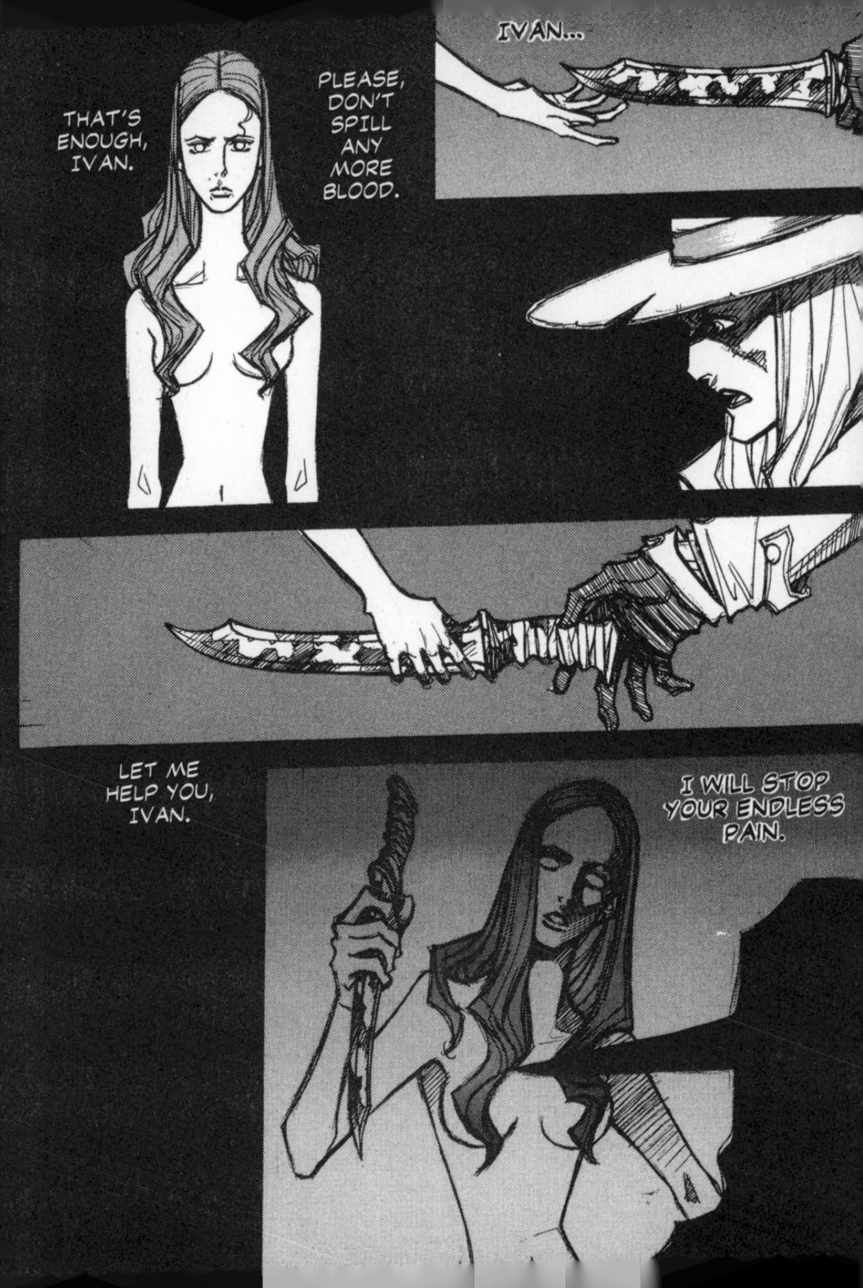
THAT'S ENOUGH, IVAN.
PLEASE, DON'T SPILL ANY MORE BLOOD.
IVAN...
LET ME HELP YOU, IVAN.
I WILL STOP YOUR ENDLESS PAIN.

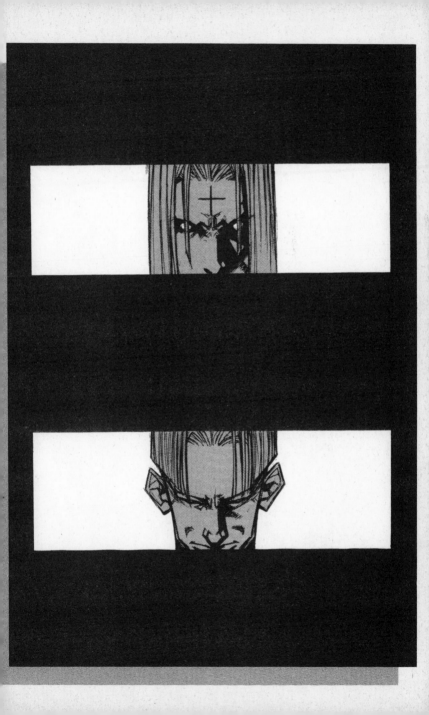

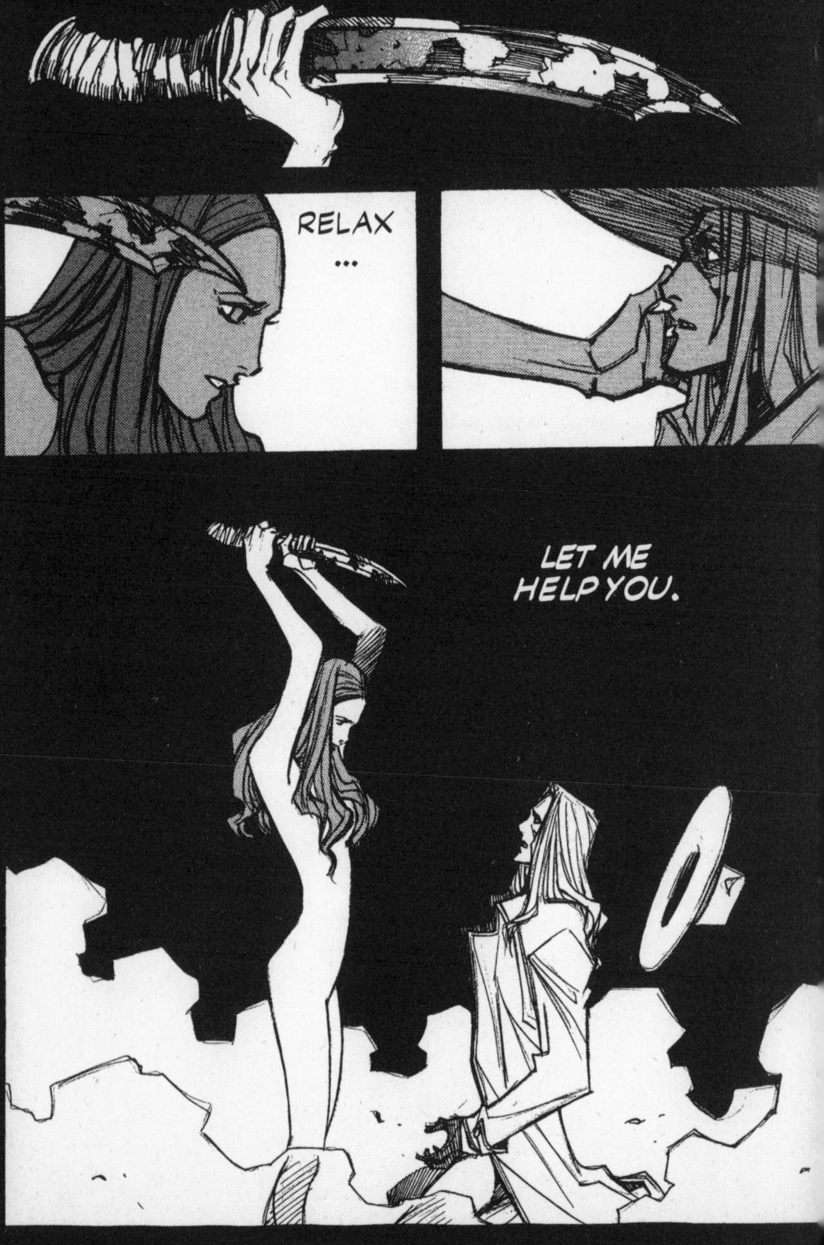
RELAX
...
LET ME
HELP YOU.

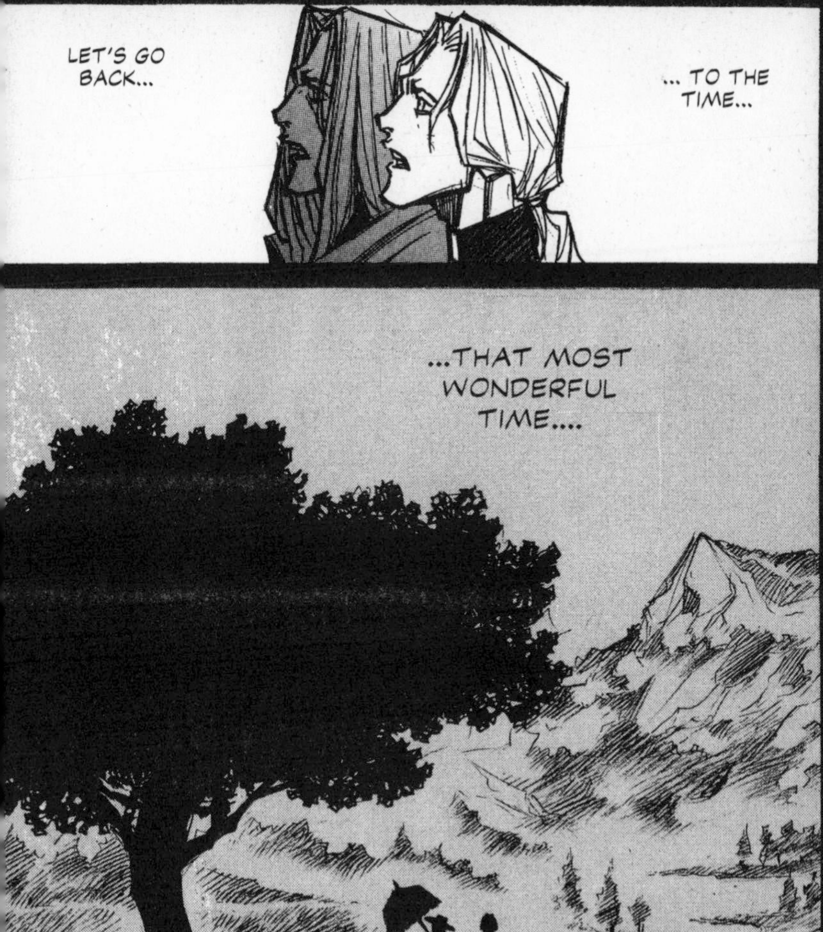
LET'S GO BACK...
... TO THE TIME...
...THAT MOST WONDERFUL TIME....
...WHEN WE WERE TOGETHER.

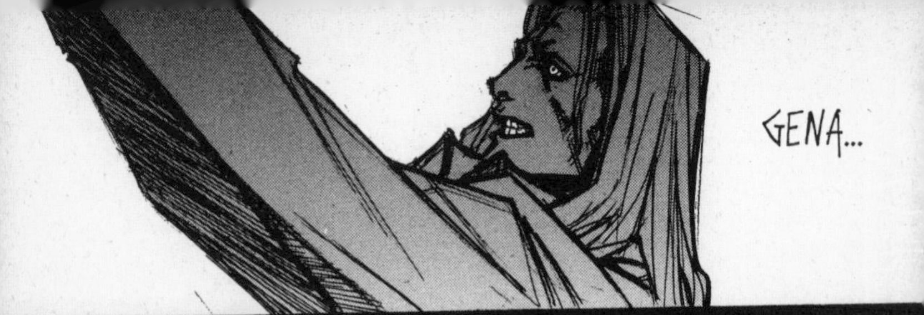
GENA...

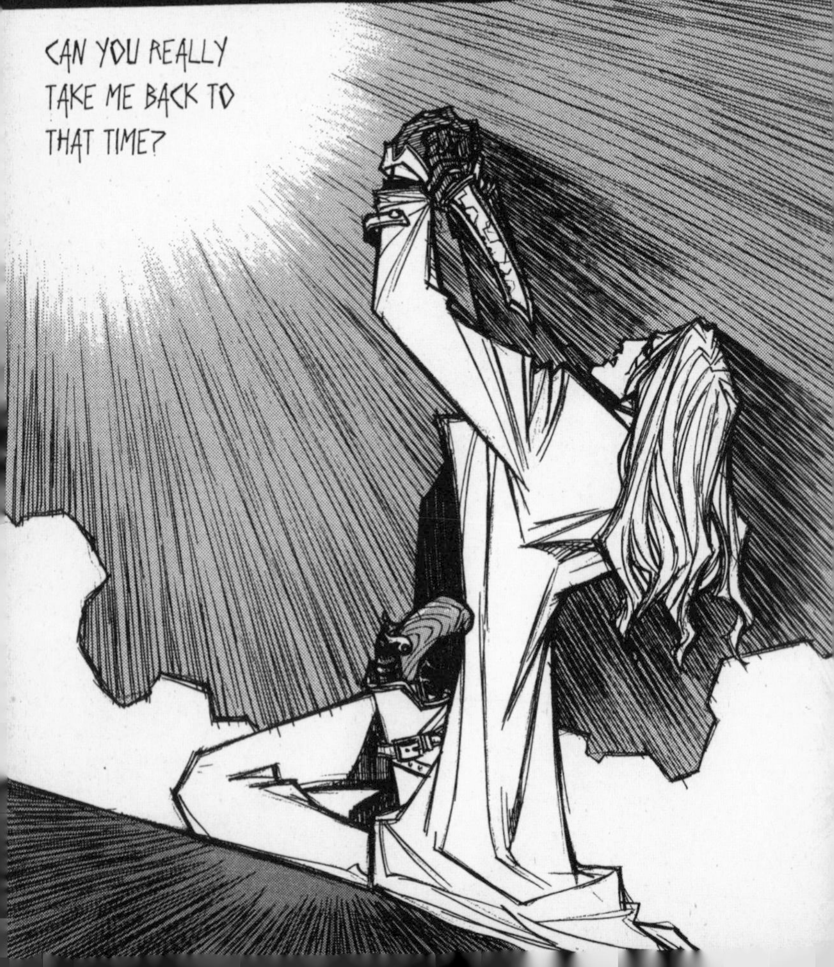
CAN YOU REALLY TAKE ME BACK TO THAT TIME?

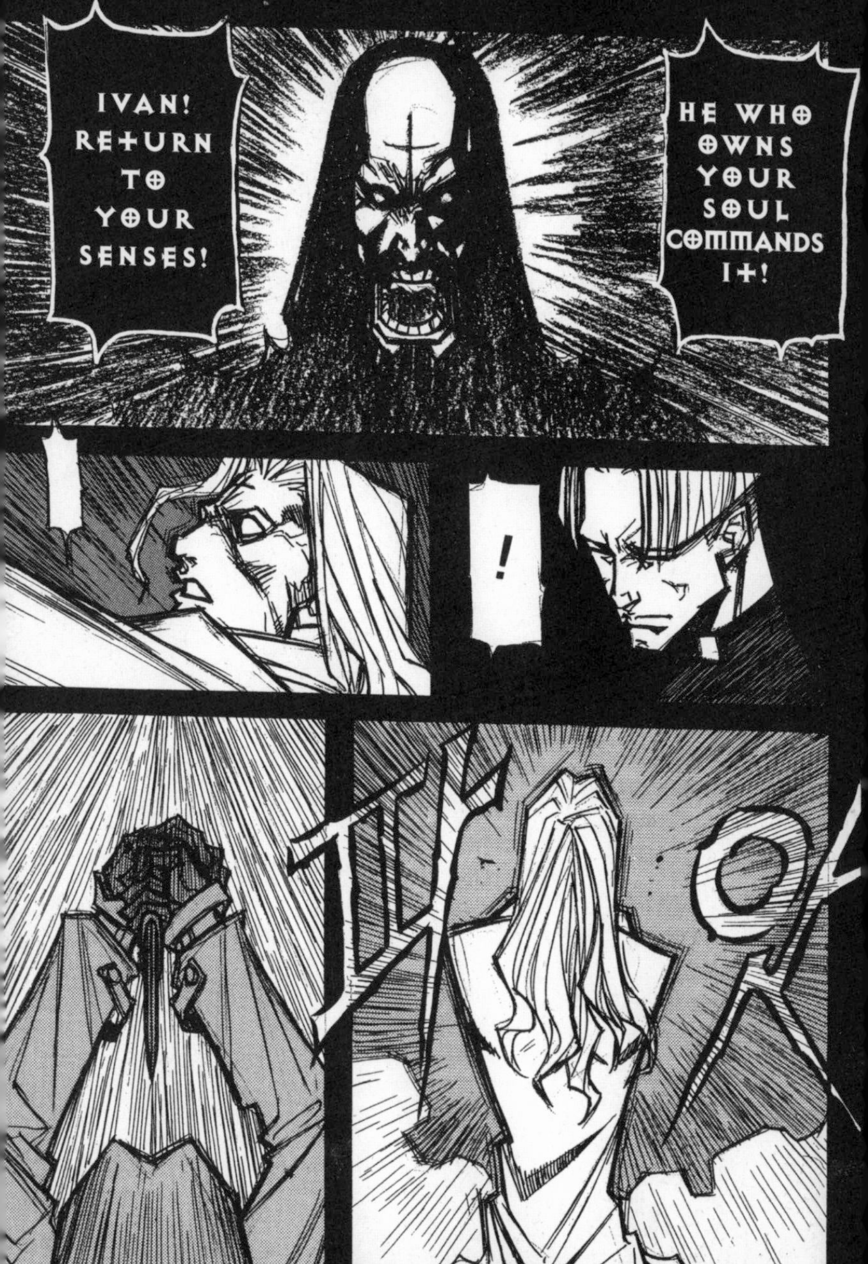
IVAN! RETURN TO YOUR SENSES!
HE WHO OWNS YOUR SOUL COMMANDS IT!
!

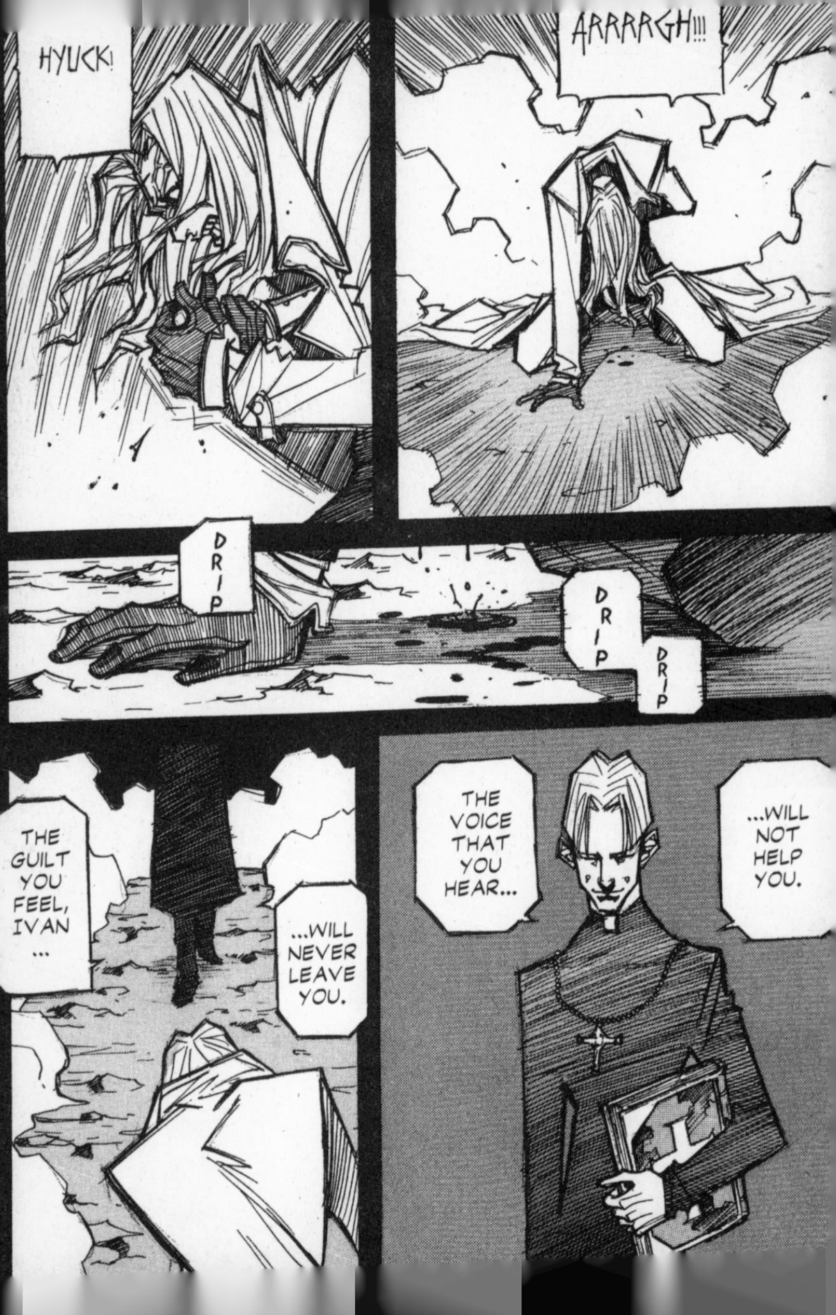
ARRRRGH!!!
HYUCK!
DRIP
DRIP
DRIP
DRIP
DRIP
DRIP
THE VOICE THAT YOU HEAR...
...WILL NOT HELP YOU.
THE GUILT YOU FEEL, IVAN ...
...WILL NEVER LEAVE YOU.

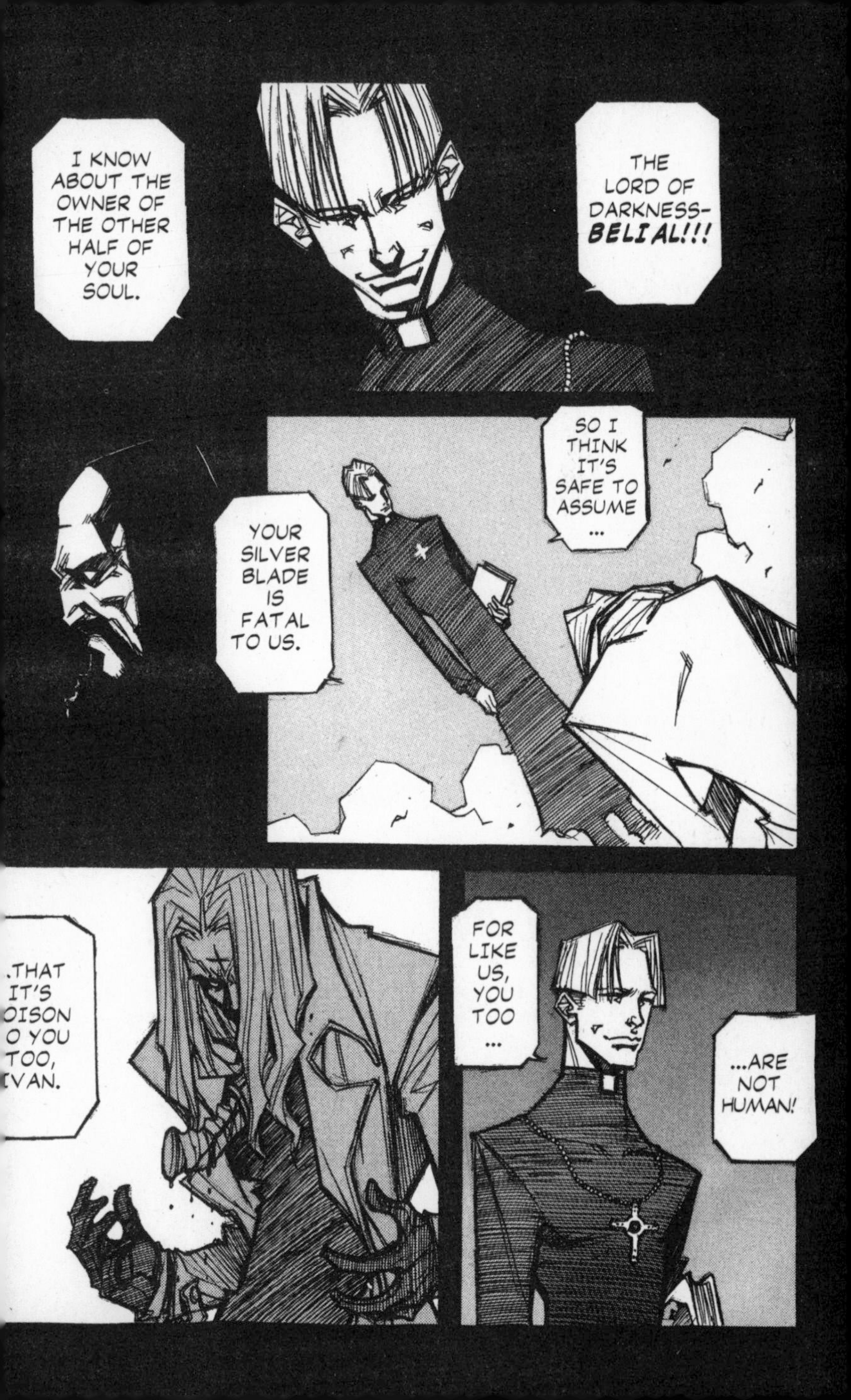
I KNOW ABOUT THE OWNER OF THE OTHER HALF OF YOUR SOUL.
THE LORD OF DARKNESS- **BELIAL!!!**
YOUR SILVER BLADE IS FATAL TO US.
SO I THINK IT'S SAFE TO ASSUME ...
.THAT IT'S OISON O YOU TOO, VAN.
FOR LIKE US, YOU TOO ...
...ARE NOT HUMAN!

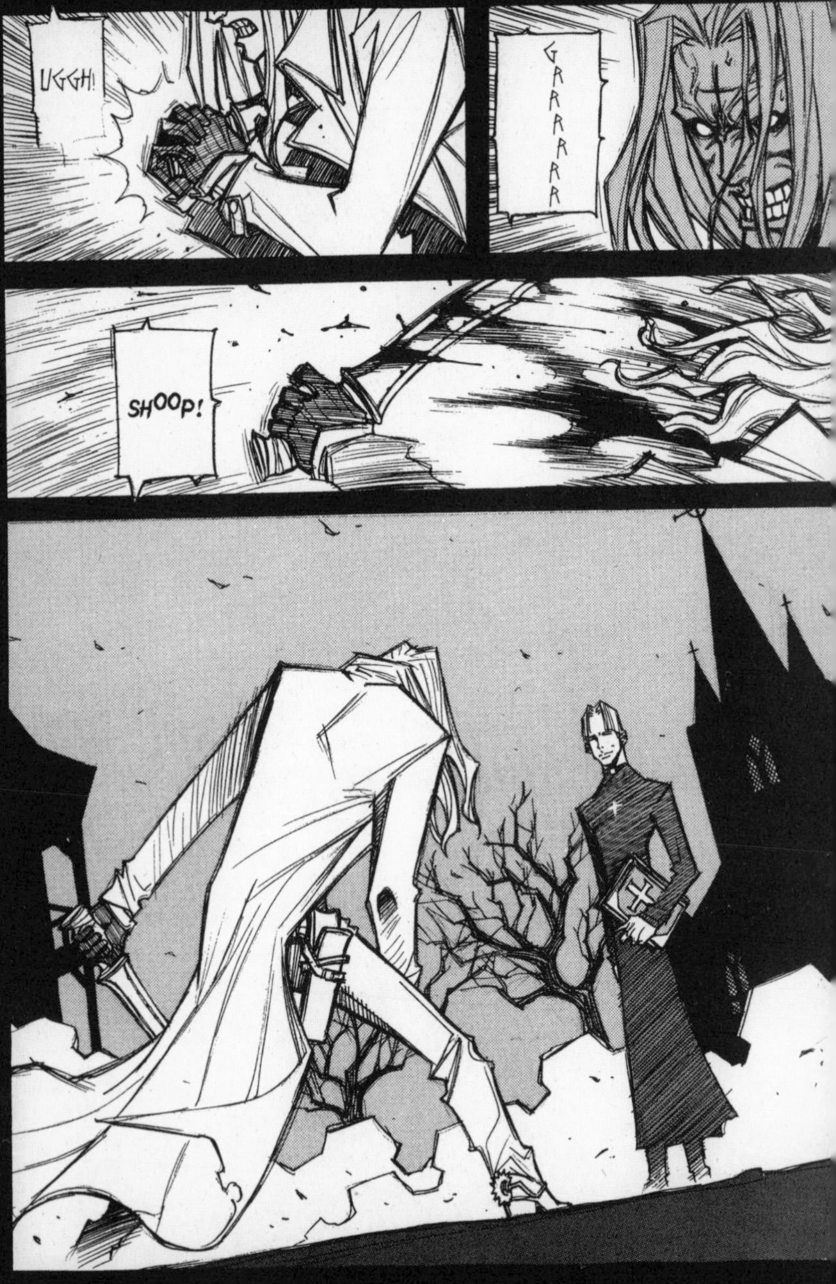
UGGH!
GRRRRRR
SHOOP!

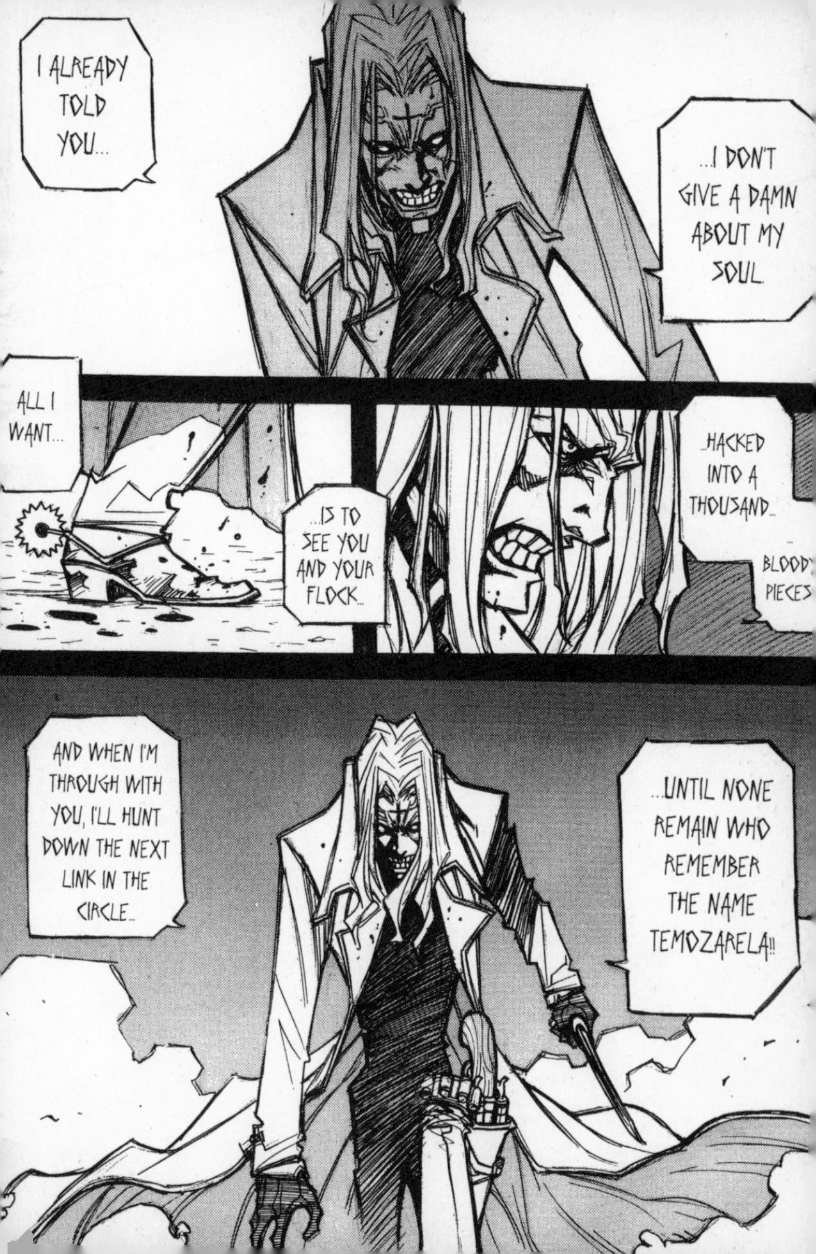
I ALREADY TOLD YOU...
...I DON'T GIVE A DAMN ABOUT MY SOUL.
ALL I WANT...
...IS TO SEE YOU AND YOUR FLOCK...
...HACKED INTO A THOUSAND...
...BLOODY PIECES
AND WHEN I'M THROUGH WITH YOU, I'LL HUNT DOWN THE NEXT LINK IN THE CIRCLE...
...UNTIL NONE REMAIN WHO REMEMBER THE NAME TEMOZARELA!!

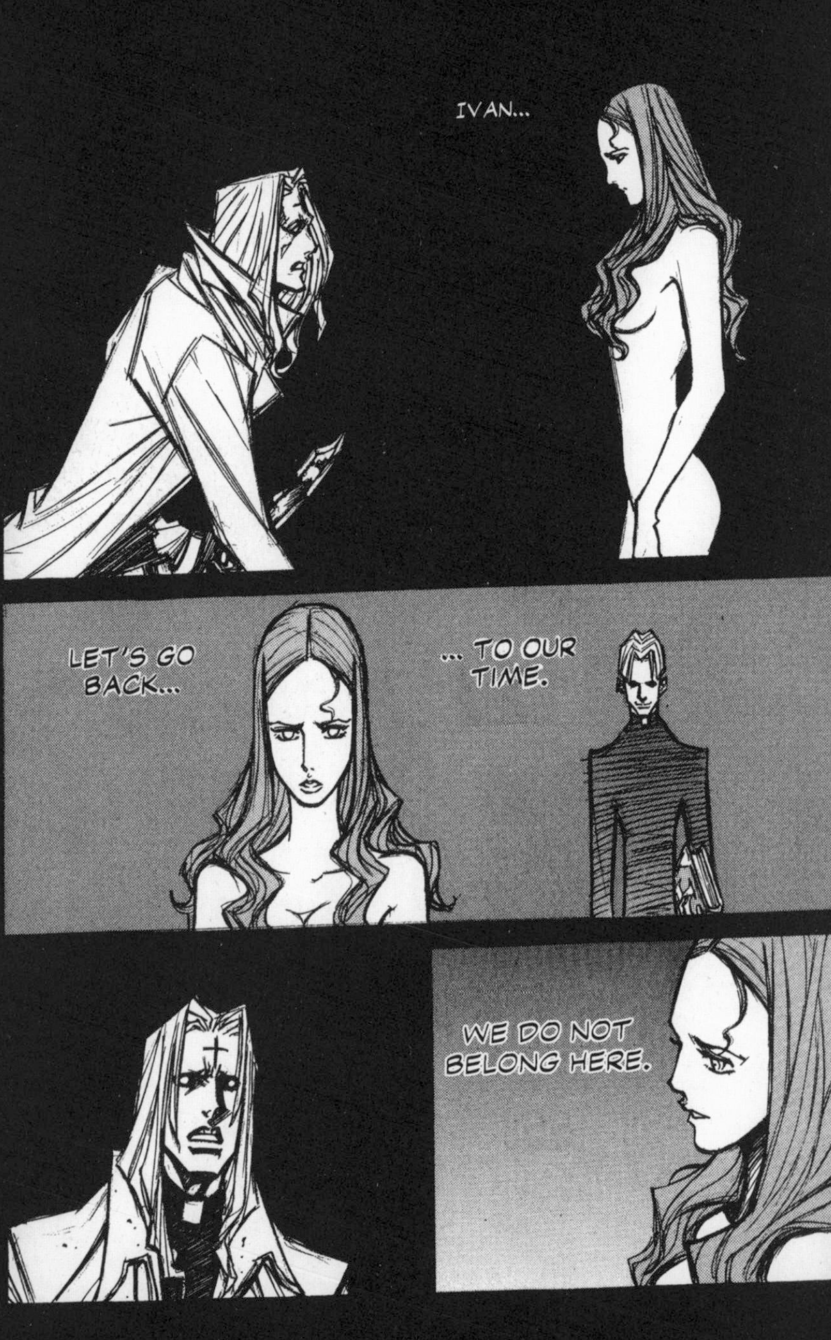
IVAN...
LET'S GO BACK...
... TO OUR TIME.
WE DO NOT BELONG HERE.

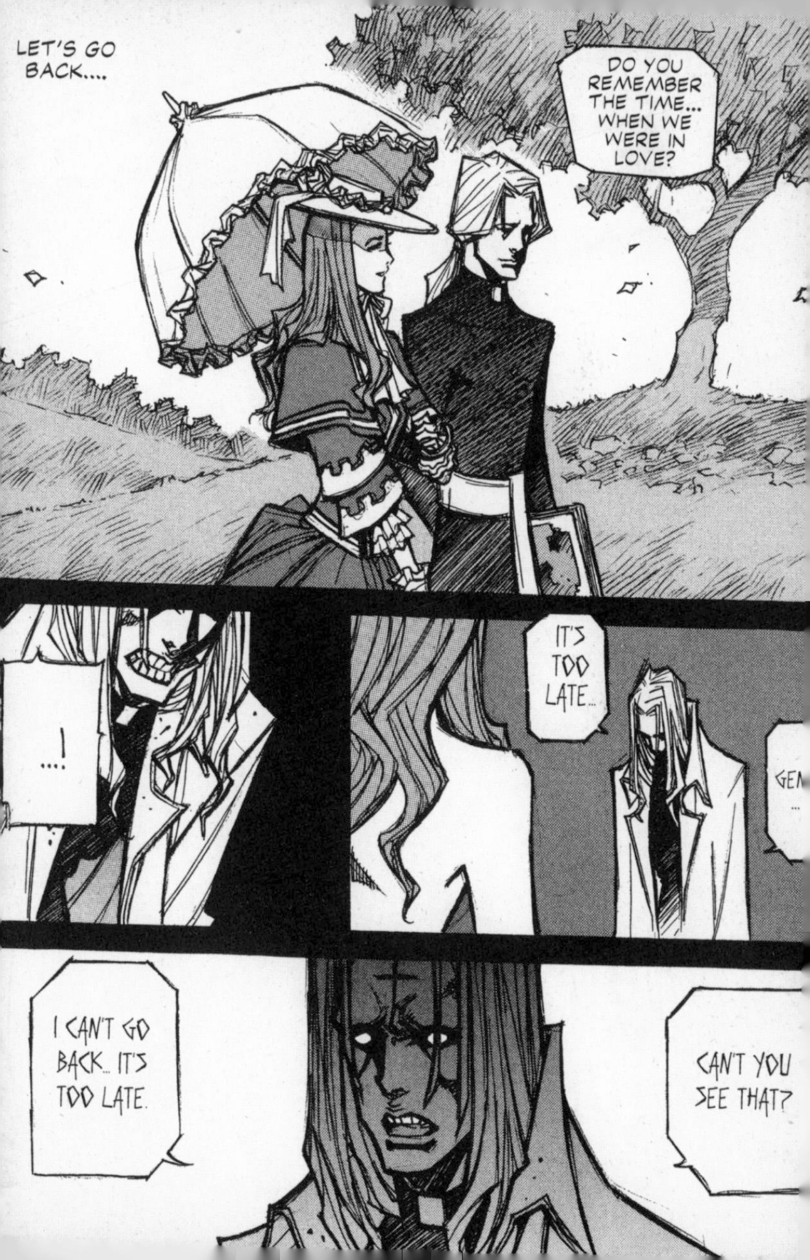
LET'S GO BACK....
DO YOU REMEMBER THE TIME... WHEN WE WERE IN LOVE?
...!
IT'S TOO LATE...
I CAN'T GO BACK... IT'S TOO LATE.
CAN'T YOU SEE THAT?

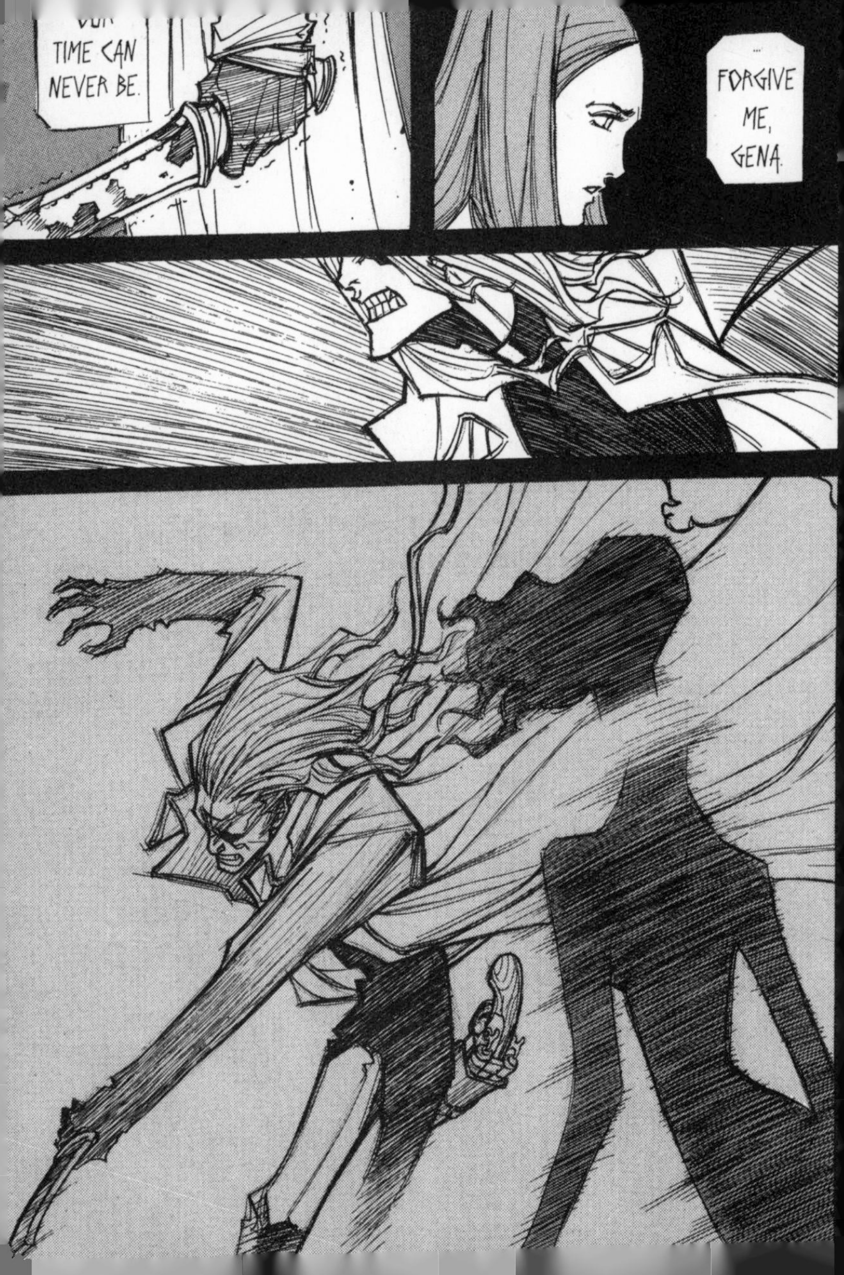
TIME CAN NEVER BE.
... FORGIVE ME, GENA.

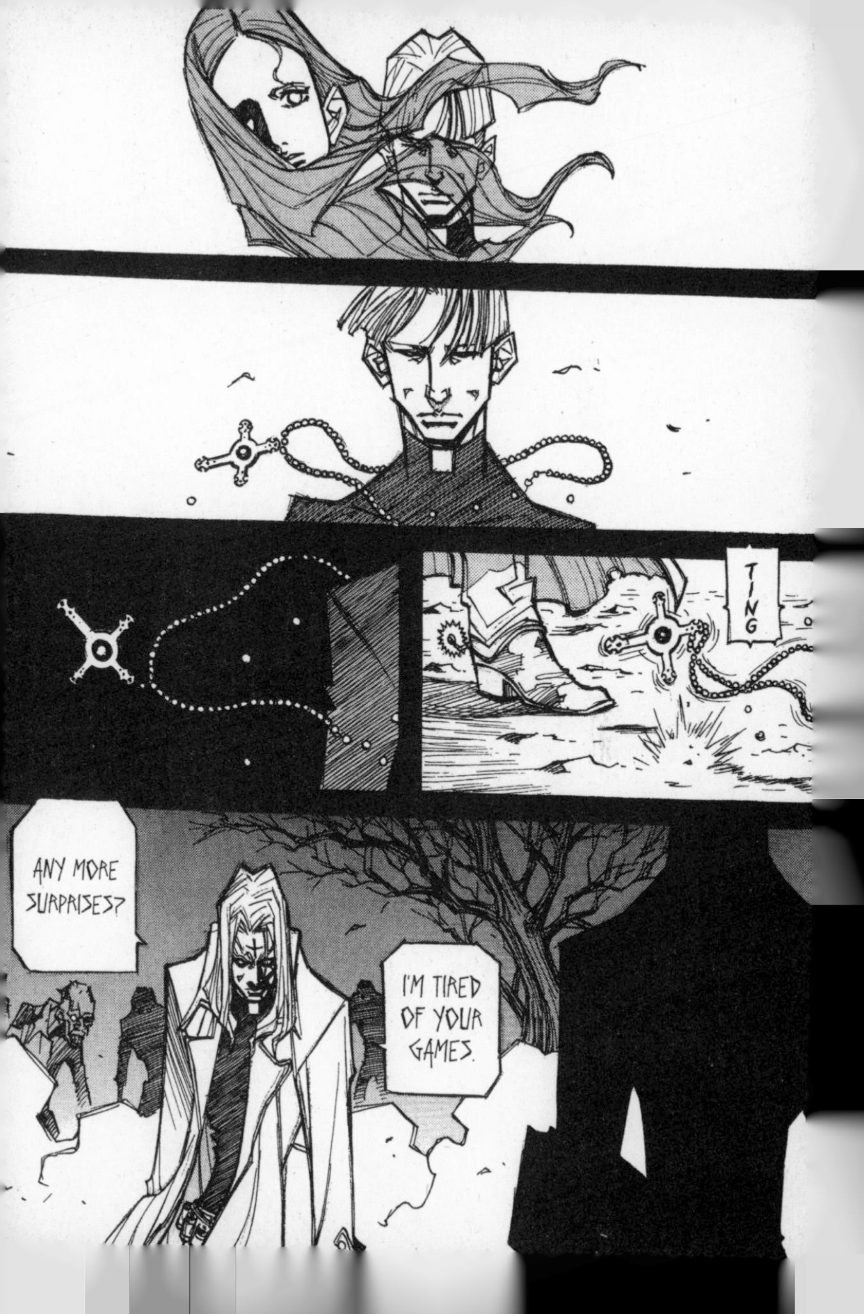
TING
ANY MORE SURPRISES?
I'M TIRED OF YOUR GAMES.

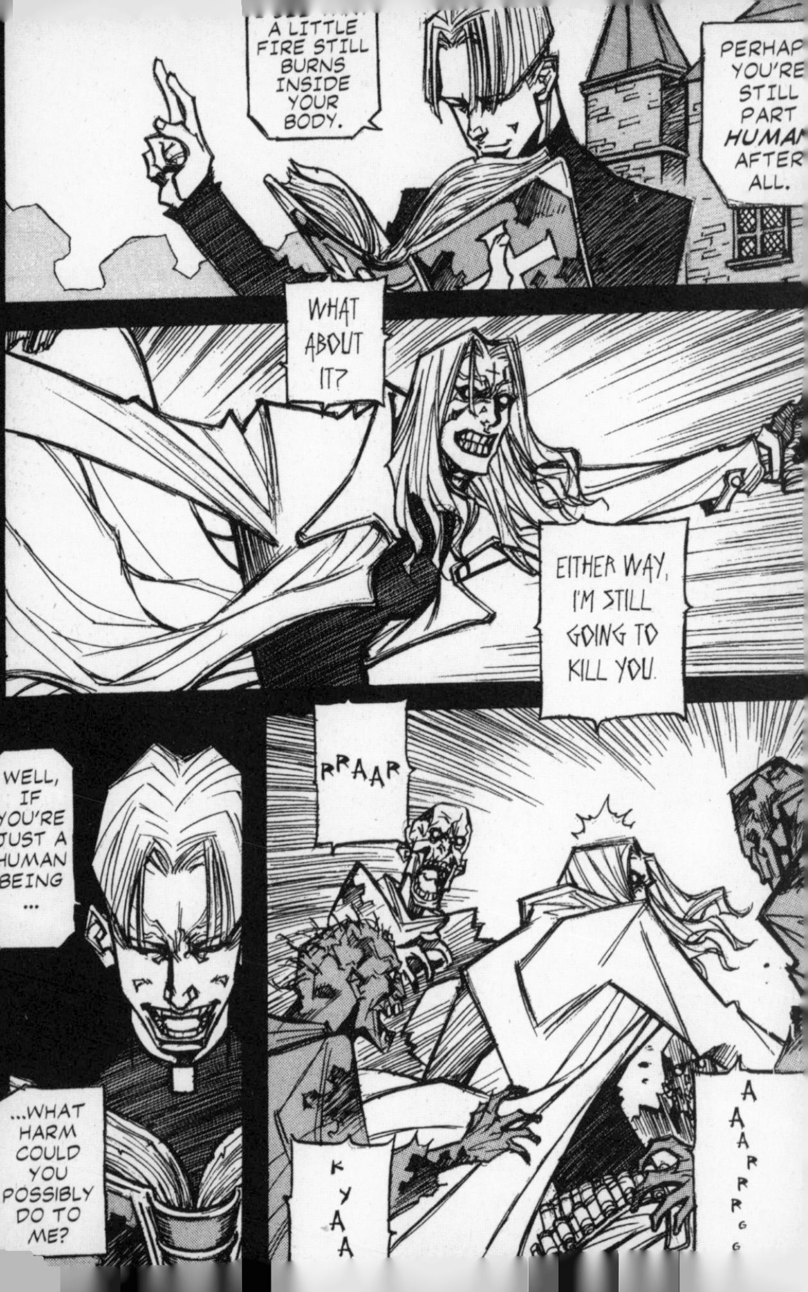
A LITTLE FIRE STILL BURNS INSIDE YOUR BODY.
PERHAP YOU'RE STILL PART HUMA AFTER ALL.
WHAT ABOUT IT?
EITHER WAY, I'M STILL GOING TO KILL YOU.
WELL, IF YOU'RE JUST A HUMAN BEING ...
...WHAT HARM COULD YOU POSSIBLY DO TO ME?
RRAAR
KYAA
AAARRGG

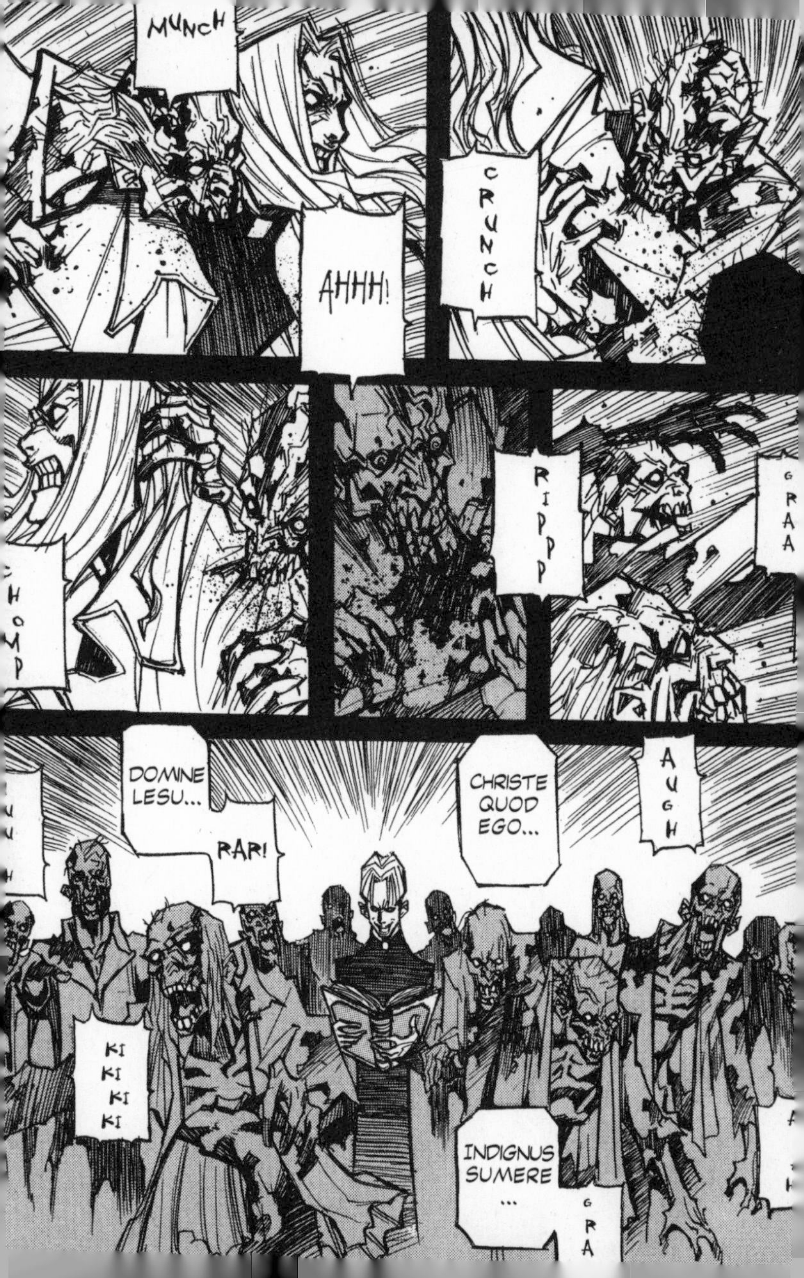
MUNCH
AHHH!
CRUNCH
CHOMP
RIPPP
GRAA
DOMINE LESU...
RAR!
CHRISTE QUOD EGO...
AUGH
KI KI KI KI
INDIGNUS SUMERE ...
GRA

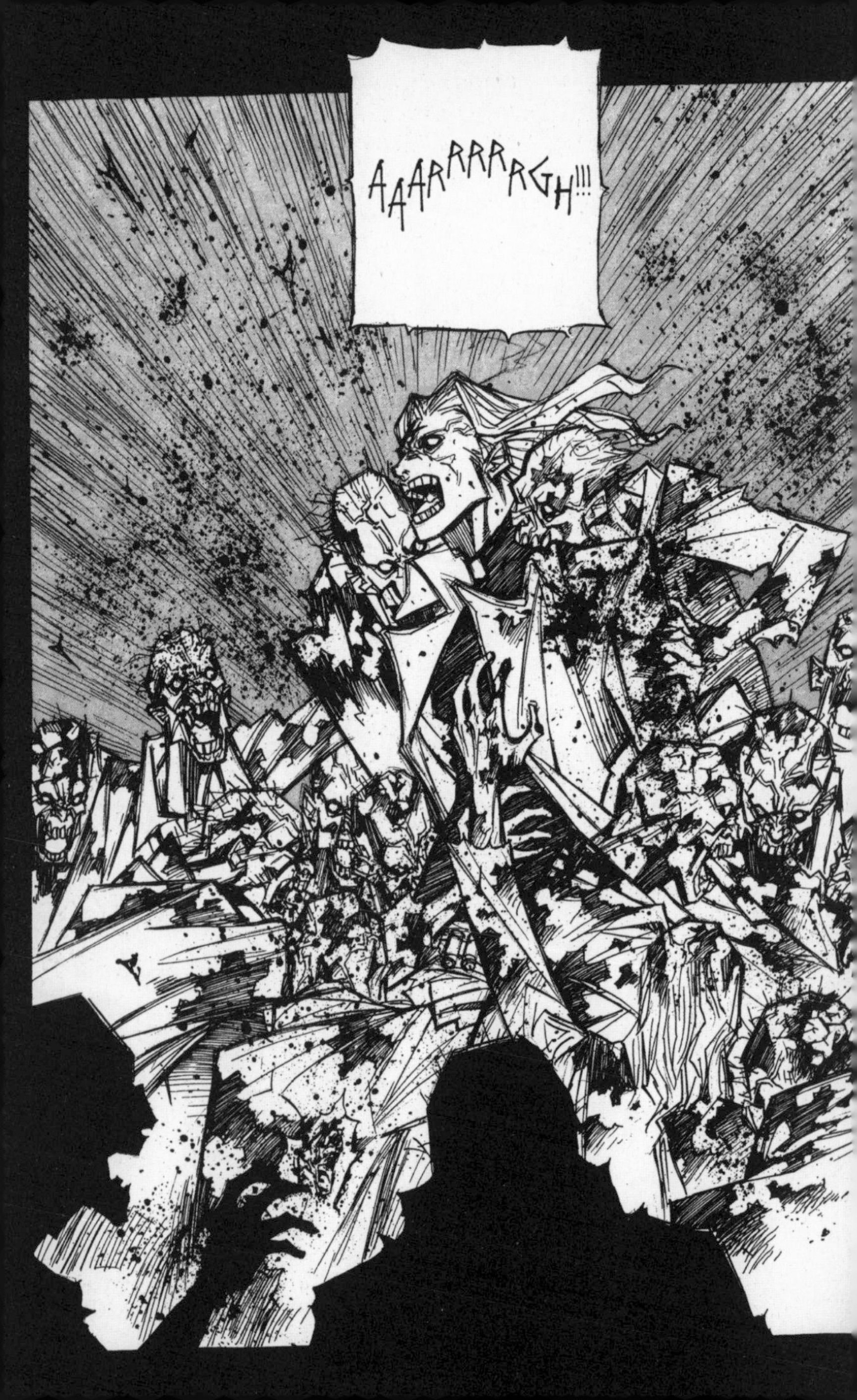
AAARRRRRRGH!!!

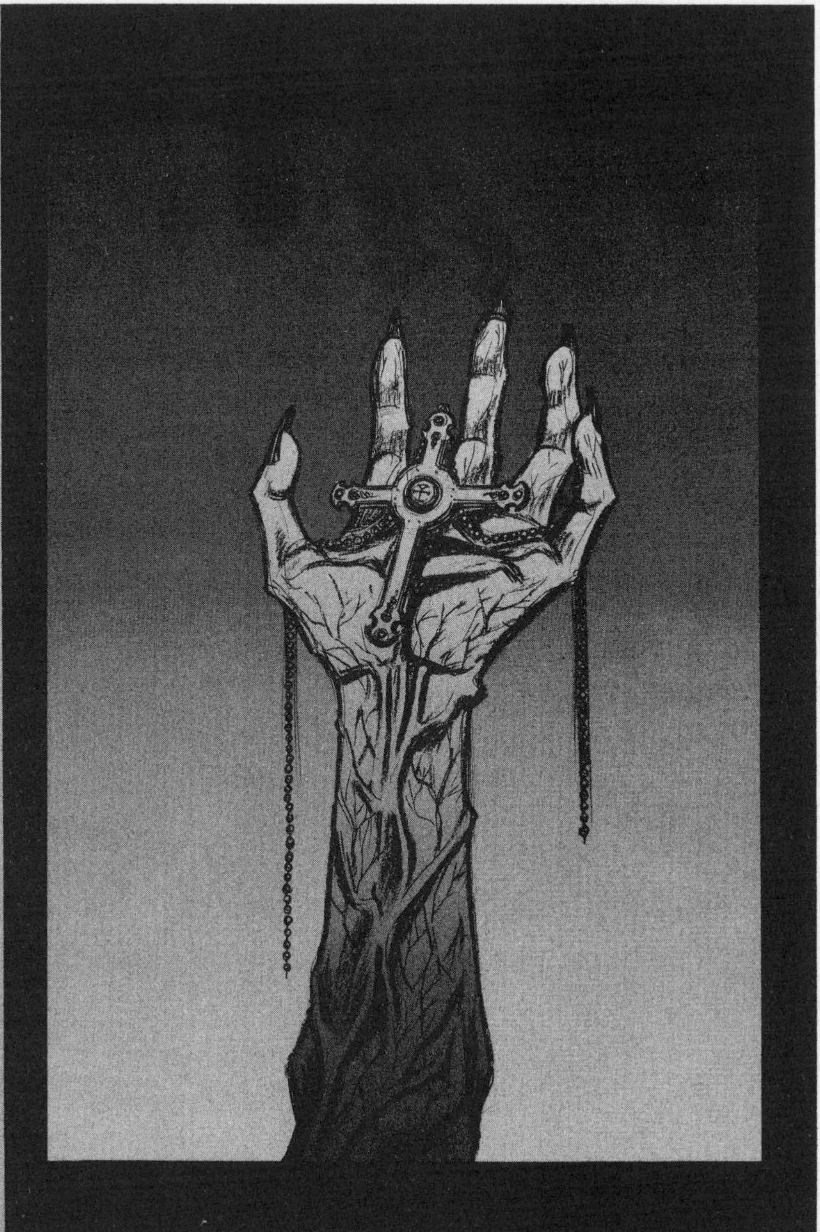

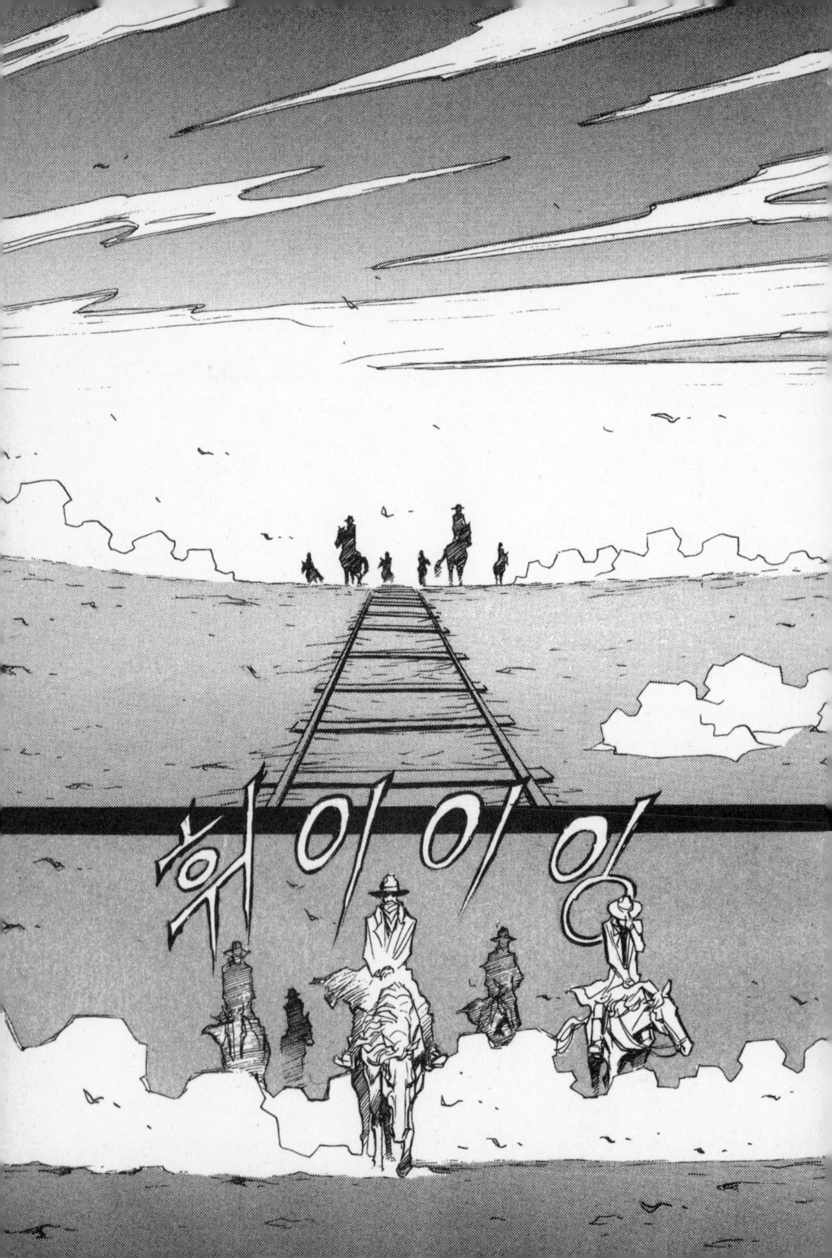
휘이이이잉

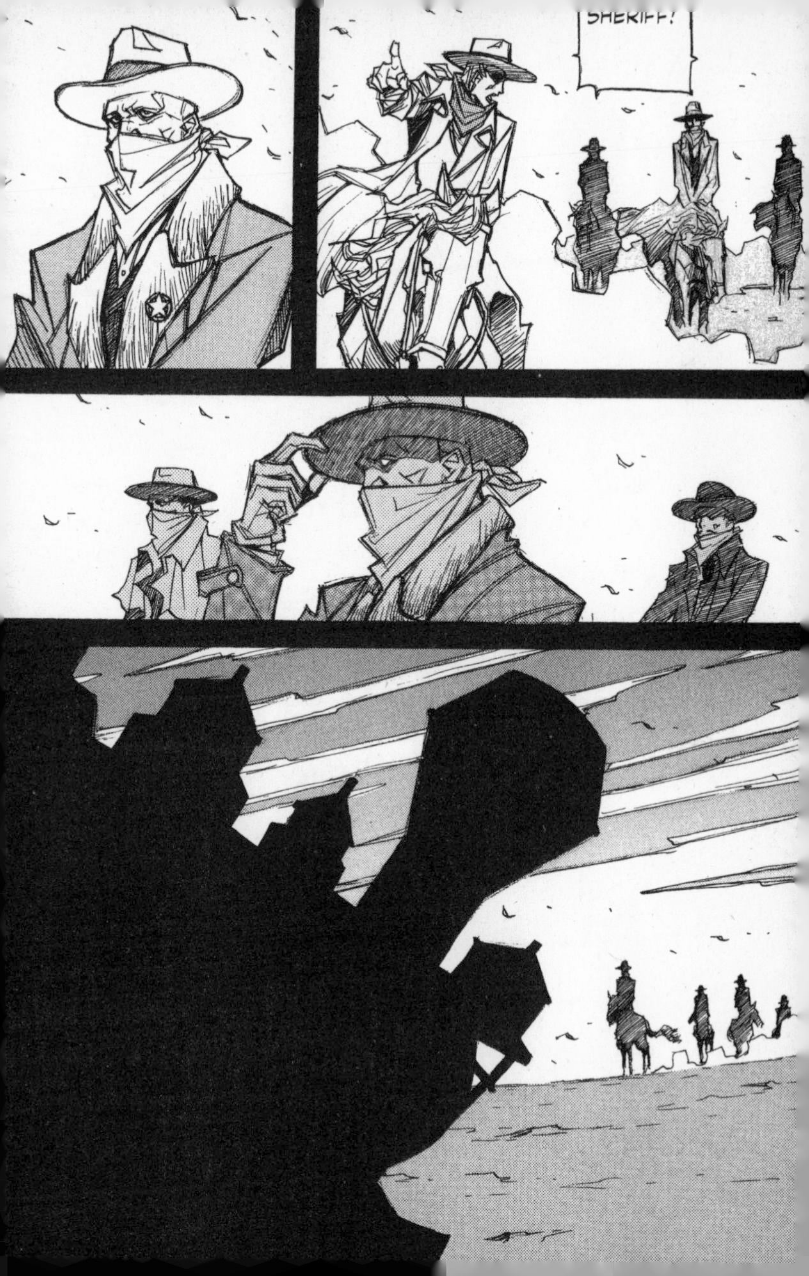
SHERIFF?

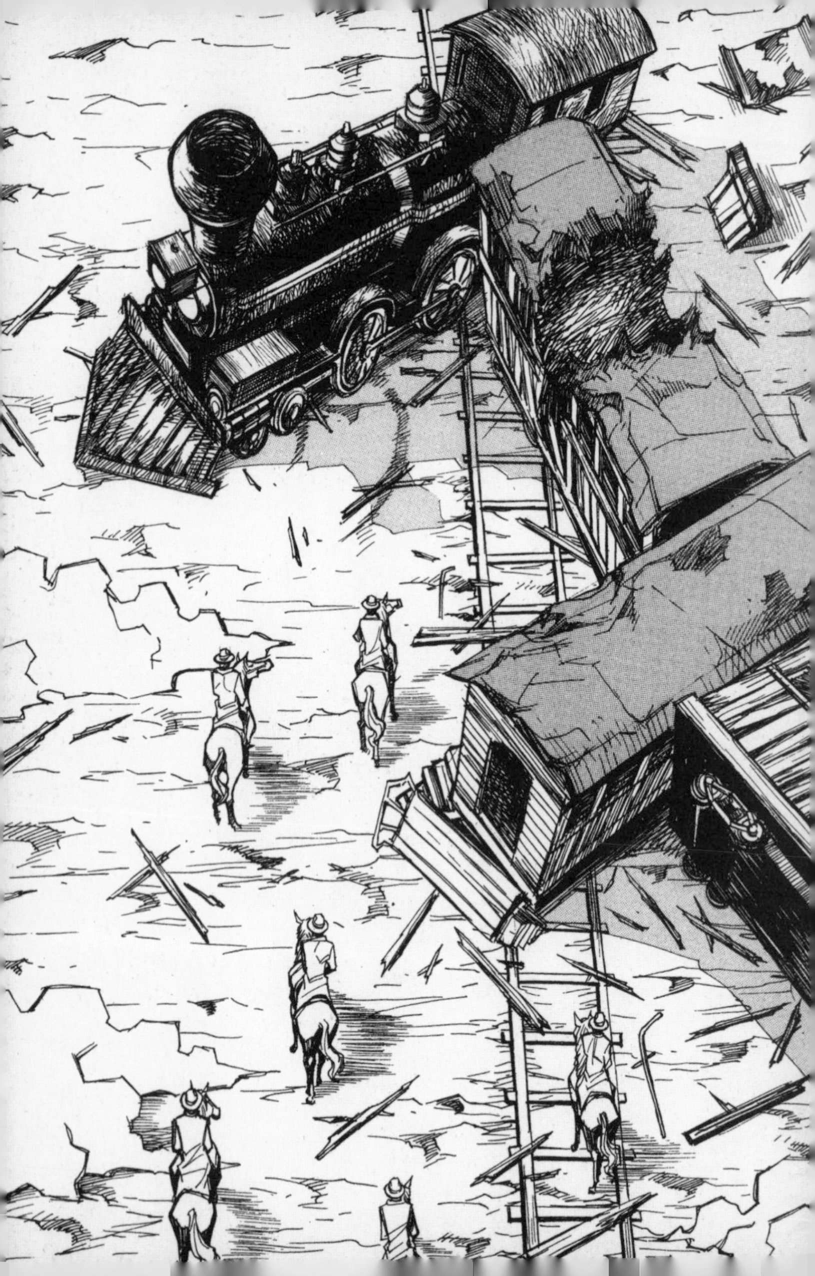

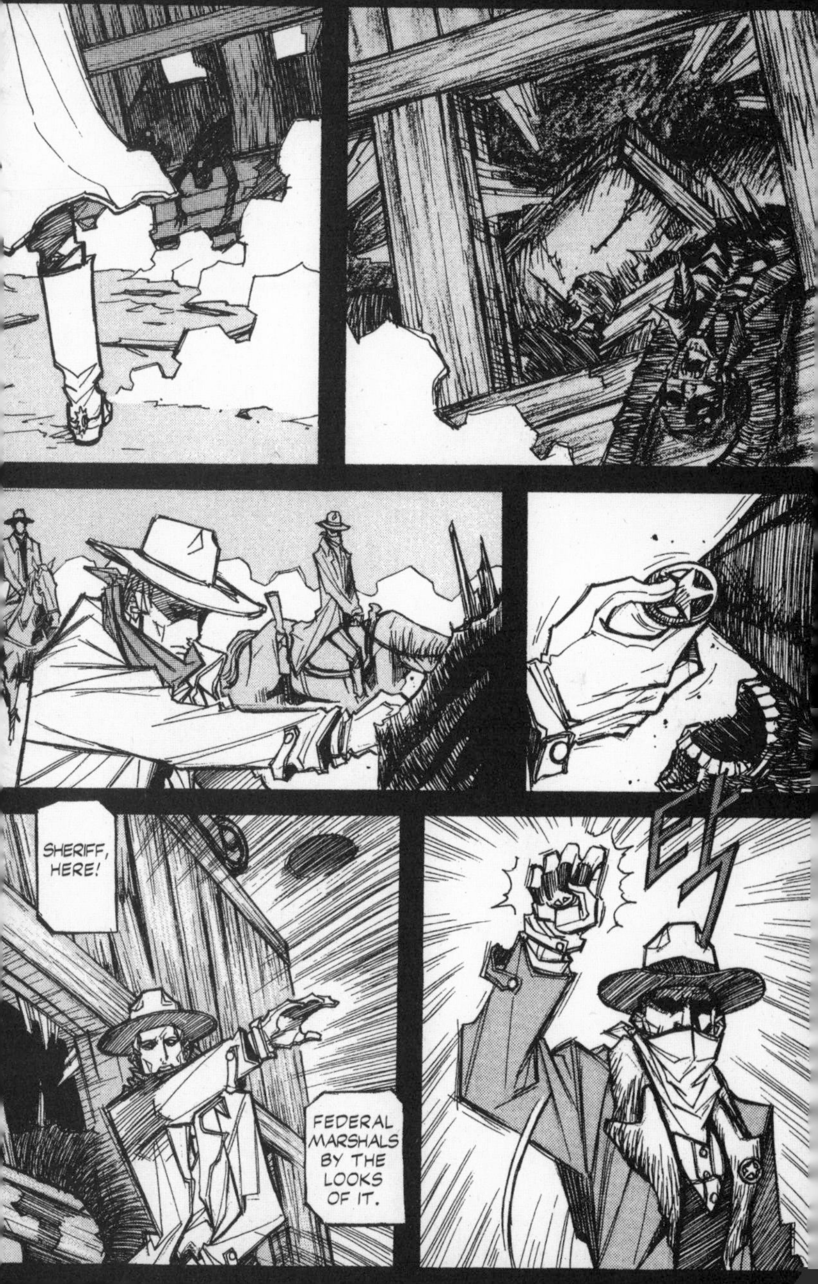
SHERIFF, HERE!
FEDERAL MARSHALS BY THE LOOKS OF IT.

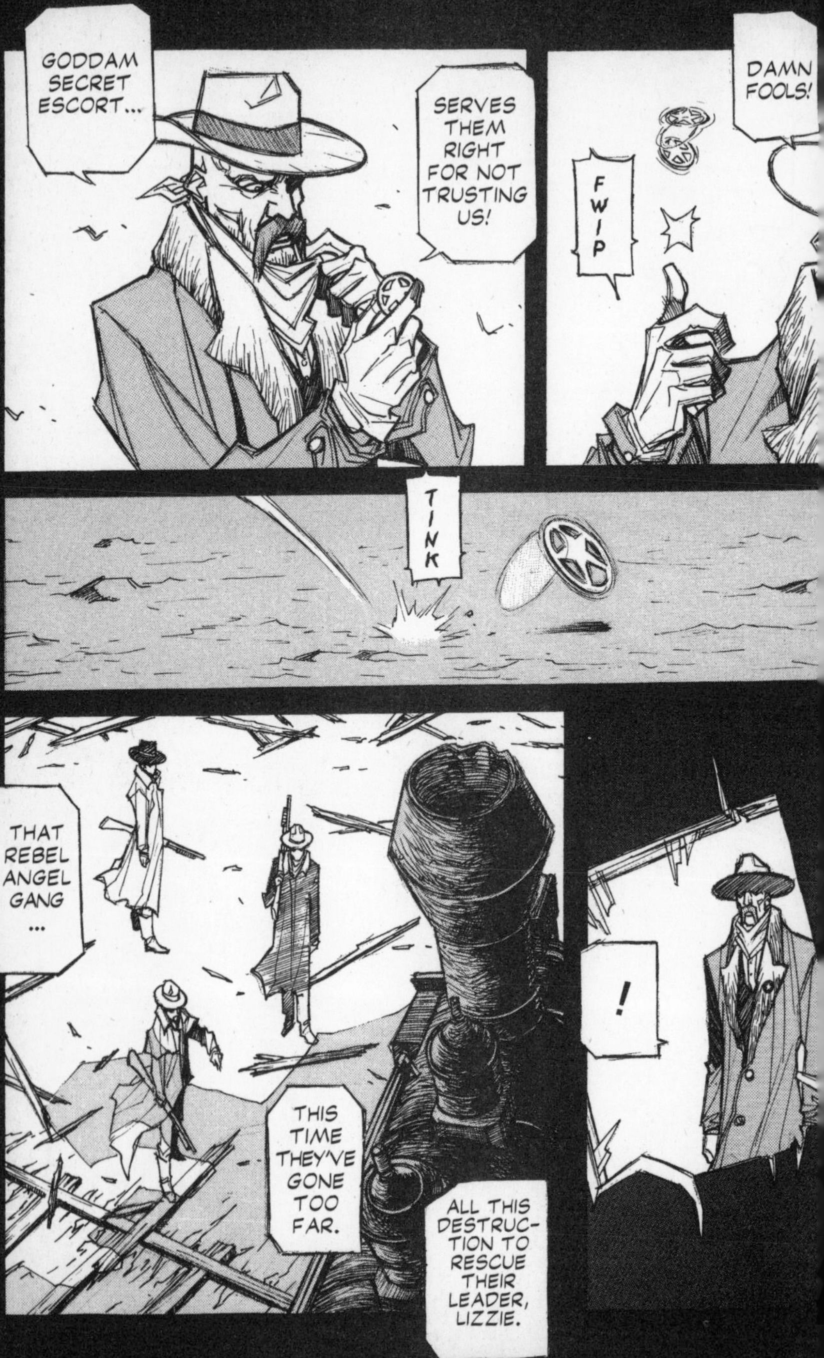
GODDAM SECRET ESCORT...
SERVES THEM RIGHT FOR NOT TRUSTING US!
DAMN FOOLS!
FWIP
TINK
THAT REBEL ANGEL GANG ...
THIS TIME THEY'VE GONE TOO FAR.
ALL THIS DESTRUCTION TO RESCUE THEIR LEADER, LIZZIE.
!

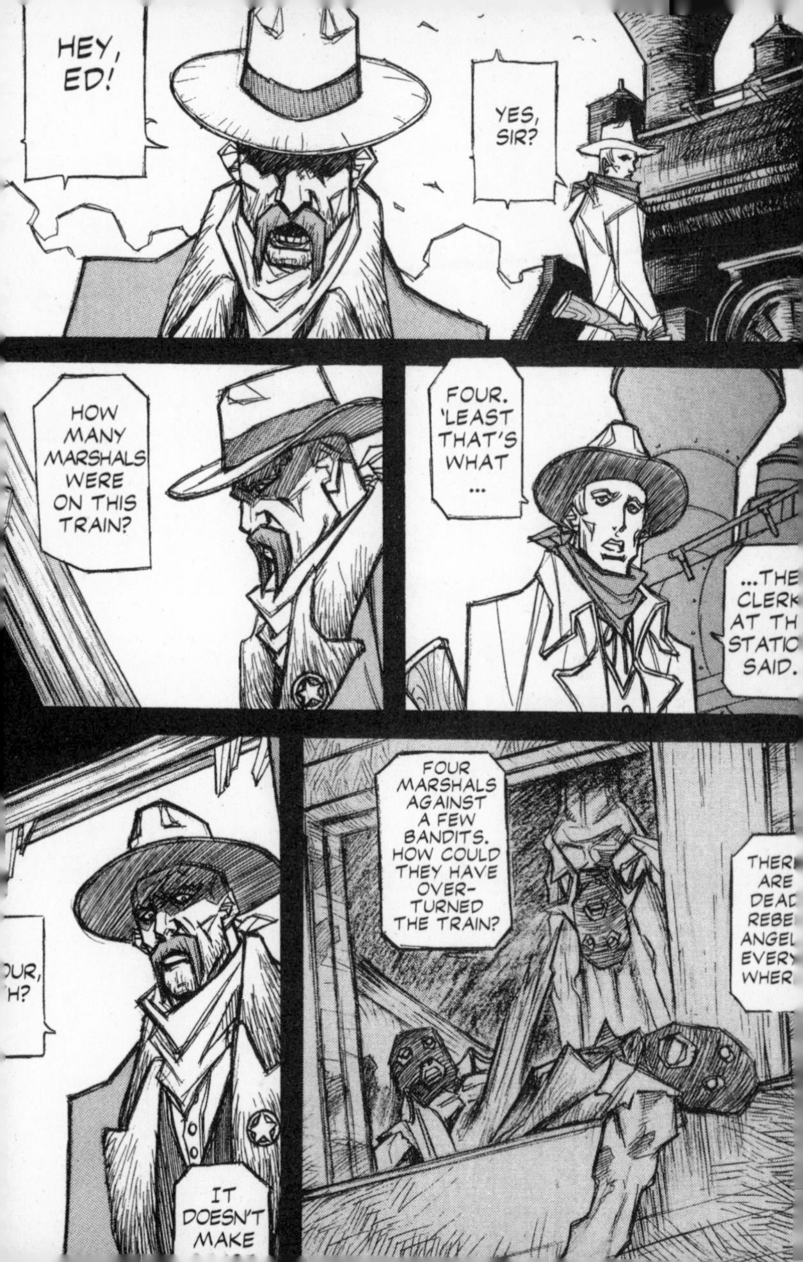

HEY, ED!
YES, SIR?
HOW MANY MARSHALS WERE ON THIS TRAIN?
FOUR. 'LEAST THAT'S WHAT ...
...THE CLERK AT TH STATIO SAID.
FOUR MARSHALS AGAINST A FEW BANDITS. HOW COULD THEY HAVE OVER-TURNED THE TRAIN?
THER ARE DEAD REBE ANGEL EVERY WHER
OUR, H?
IT DOESN'T MAKE

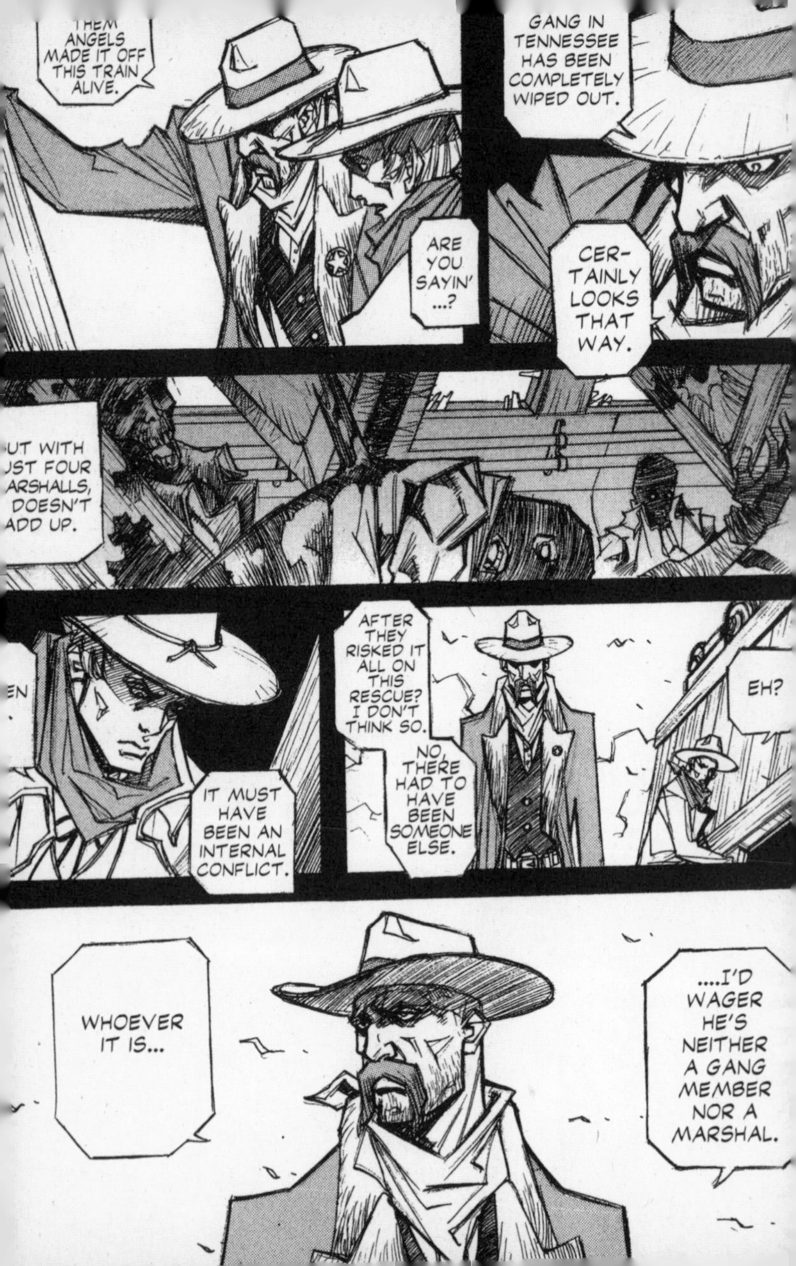
THEM ANGELS MADE IT OFF THIS TRAIN ALIVE.
ARE YOU SAYIN' ...?
GANG IN TENNESSEE HAS BEEN COMPLETELY WIPED OUT.
CER-TAINLY LOOKS THAT WAY.
UT WITH UST FOUR ARSHALLS, DOESN'T ADD UP.
EN
IT MUST HAVE BEEN AN INTERNAL CONFLICT.
AFTER THEY RISKED IT ALL ON THIS RESCUE? I DON'T THINK SO.
NO, THERE HAD TO HAVE BEEN SOMEONE ELSE.
EH?
WHOEVER IT IS...
....I'D WAGER HE'S NEITHER A GANG MEMBER NOR A MARSHAL.

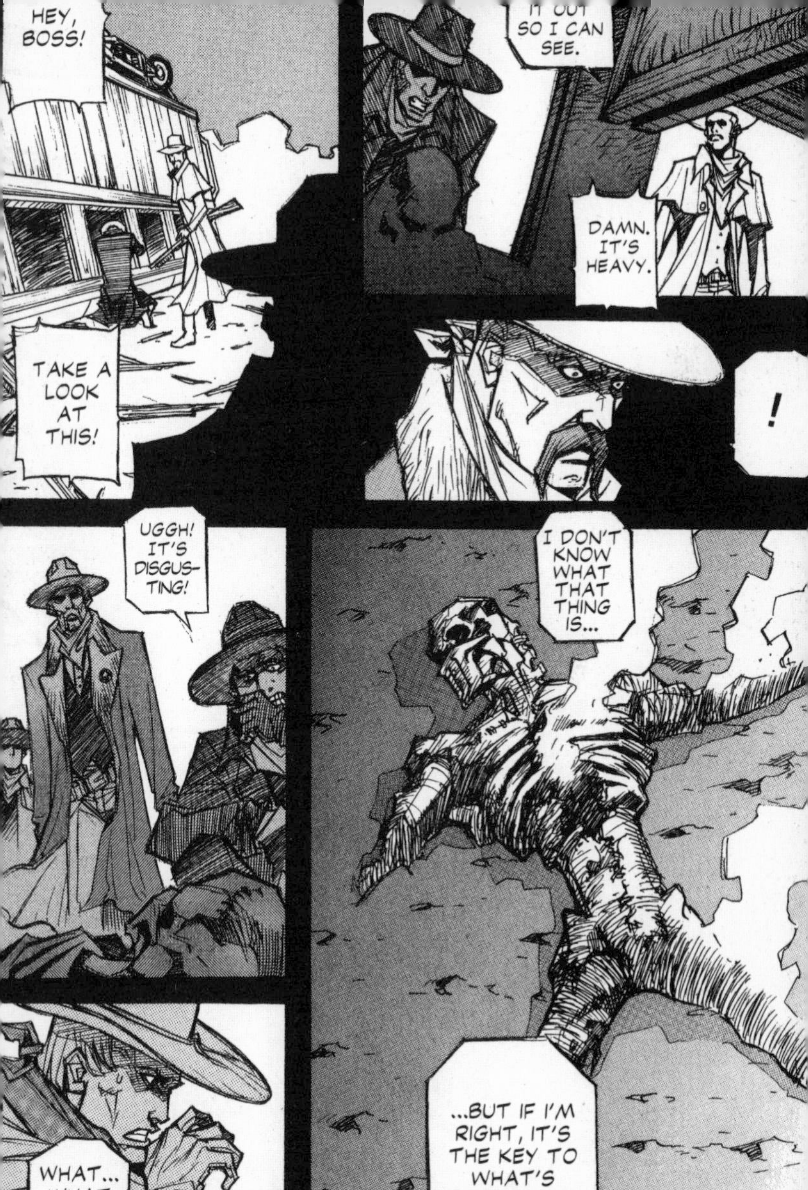

HEY, BOSS!
TAKE A LOOK AT THIS!
IT OUT SO I CAN SEE.
DAMN. IT'S HEAVY.
!
UGGH! IT'S DISGUSTING!
WHAT... WHAT THE HELL IS
I DON'T KNOW WHAT THAT THING IS...
...BUT IF I'M RIGHT, IT'S THE KEY TO WHAT'S BEHIND THIS MASSACRE.

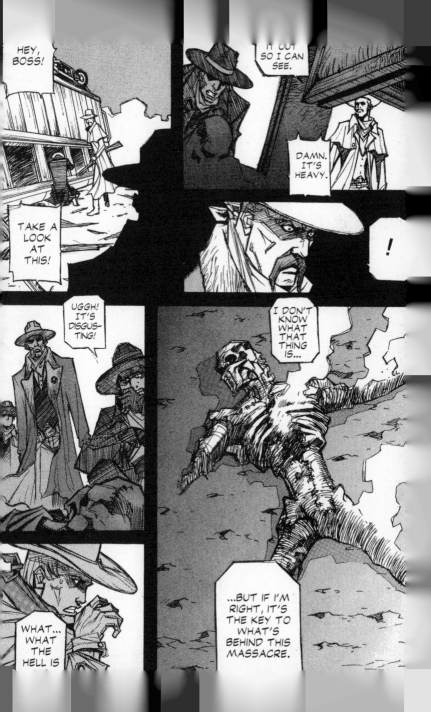

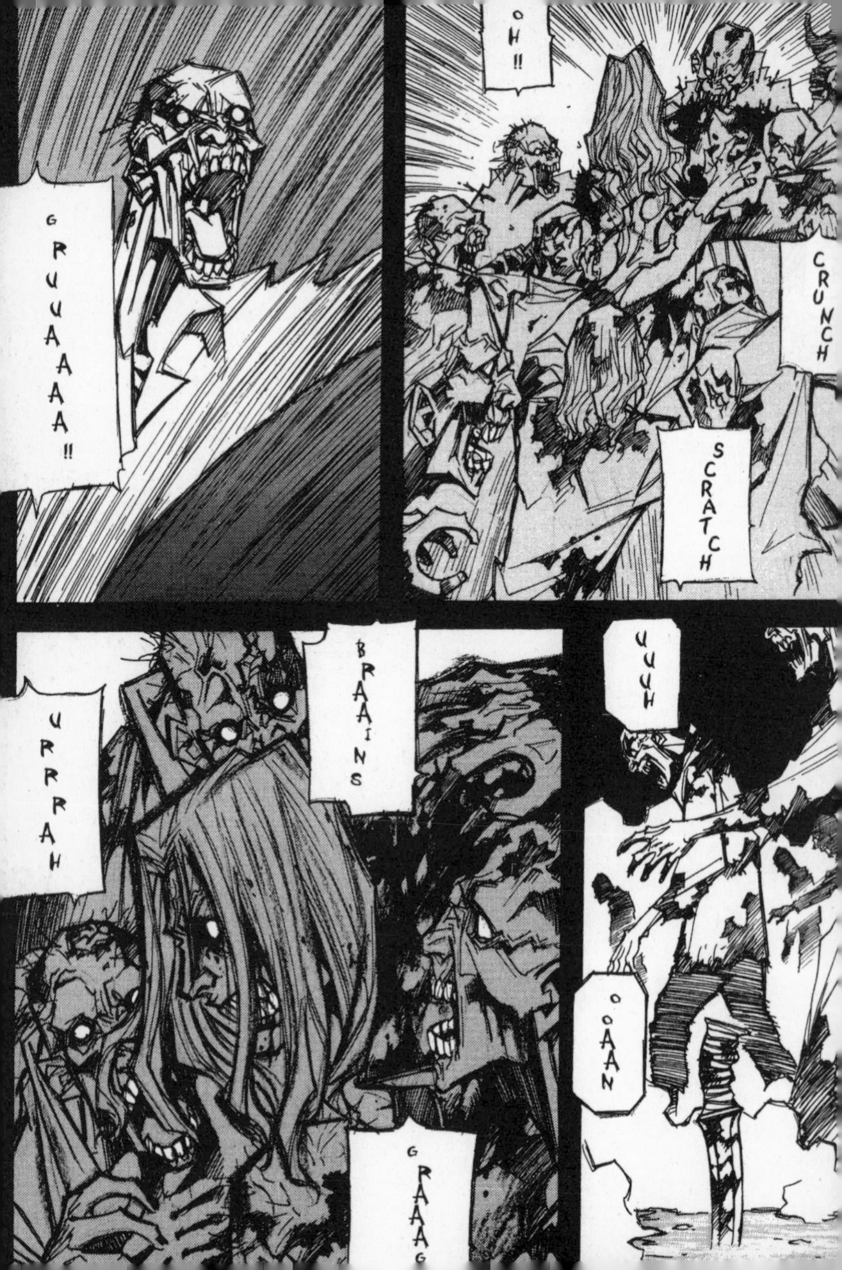
GRUUAAAA!!
OH!!
CRUNCH
SCRATCH
URRRAH
BRAAINS
GRAAAG
UUUH
OOAAN

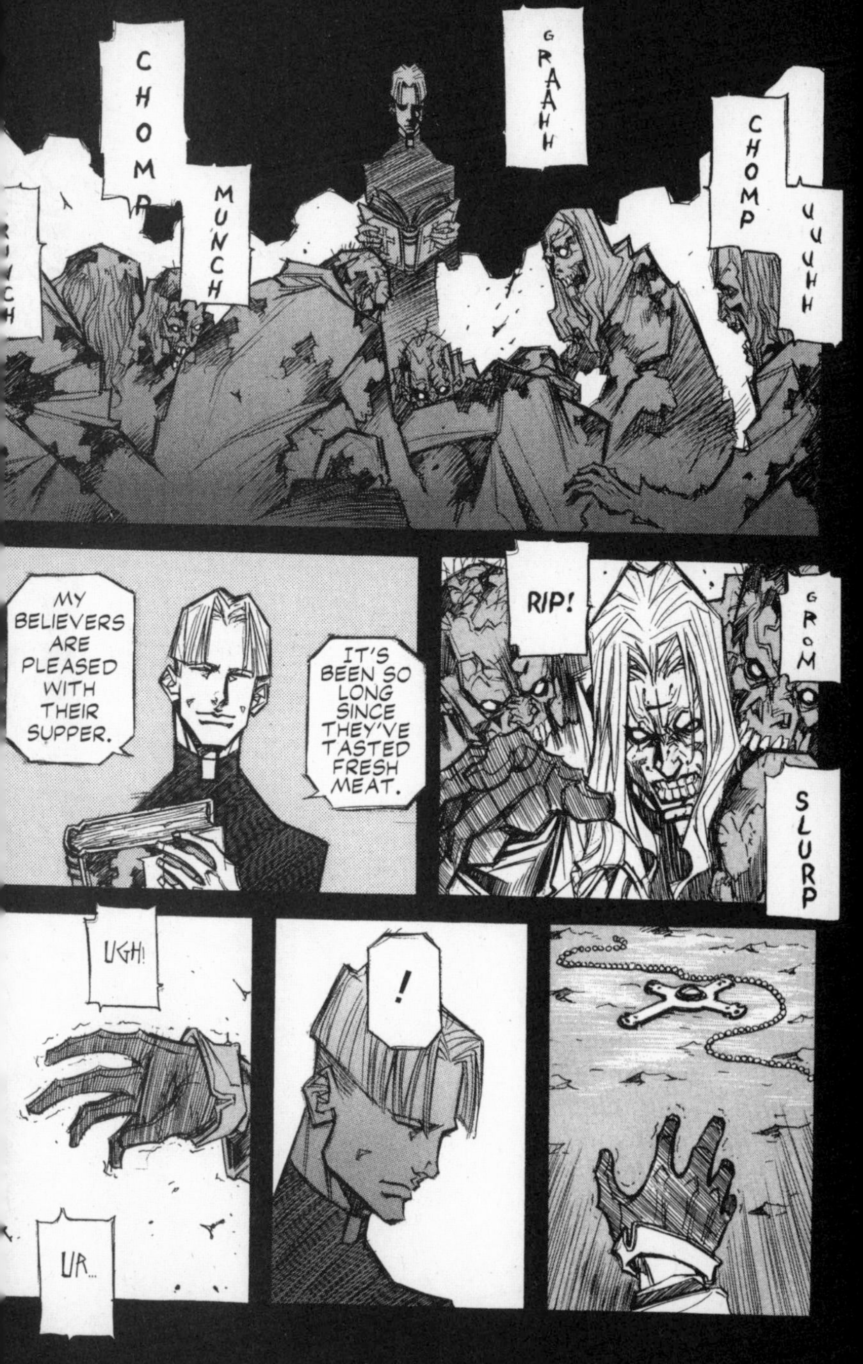
CHOMP
MUNCH
GRAAHH
CHOMP
UUUHH
MY BELIEVERS ARE PLEASED WITH THEIR SUPPER.
IT'S BEEN SO LONG SINCE THEY'VE TASTED FRESH MEAT.
RIP!
GROM
SLURP
UGH!
UR...
!

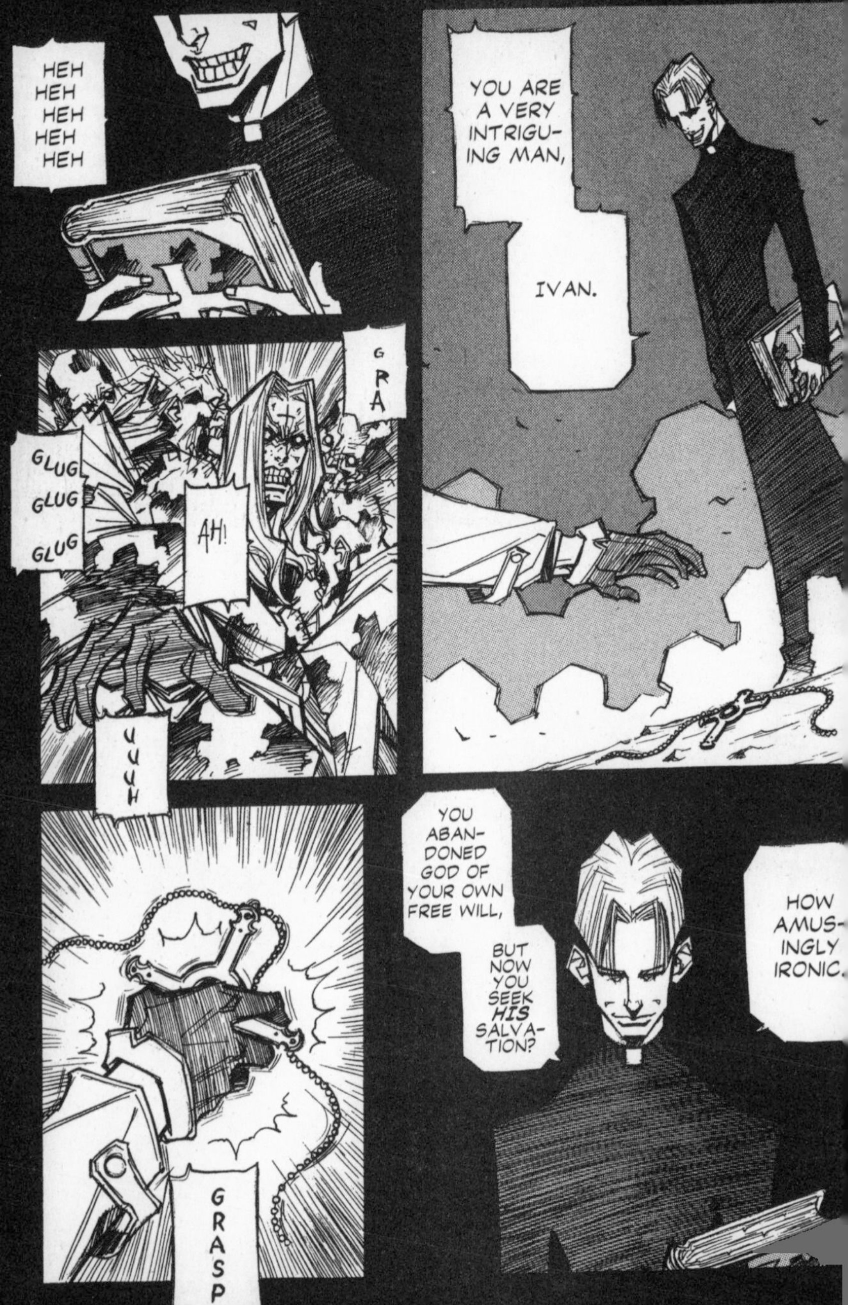
HEH HEH HEH HEH HEH
GRA
GLUG GLUG GLUG
AH!
UUUH
YOU ARE A VERY INTRIGUING MAN,
IVAN.
GRASP
YOU ABANDONED GOD OF YOUR OWN FREE WILL,
BUT NOW YOU SEEK ***HIS*** SALVATION?
HOW AMUSINGLY IRONIC.

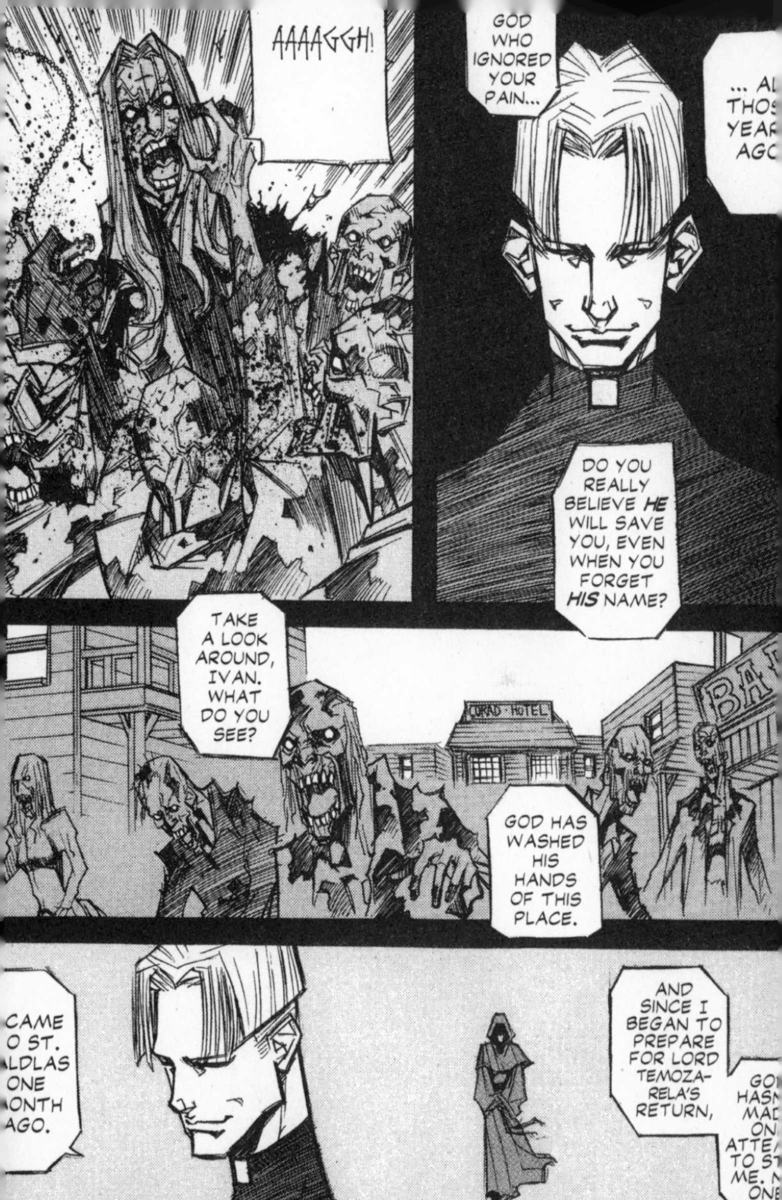
AAAAGGH!
GOD WHO IGNORED YOUR PAIN...
... AL THOS YEAR AGO
DO YOU REALLY BELIEVE HE WILL SAVE YOU, EVEN WHEN YOU FORGET HIS NAME?
TAKE A LOOK AROUND, IVAN. WHAT DO YOU SEE?
CURAD HOTEL
GOD HAS WASHED HIS HANDS OF THIS PLACE.
CAME O ST. ALDLAS ONE ONTH AGO.
AND SINCE I BEGAN TO PREPARE FOR LORD TEMOZA-RELA'S RETURN,
GO HASN MAD ON ATTEN TO ST ME. N ONE

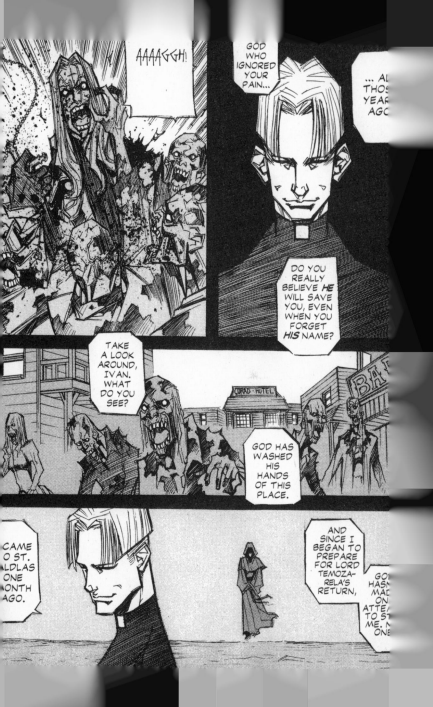

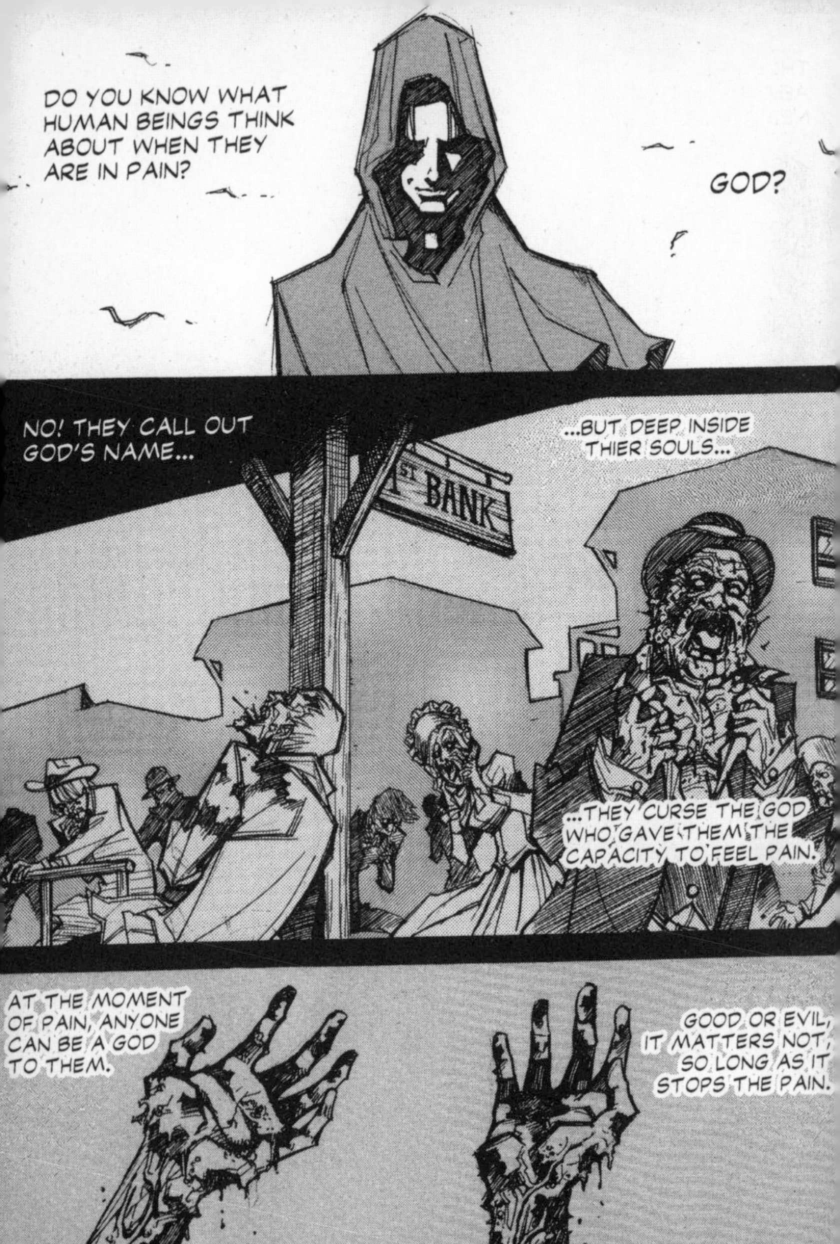
DO YOU KNOW WHAT HUMAN BEINGS THINK ABOUT WHEN THEY ARE IN PAIN?
GOD?
NO! THEY CALL OUT GOD'S NAME...
...BUT DEEP INSIDE THIER SOULS...
1ST BANK
...THEY CURSE THE GOD WHO GAVE THEM THE CAPACITY TO FEEL PAIN.
AT THE MOMENT OF PAIN, ANYONE CAN BE A GOD TO THEM.
GOOD OR EVIL, IT MATTERS NOT, SO LONG AS IT STOPS THE PAIN.

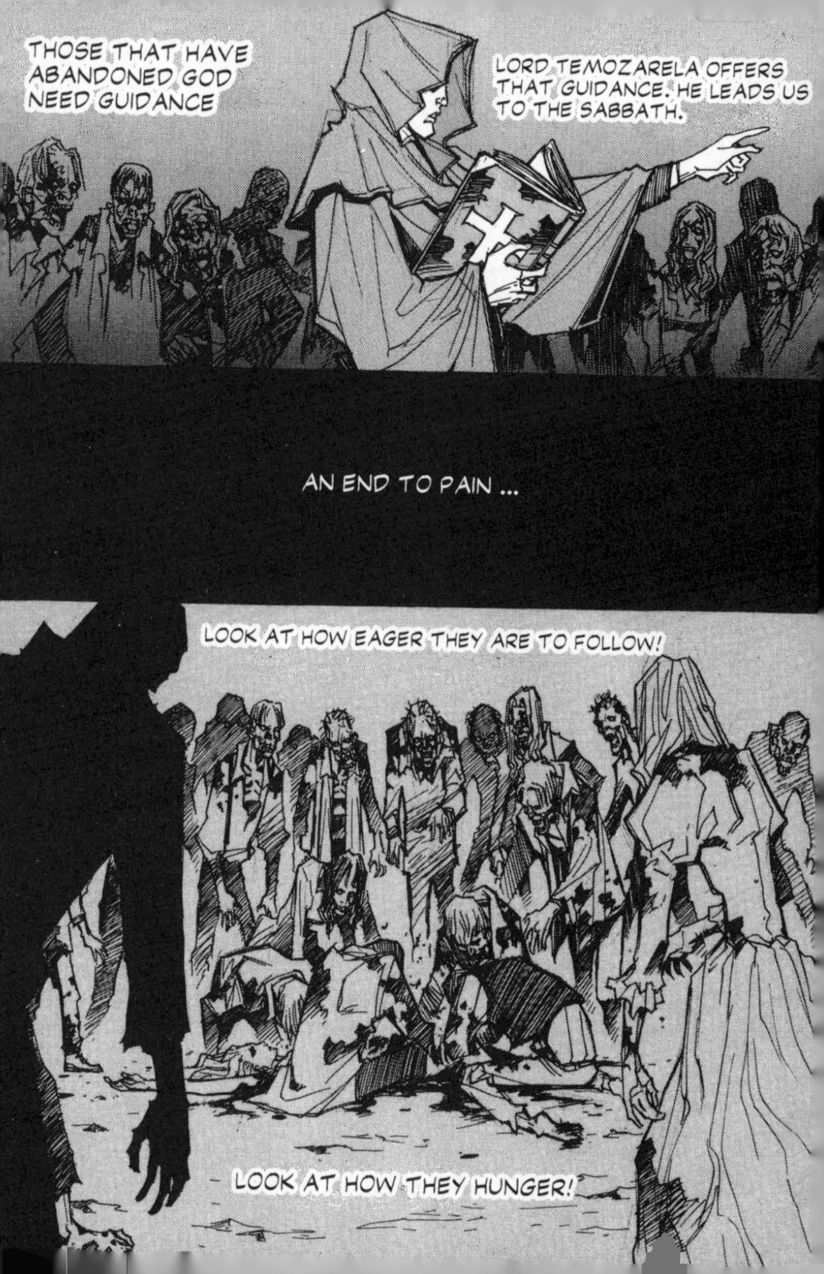
THOSE THAT HAVE ABANDONED GOD NEED GUIDANCE
LORD TEMOZARELA OFFERS THAT GUIDANCE. HE LEADS US TO THE SABBATH.
AN END TO PAIN ...
LOOK AT HOW EAGER THEY ARE TO FOLLOW!
LOOK AT HOW THEY HUNGER!

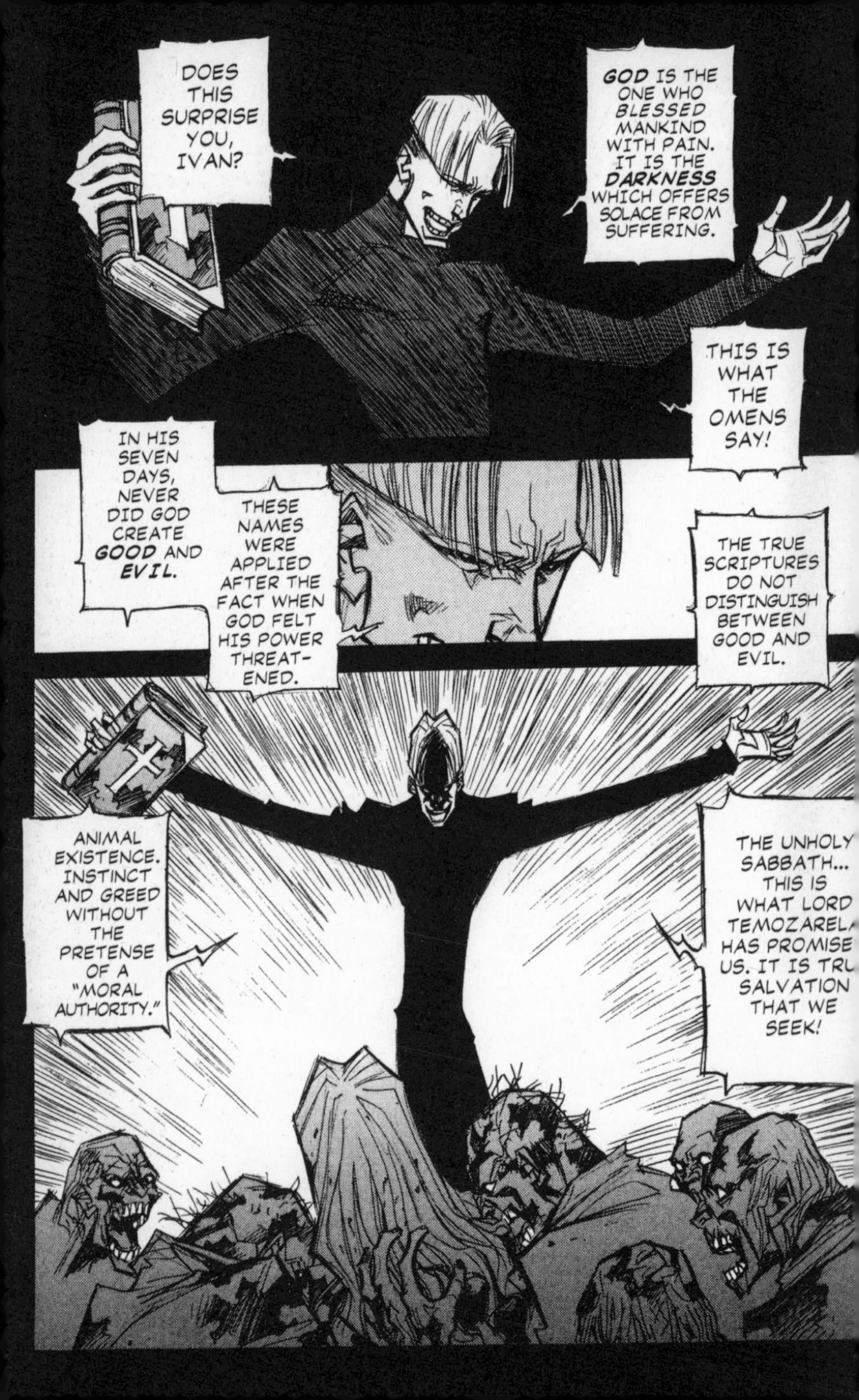
DOES THIS SURPRISE YOU, IVAN?
GOD IS THE ONE WHO BLESSED MANKIND WITH PAIN. IT IS THE DARKNESS WHICH OFFERS SOLACE FROM SUFFERING.
THIS IS WHAT THE OMENS SAY!
IN HIS SEVEN DAYS, NEVER DID GOD CREATE GOOD AND EVIL.
THESE NAMES WERE APPLIED AFTER THE FACT WHEN GOD FELT HIS POWER THREAT-ENED.
THE TRUE SCRIPTURES DO NOT DISTINGUISH BETWEEN GOOD AND EVIL.
ANIMAL EXISTENCE. INSTINCT AND GREED WITHOUT THE PRETENSE OF A "MORAL AUTHORITY."
THE UNHOLY SABBATH... THIS IS WHAT LORD TEMOZAREL HAS PROMISE US. IT IS TRU SALVATION THAT WE SEEK!

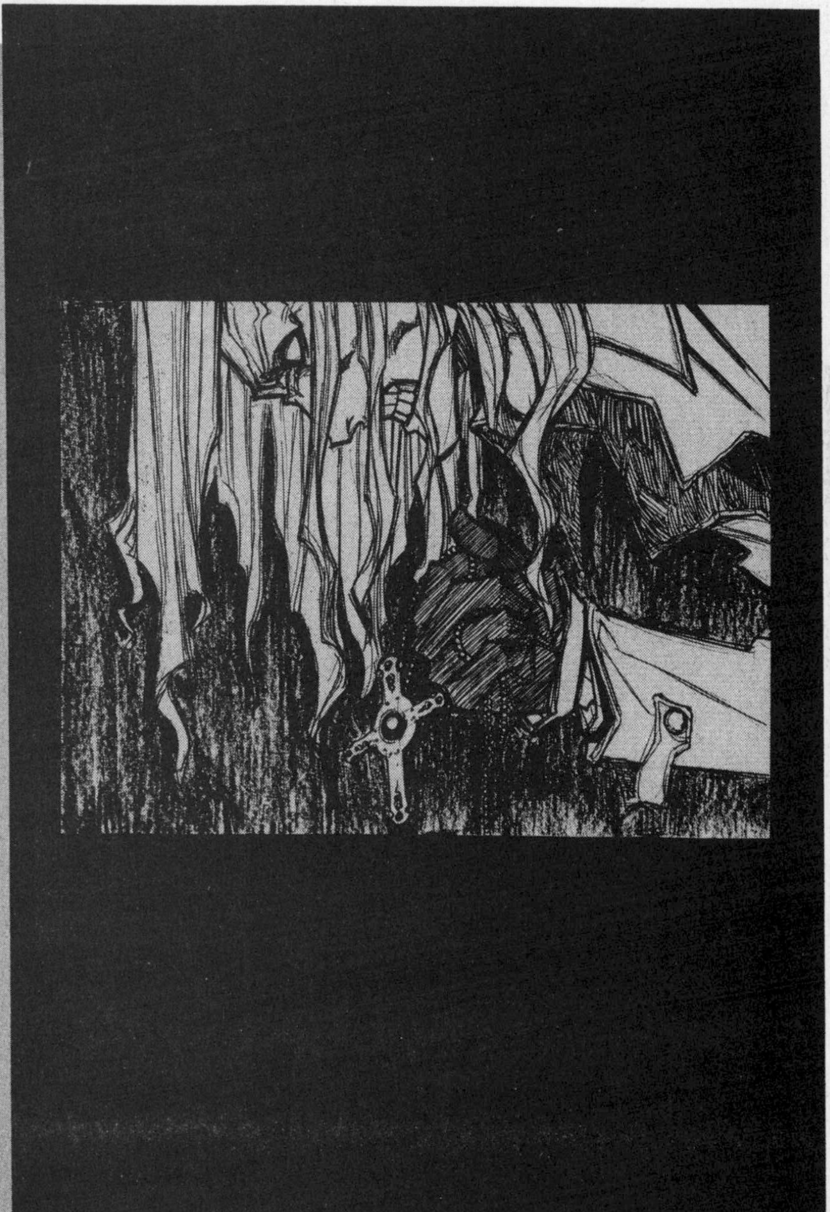

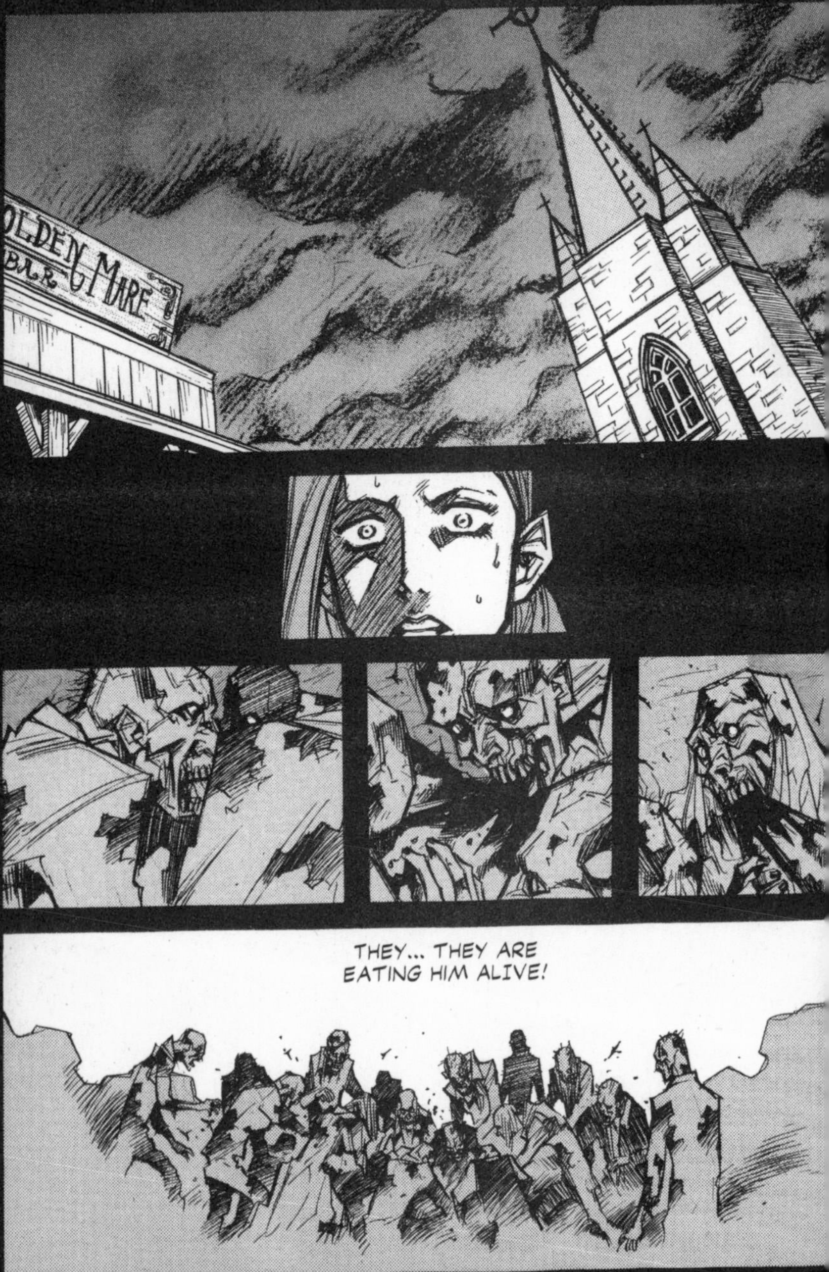
OLDEN MARE
BAR
THEY... THEY ARE EATING HIM ALIVE!

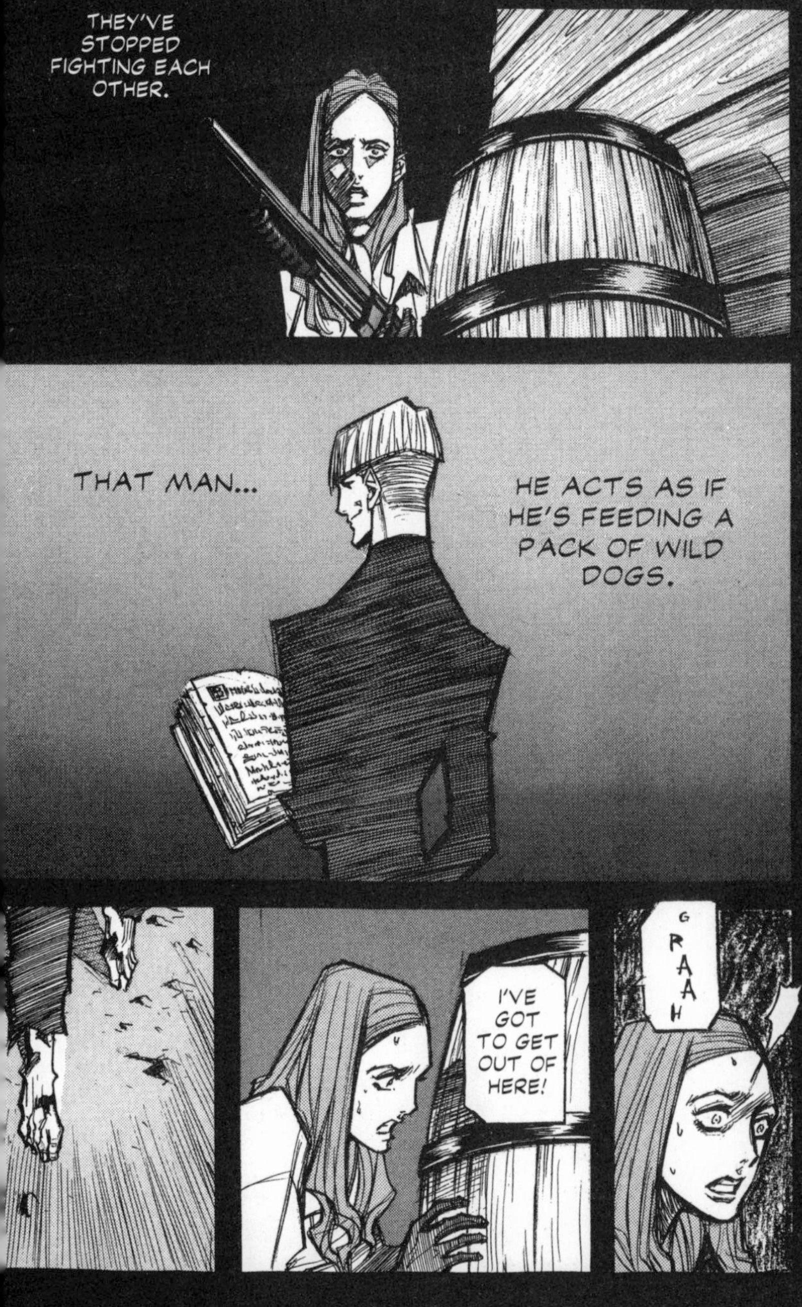
THEY'VE STOPPED FIGHTING EACH OTHER.
THAT MAN...
HE ACTS AS IF HE'S FEEDING A PACK OF WILD DOGS.
I'VE GOT TO GET OUT OF HERE!
GRAAH

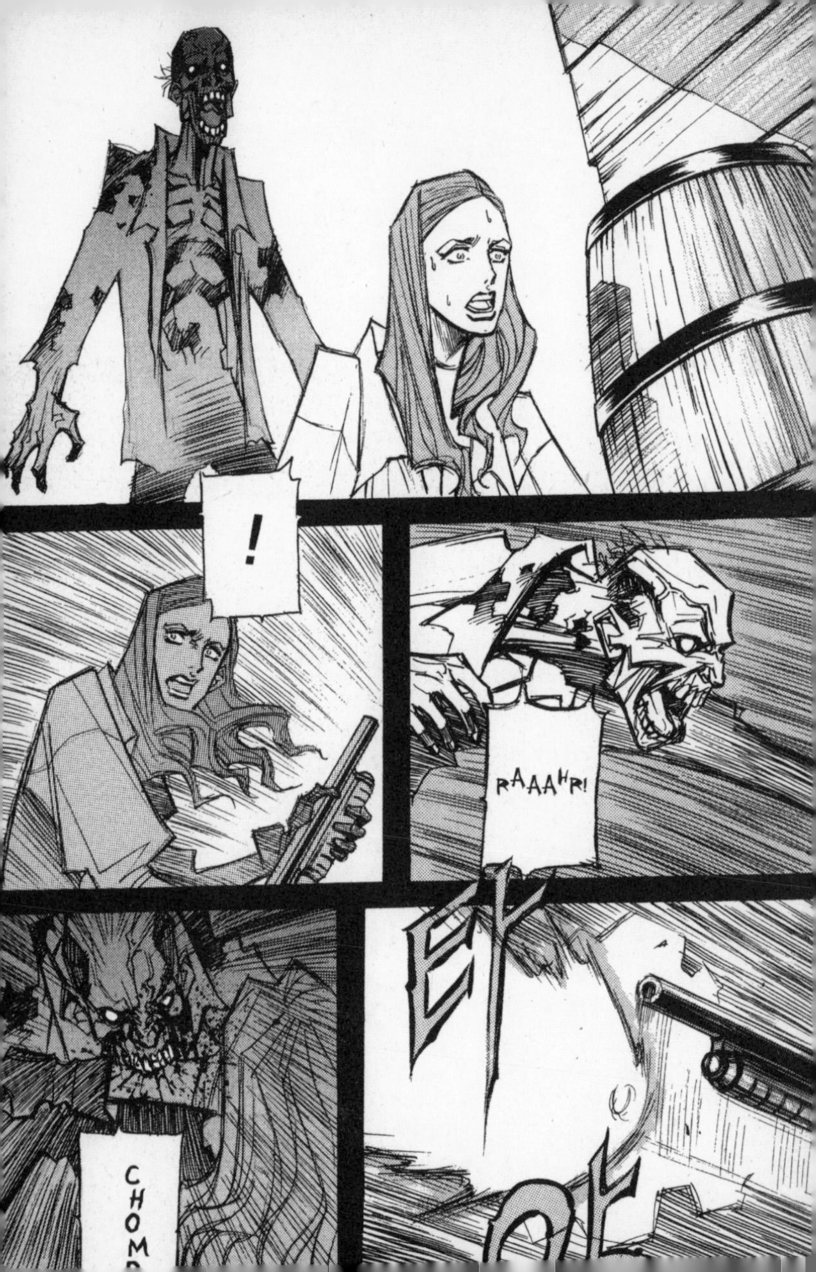
!
RAAAHR!
CHOM

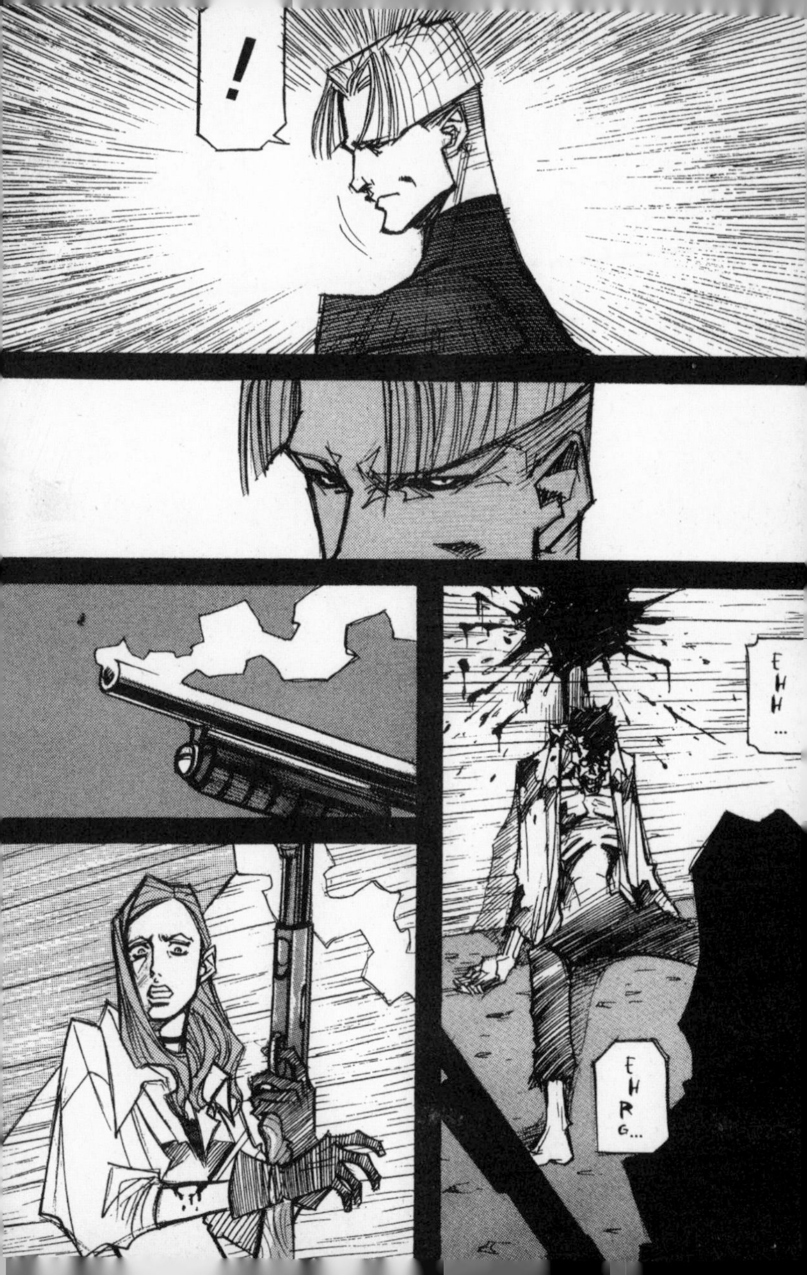
!
EHH...
EHRG...

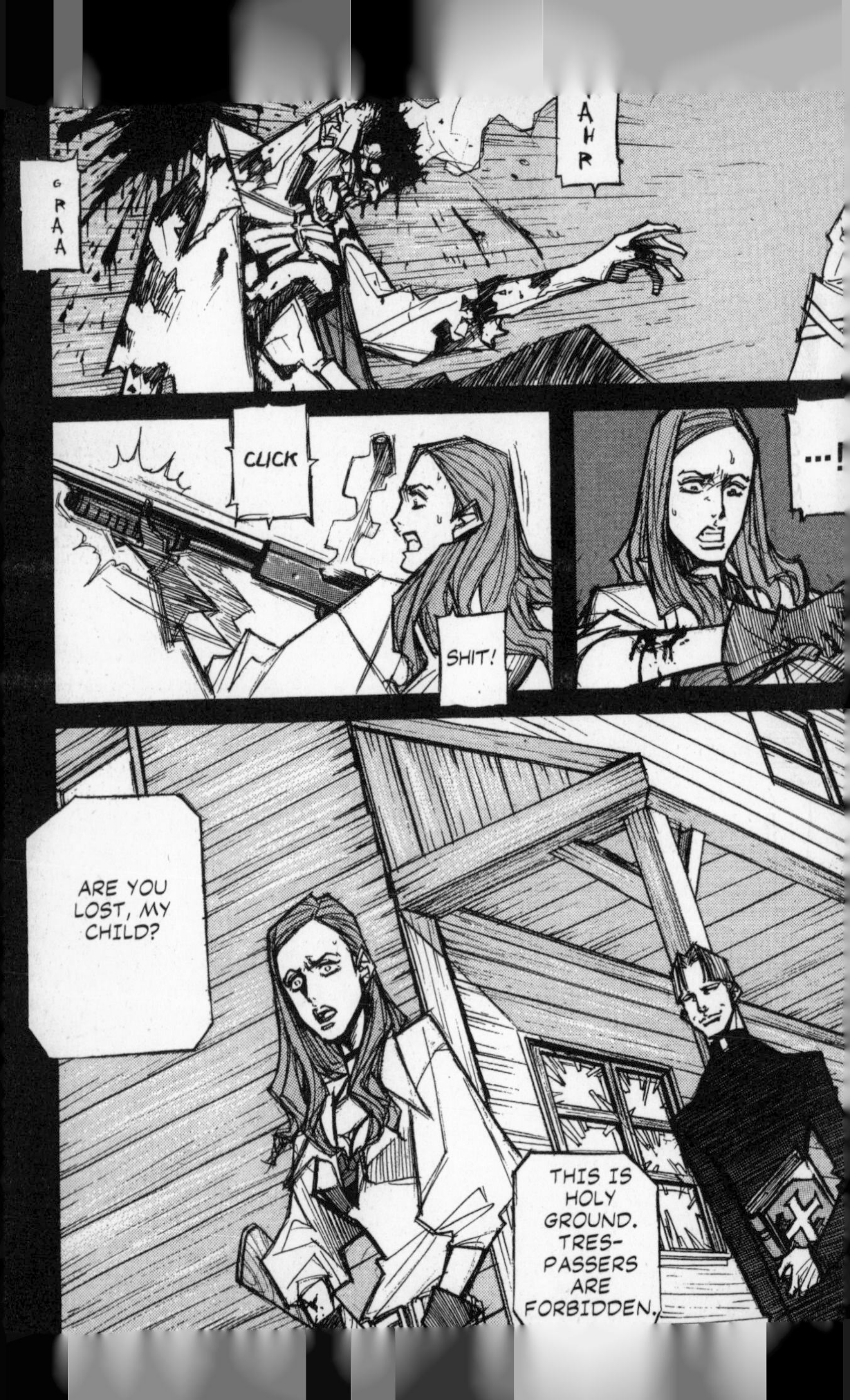
GRAA
AHR
CLICK
SHIT!
...!
ARE YOU LOST, MY CHILD?
THIS IS HOLY GROUND. TRES-PASSERS ARE FORBIDDEN.

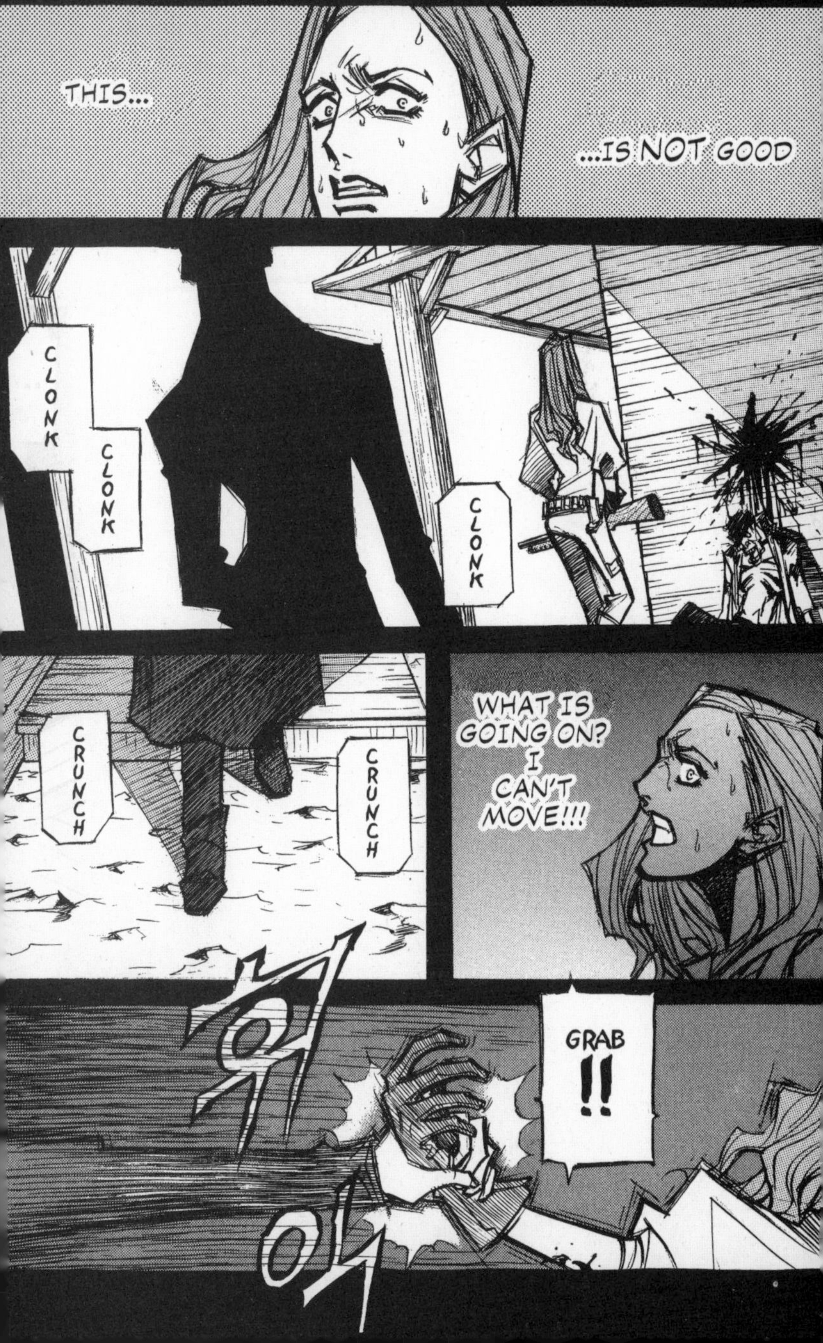
THIS...
...IS NOT GOOD
CLONK
CLONK
CLONK
CRUNCH
CRUNCH
WHAT IS GOING ON? I CAN'T MOVE!!!
GRAB !!

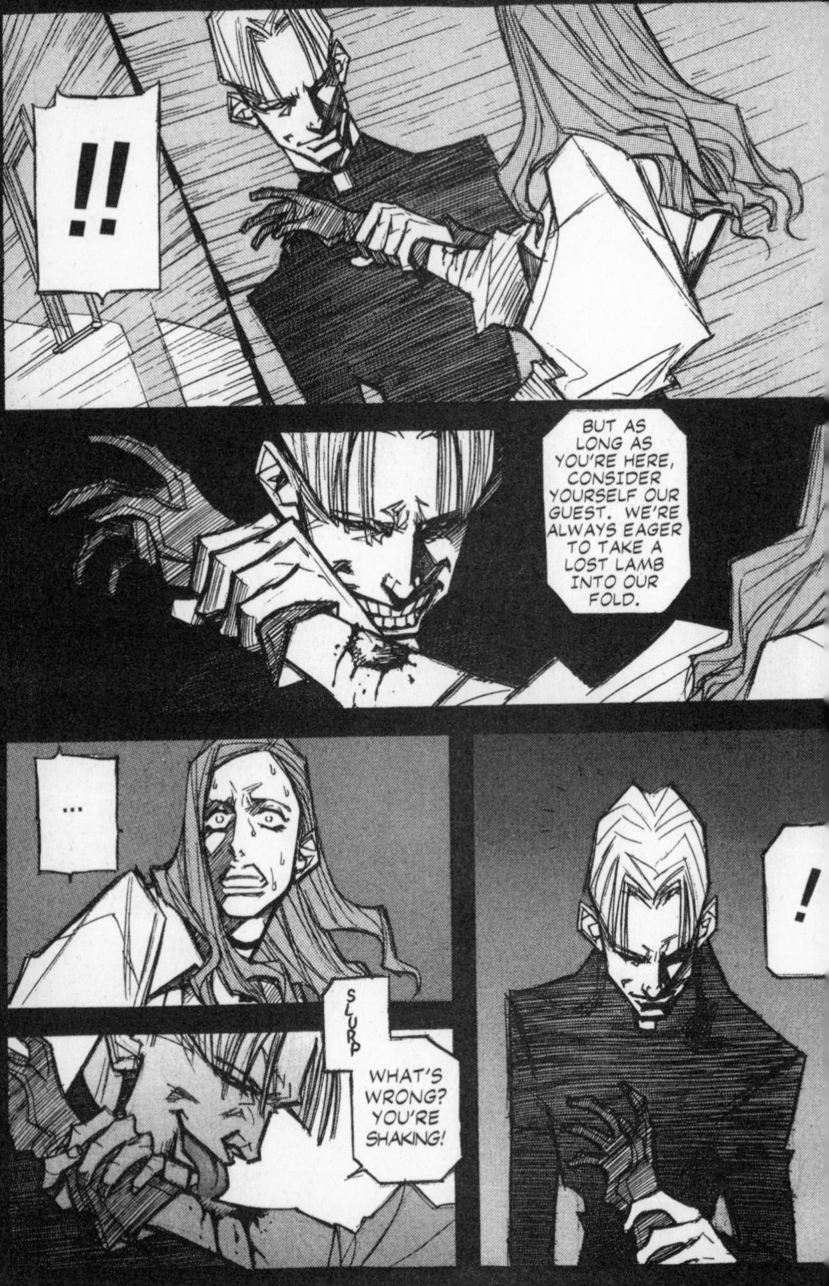
!!
BUT AS LONG AS YOU'RE HERE, CONSIDER YOURSELF OUR GUEST. WE'RE ALWAYS EAGER TO TAKE A LOST LAMB INTO OUR FOLD.
...
SLURP
WHAT'S WRONG? YOU'RE SHAKING!
!

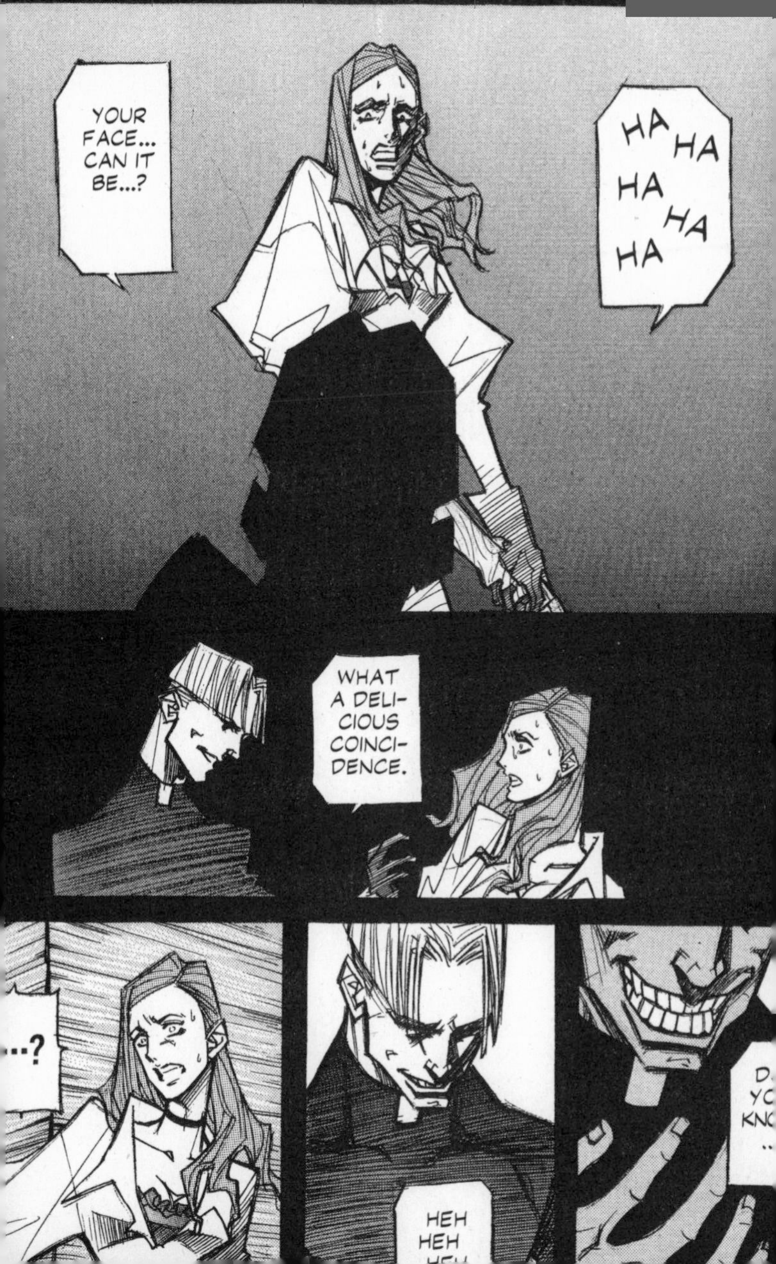
YOUR FACE... CAN IT BE...?
HA HA HA HA HA
WHAT A DELICIOUS COINCIDENCE.
...?
HEH HEH

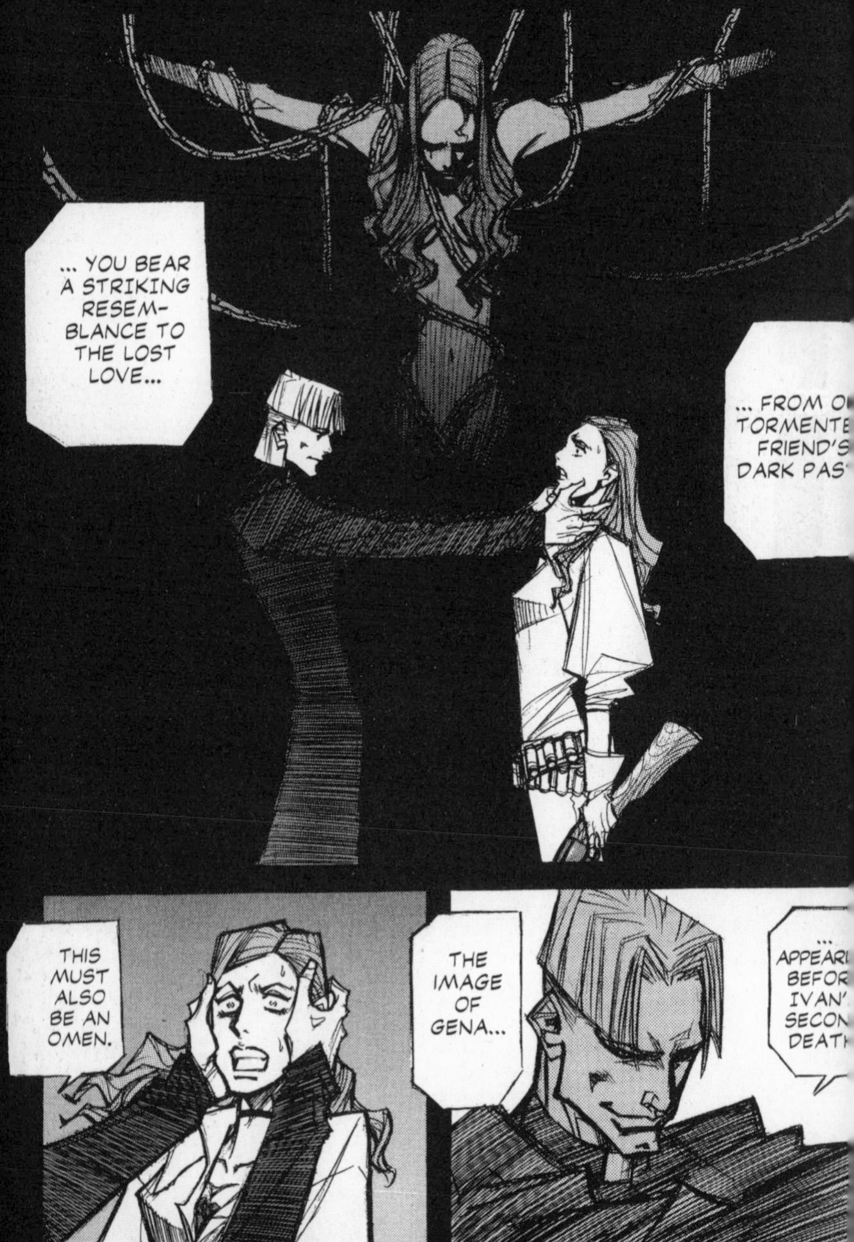
... YOU BEAR A STRIKING RESEM-BLANCE TO THE LOST LOVE...
... FROM O TORMENTE FRIEND'S DARK PAS
THIS MUST ALSO BE AN OMEN.
THE IMAGE OF GENA...
... APPEAR BEFOR IVAN' SECON DEATH

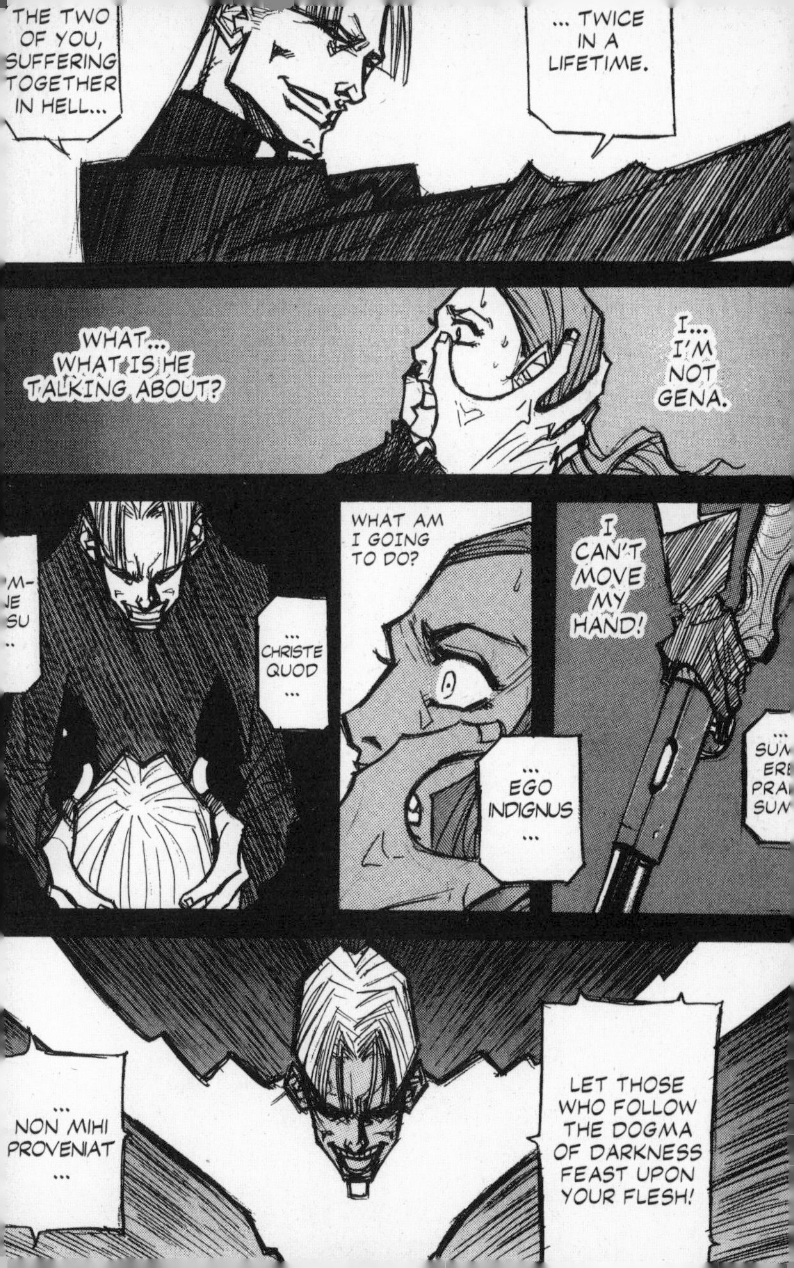
THE TWO OF YOU, SUFFERING TOGETHER IN HELL...
... TWICE IN A LIFETIME.
WHAT... WHAT IS HE TALKING ABOUT?
I... I'M NOT GENA.
... CHRISTE QUOD ...
WHAT AM I GOING TO DO?
... EGO INDIGNUS ...
I CAN'T MOVE MY HAND!
... NON MIHI PROVENIAT ...
LET THOSE WHO FOLLOW THE DOGMA OF DARKNESS FEAST UPON YOUR FLESH!

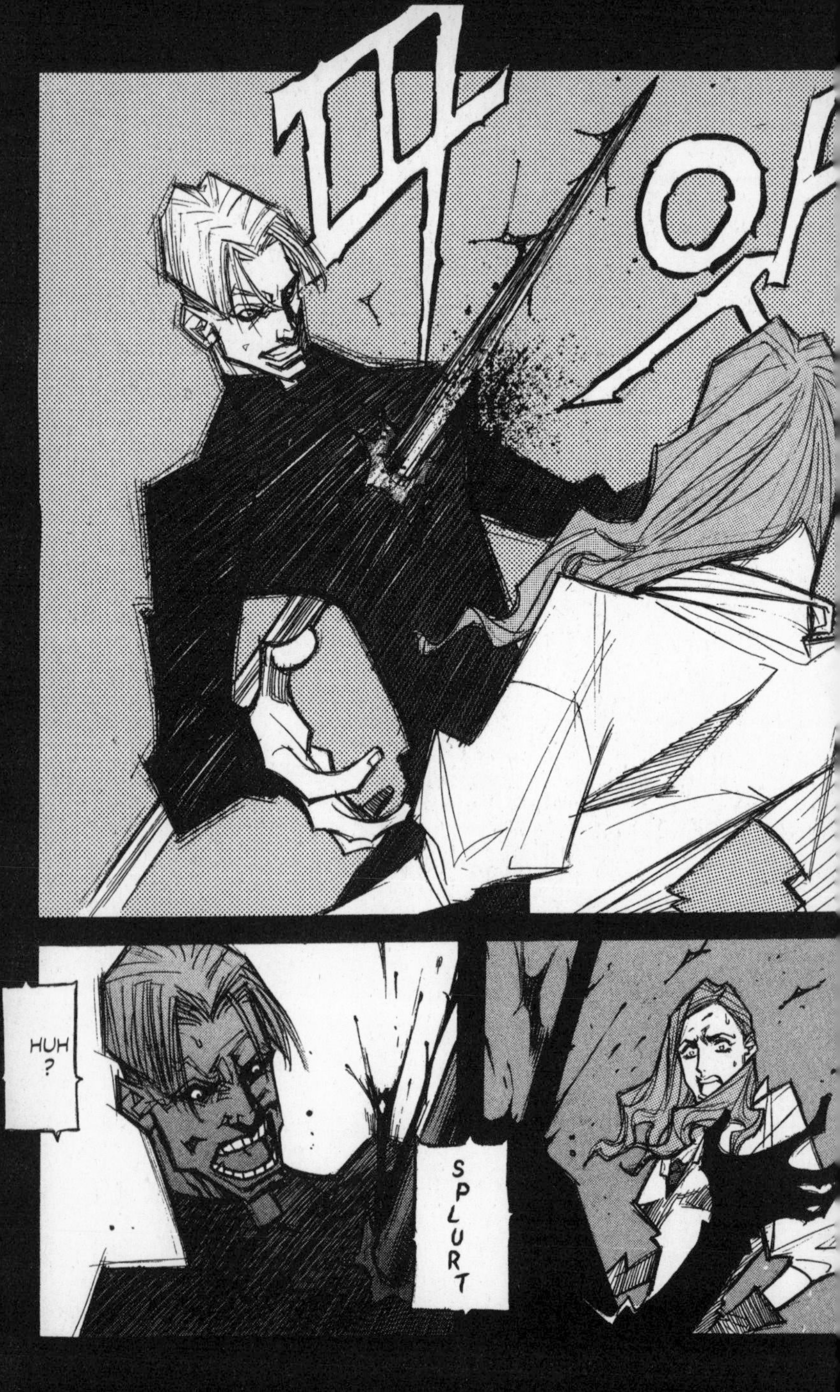
HUH ?
SPLURT

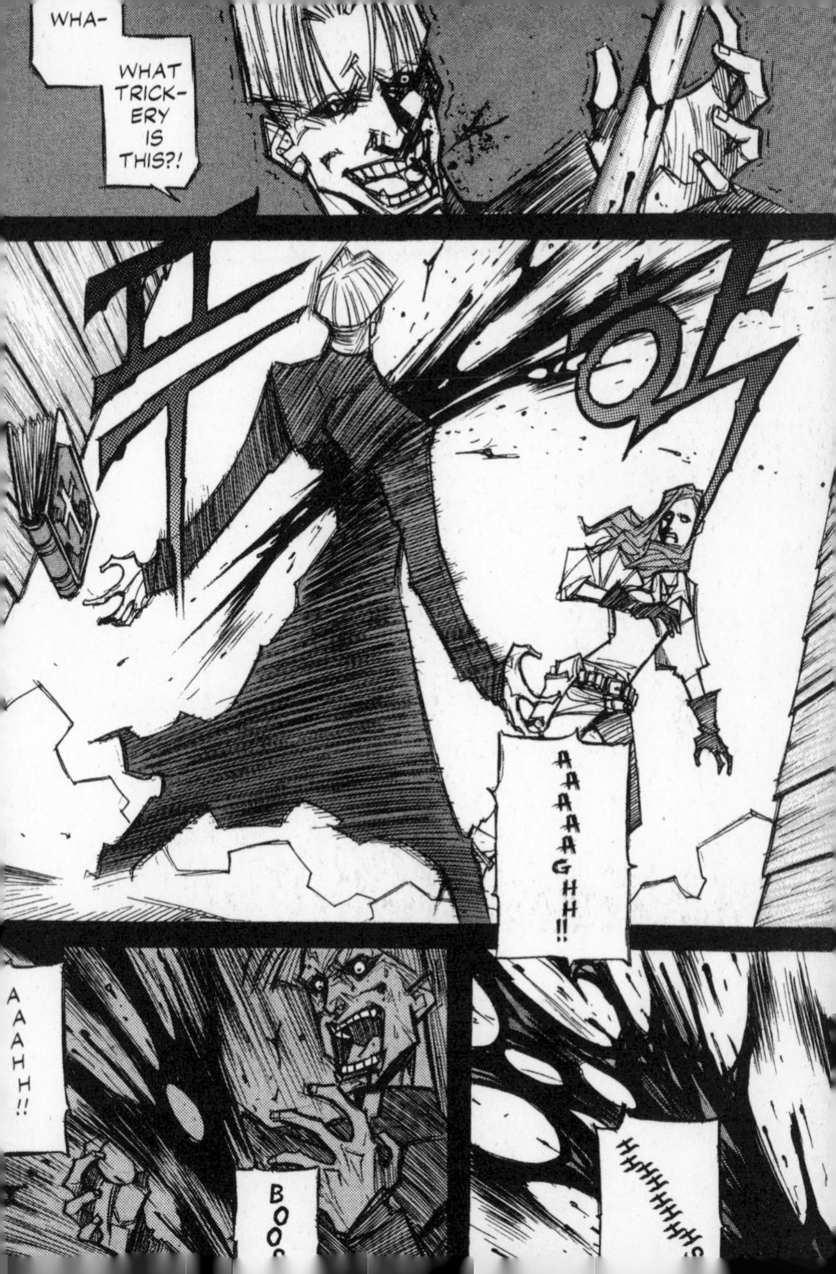
WHA-
WHAT TRICK-ERY IS THIS?!
AAAAAAGHH!!
AAAHH!!
BOO
HHHHHHHHH

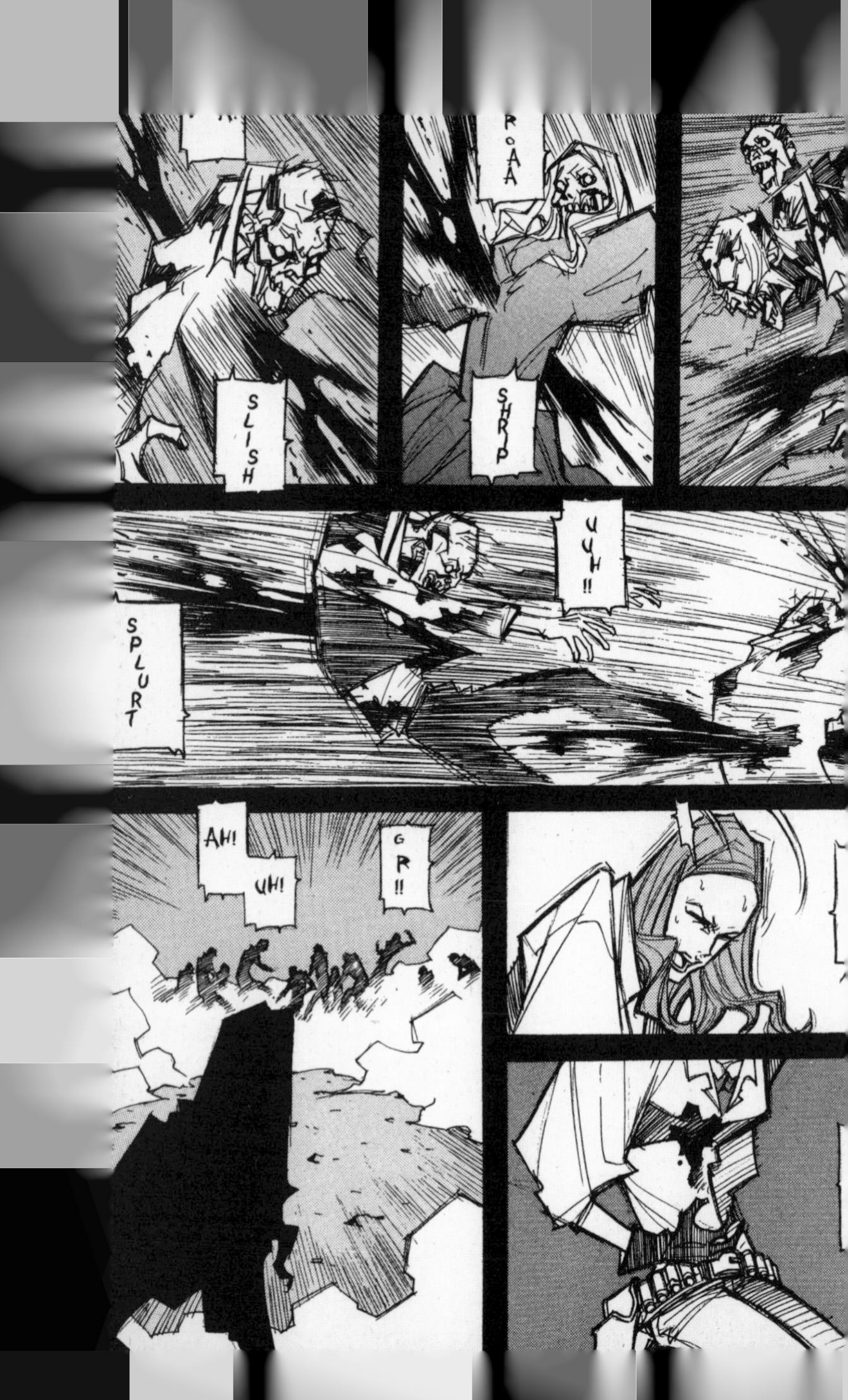
SLISH
ROAA
SHRIP
SPLURT
UUH!!
AH!
UH!
GR!!

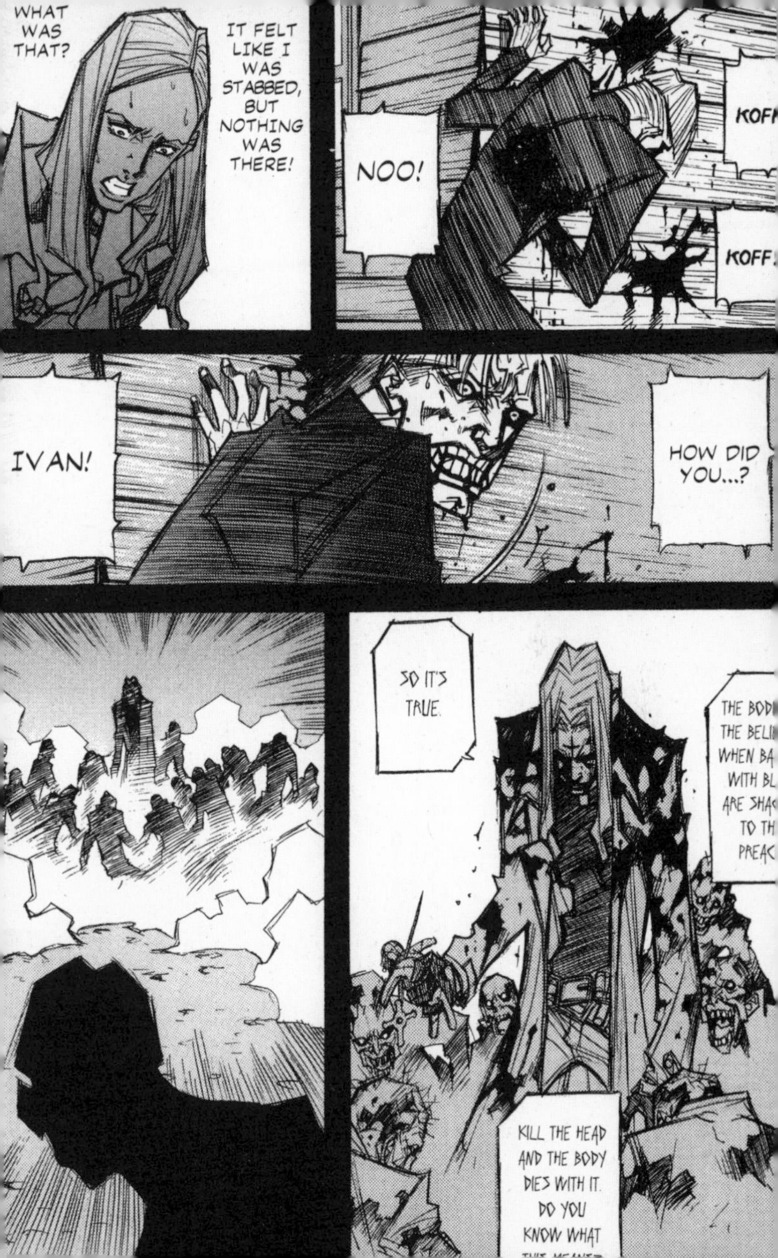
NOO!
KOFF
KOFF!
WHAT WAS THAT?
IT FELT LIKE I WAS STABBED, BUT NOTHING WAS THERE!
HOW DID YOU...?
IVAN!
SO IT'S TRUE.
THE BOD
THE BELI
WHEN BA
WITH BL
ARE SHAC
TO TH
PREAC
KILL THE HEAD AND THE BODY DIES WITH IT. DO YOU KNOW WHAT

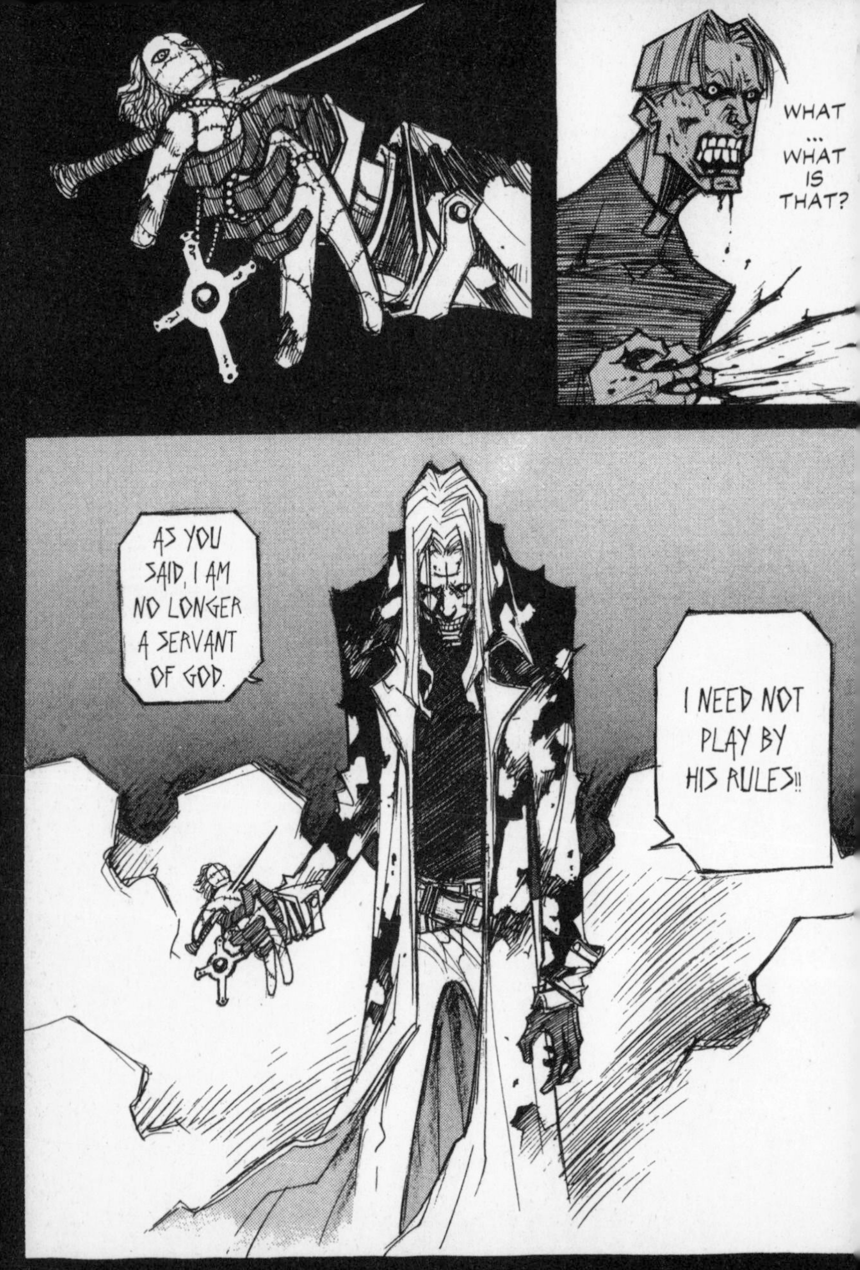
WHAT ... WHAT IS THAT?
AS YOU SAID, I AM NO LONGER A SERVANT OF GOD.
I NEED NOT PLAY BY HIS RULES!!

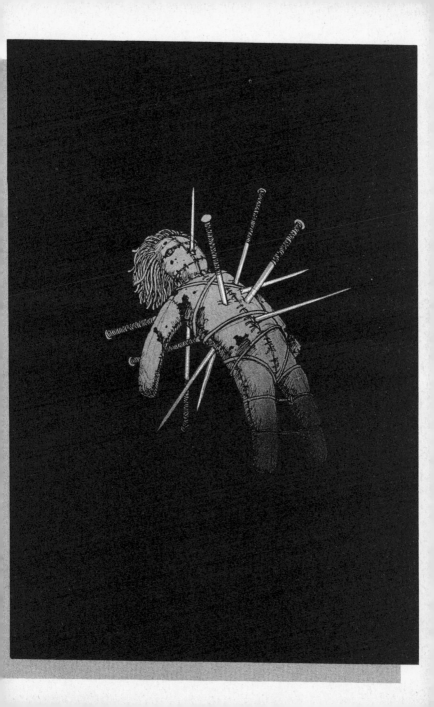

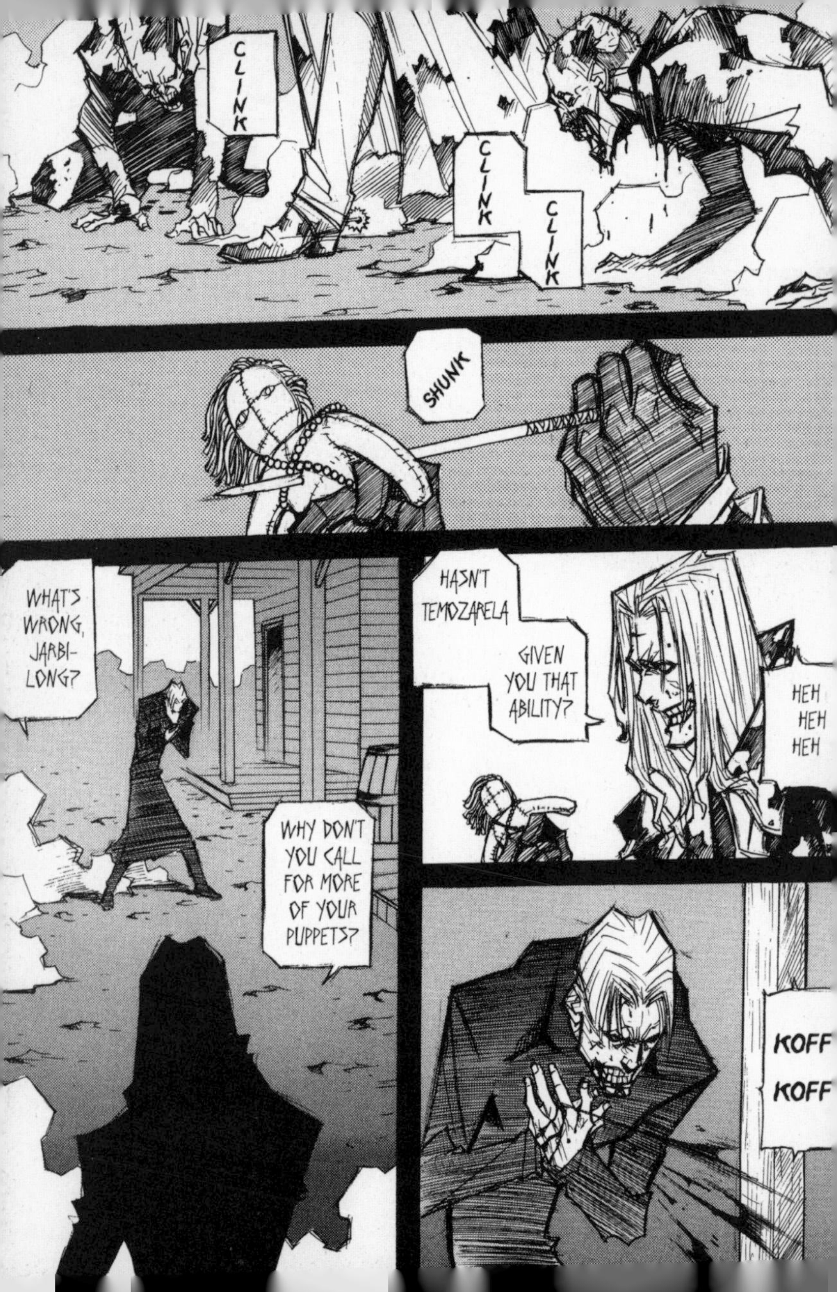
CLINK
CLINK
CLINK
SHUNK
WHAT'S WRONG, JARBI-LONG?
WHY DON'T YOU CALL FOR MORE OF YOUR PUPPETS?
HASN'T TEMOZARELA
GIVEN YOU THAT ABILITY?
HEH HEH HEH
KOFF KOFF

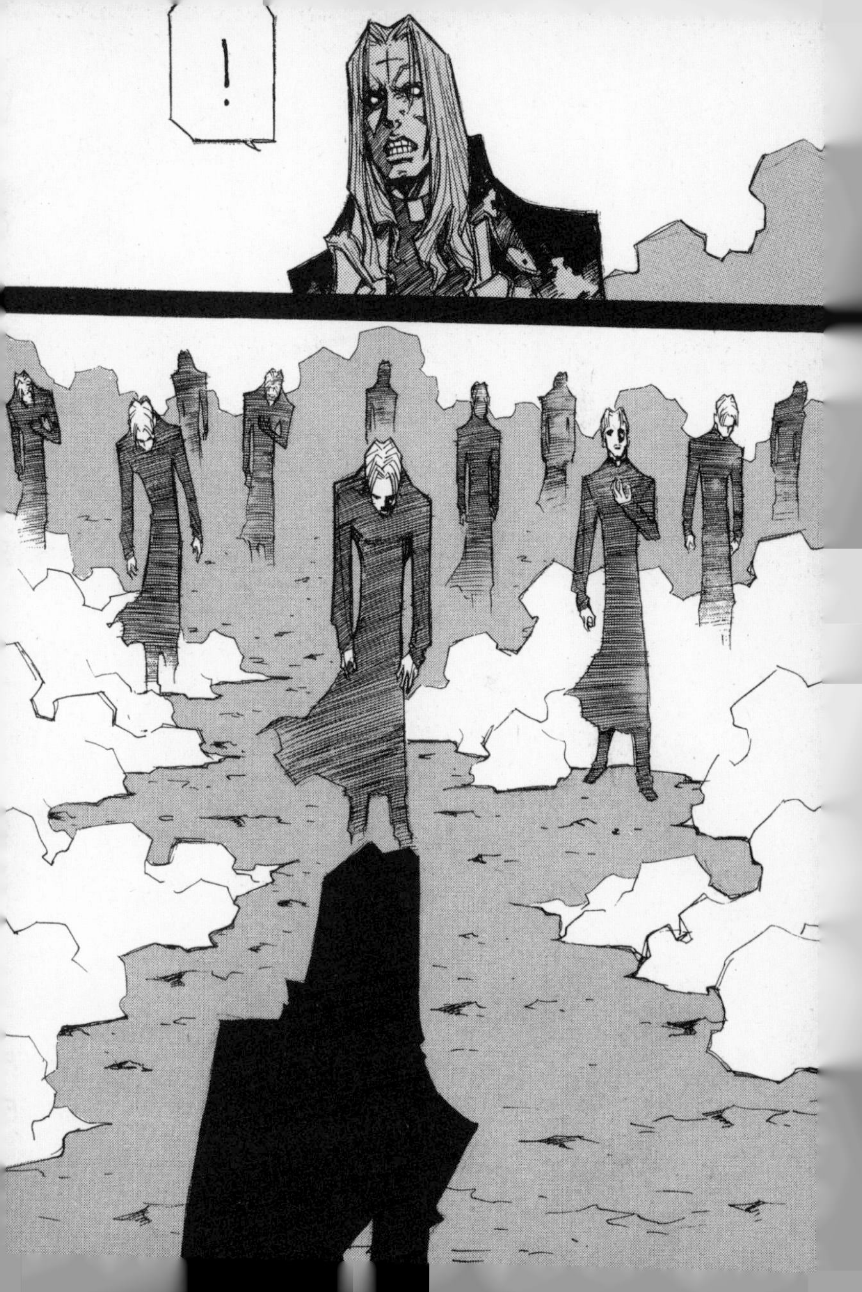
!

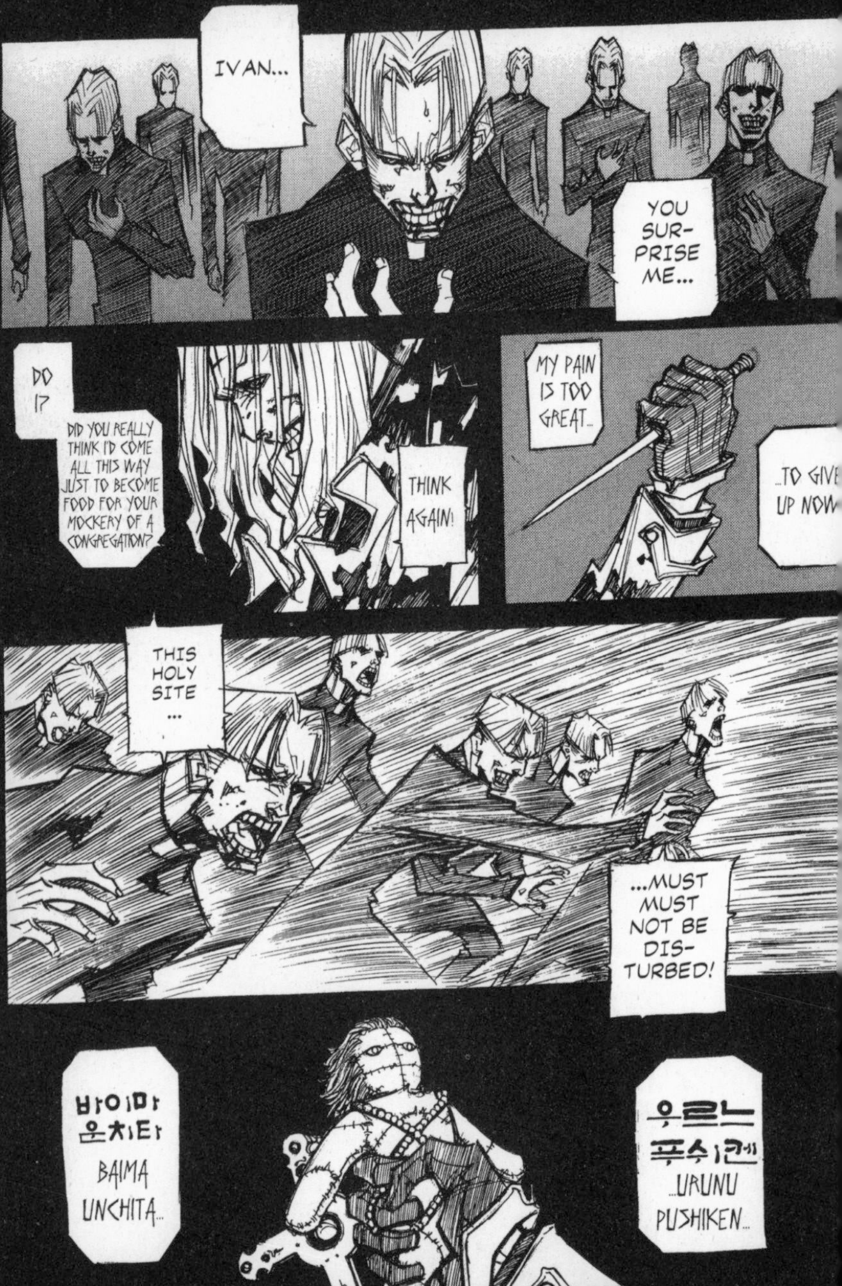
IVAN...
YOU SUR-PRISE ME...
DO I?
DID YOU REALLY THINK I'D COME ALL THIS WAY JUST TO BECOME FOOD FOR YOUR MOCKERY OF A CONGREGATION?
THINK AGAIN!
MY PAIN IS TOO GREAT...
...TO GIVE UP NOW
THIS HOLY SITE ...
...MUST MUST NOT BE DIS-TURBED!
BAIMA UNCHITA...
...URUNU PUSHIKEN...

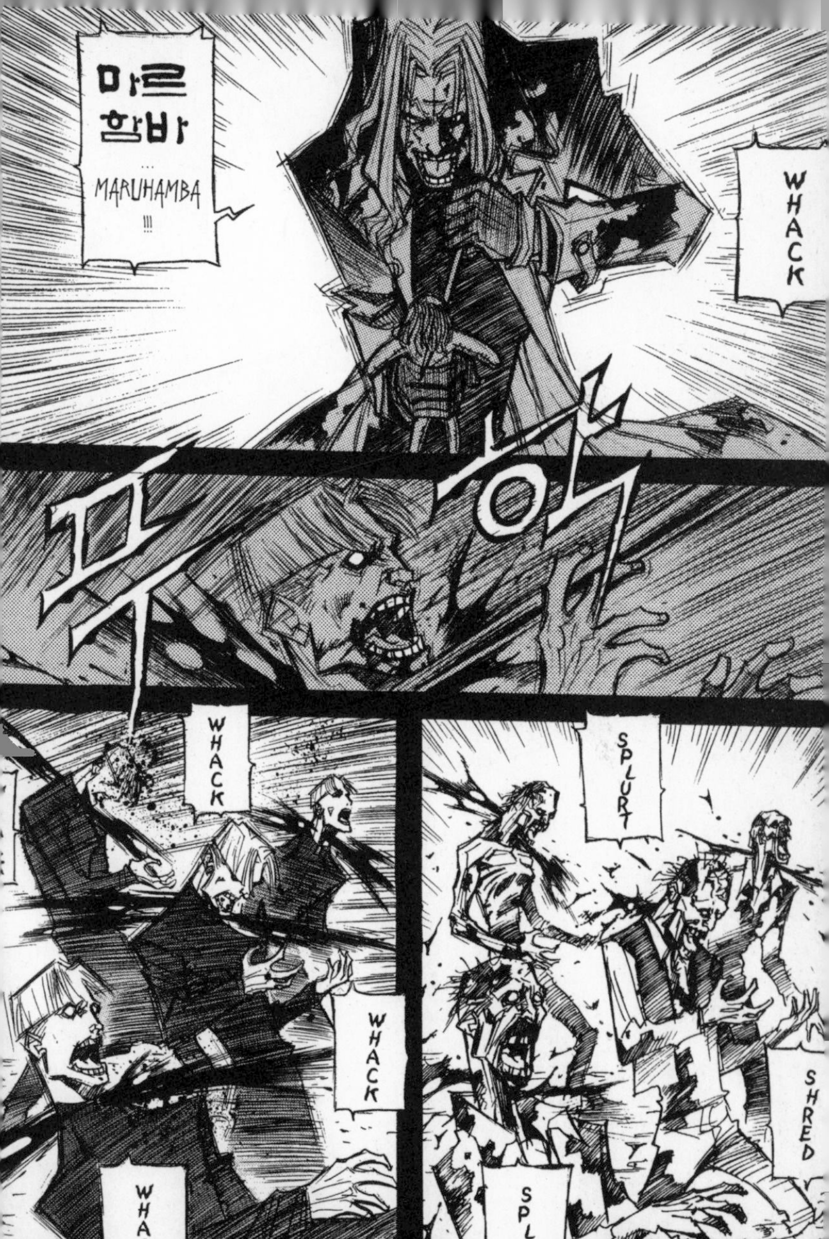
마르 함바
...
MARUHAMBA
!!!
WHACK
WHACK
WHACK
SPLURT
SHRED

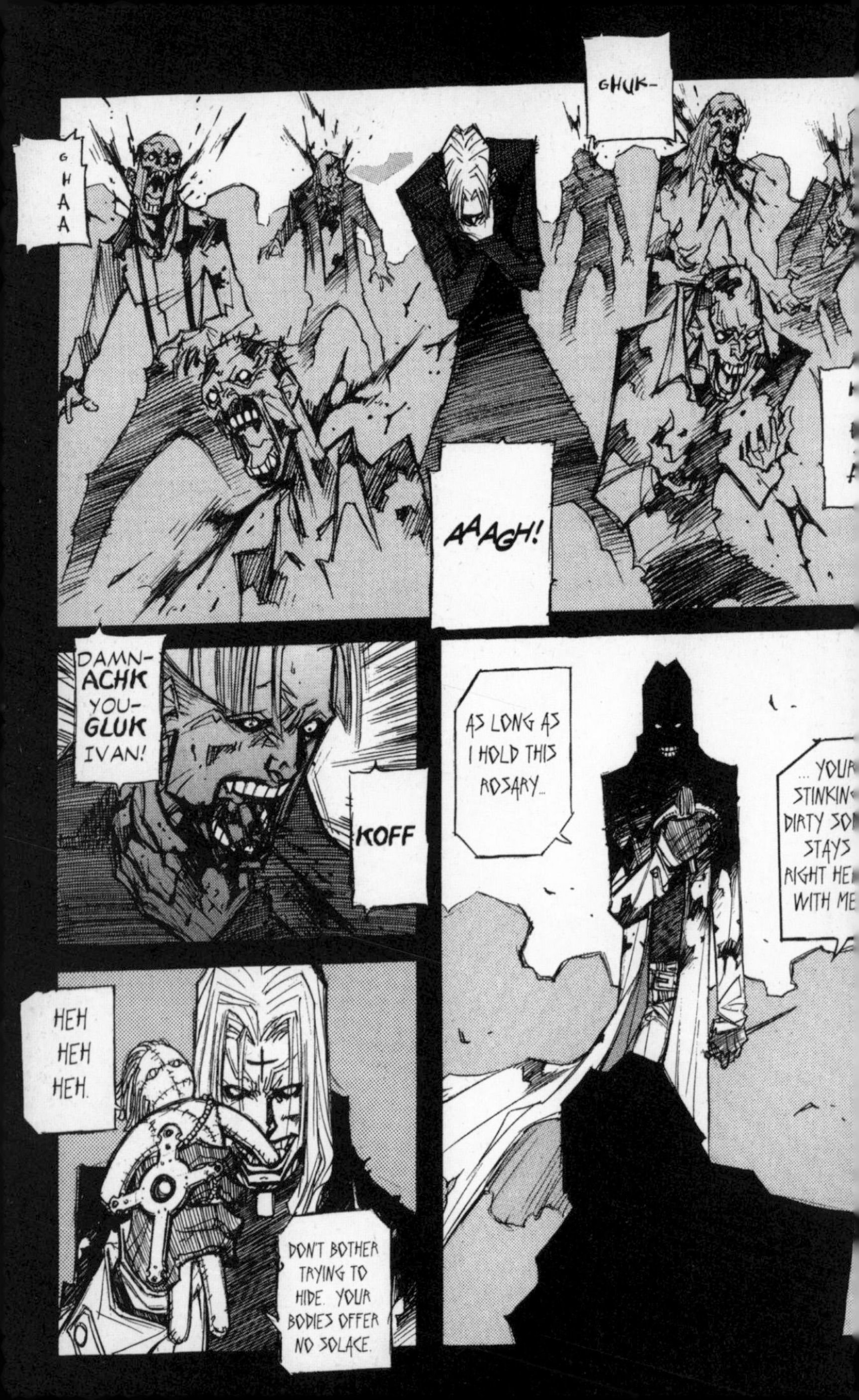
GHAA
GHUK-
AAAGH!
DAMN- ACHK YOU- GLUK IVAN!
KOFF
HEH HEH HEH.
DON'T BOTHER TRYING TO HIDE. YOUR BODIES OFFER NO SOLACE.
AS LONG AS I HOLD THIS ROSARY...
... YOUR STINKIN DIRTY SO STAYS RIGHT HE WITH ME

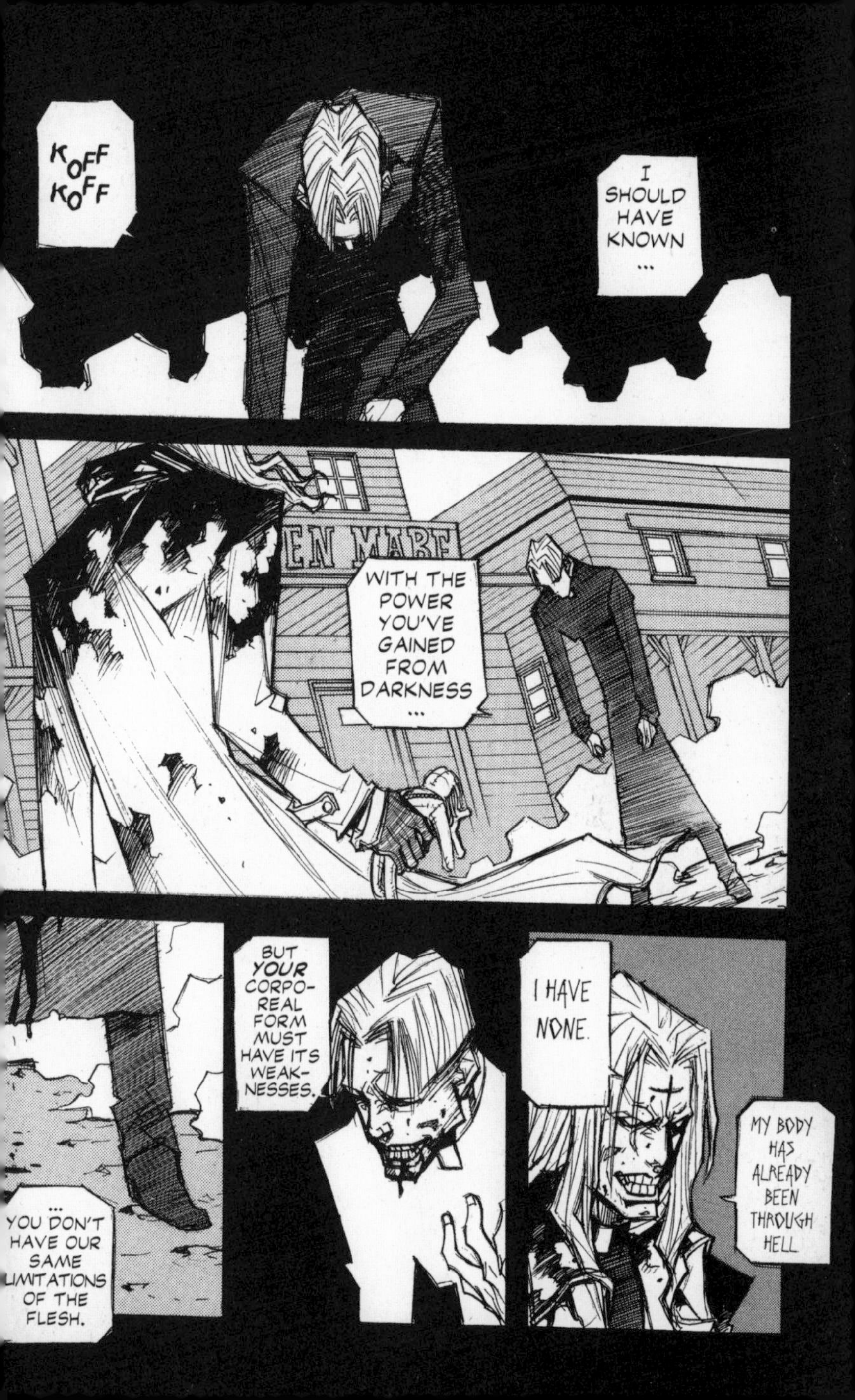
KOFF KOFF
I SHOULD HAVE KNOWN ...
EN MARE
WITH THE POWER YOU'VE GAINED FROM DARKNESS ...
... YOU DON'T HAVE OUR SAME LIMITATIONS OF THE FLESH.
BUT *YOUR* CORPO-REAL FORM MUST HAVE ITS WEAK-NESSES.
I HAVE NONE.
MY BODY HAS ALREADY BEEN THROUGH HELL

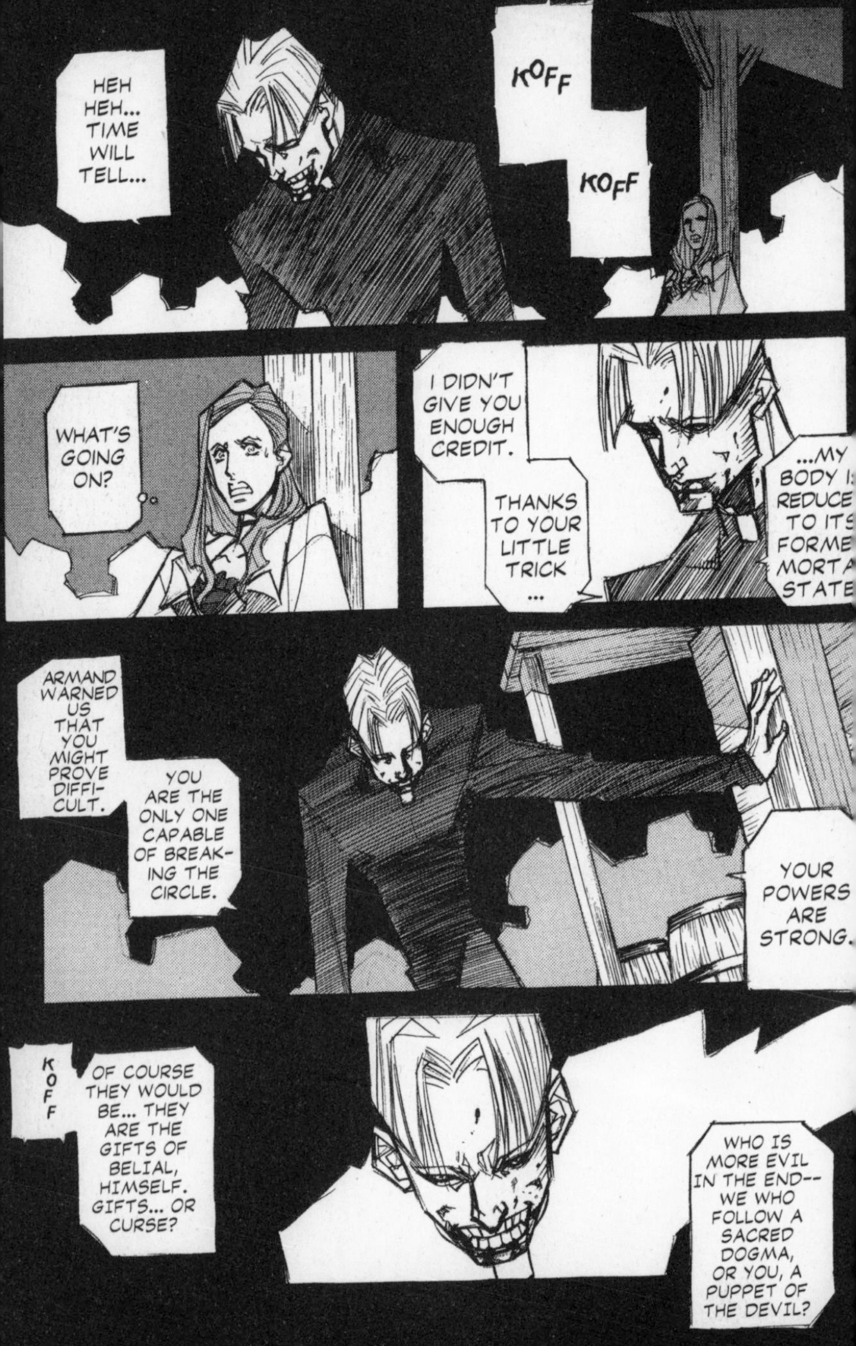
HEH HEH... TIME WILL TELL...
KOFF
KOFF
WHAT'S GOING ON?
I DIDN'T GIVE YOU ENOUGH CREDIT.
THANKS TO YOUR LITTLE TRICK ...
...MY BODY I REDUCE TO ITS FORME MORTA STATE
ARMAND WARNED US THAT YOU MIGHT PROVE DIFFI-CULT.
YOU ARE THE ONLY ONE CAPABLE OF BREAK-ING THE CIRCLE.
YOUR POWERS ARE STRONG.
KOFF
OF COURSE THEY WOULD BE... THEY ARE THE GIFTS OF BELIAL, HIMSELF. GIFTS... OR CURSE?
WHO IS MORE EVIL IN THE END-- WE WHO FOLLOW A SACRED DOGMA, OR YOU, A PUPPET OF THE DEVIL?

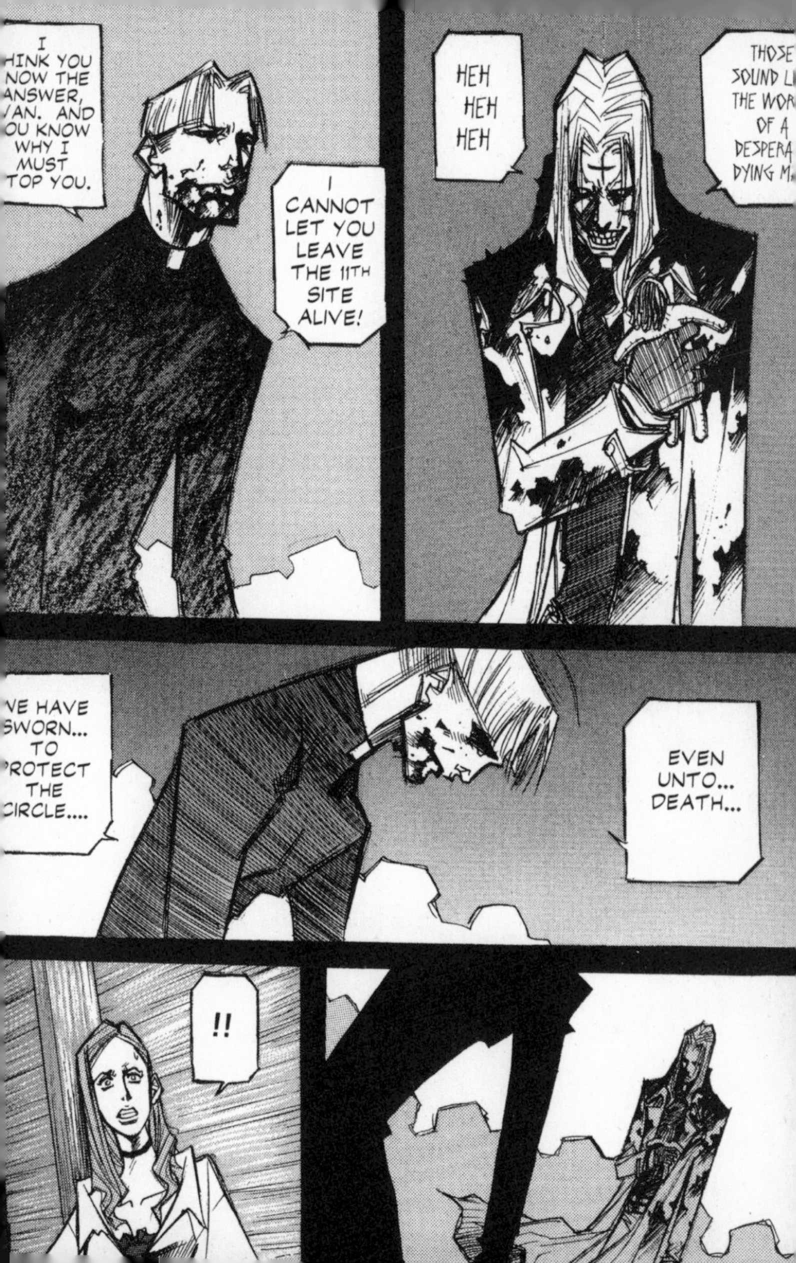
I HINK YOU NOW THE ANSWER, VAN. AND OU KNOW WHY I MUST TOP YOU.
I CANNOT LET YOU LEAVE THE 11TH SITE ALIVE!
HEH HEH HEH
THOSE SOUND L THE WOR OF A DESPERA DYING MA
VE HAVE SWORN... TO PROTECT THE CIRCLE....
EVEN UNTO... DEATH...
!!

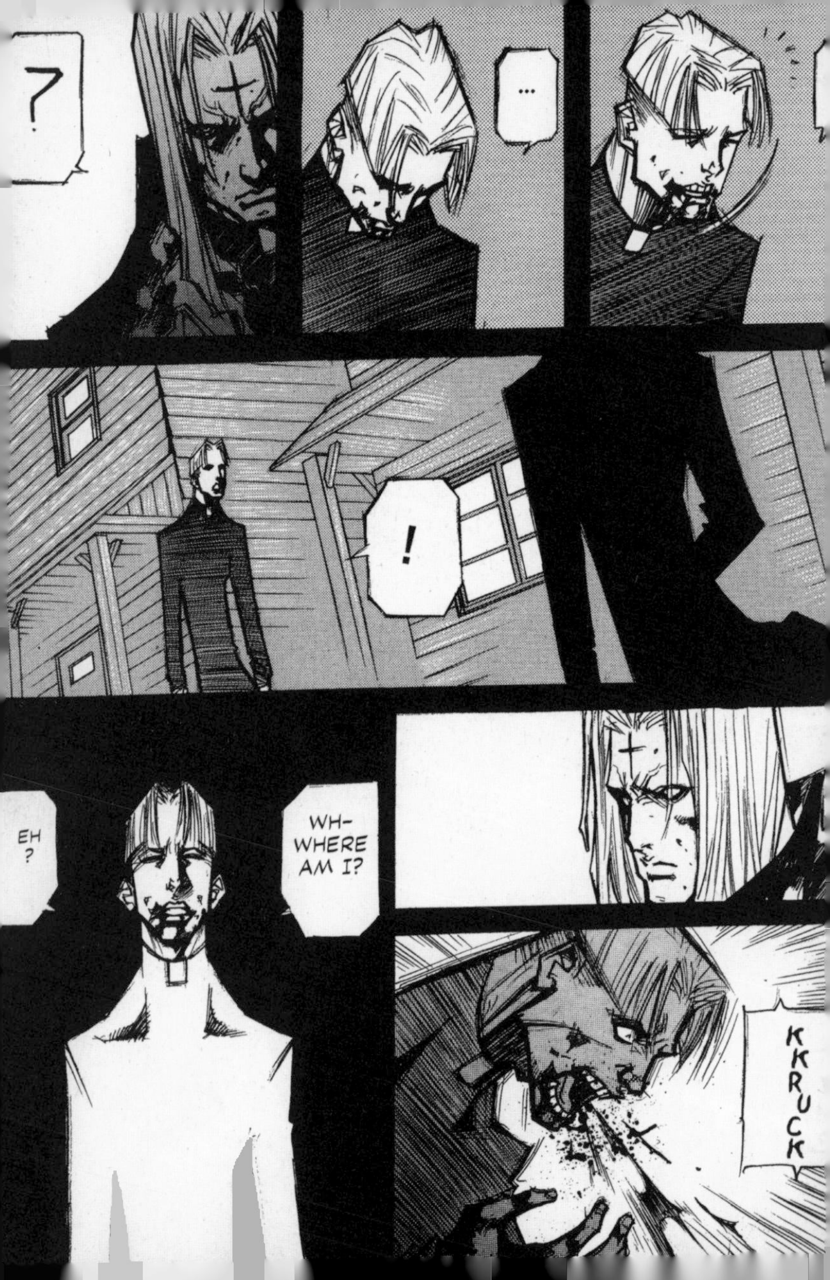
?
...
!
EH ?
WH- WHERE AM I?
KKRUCK

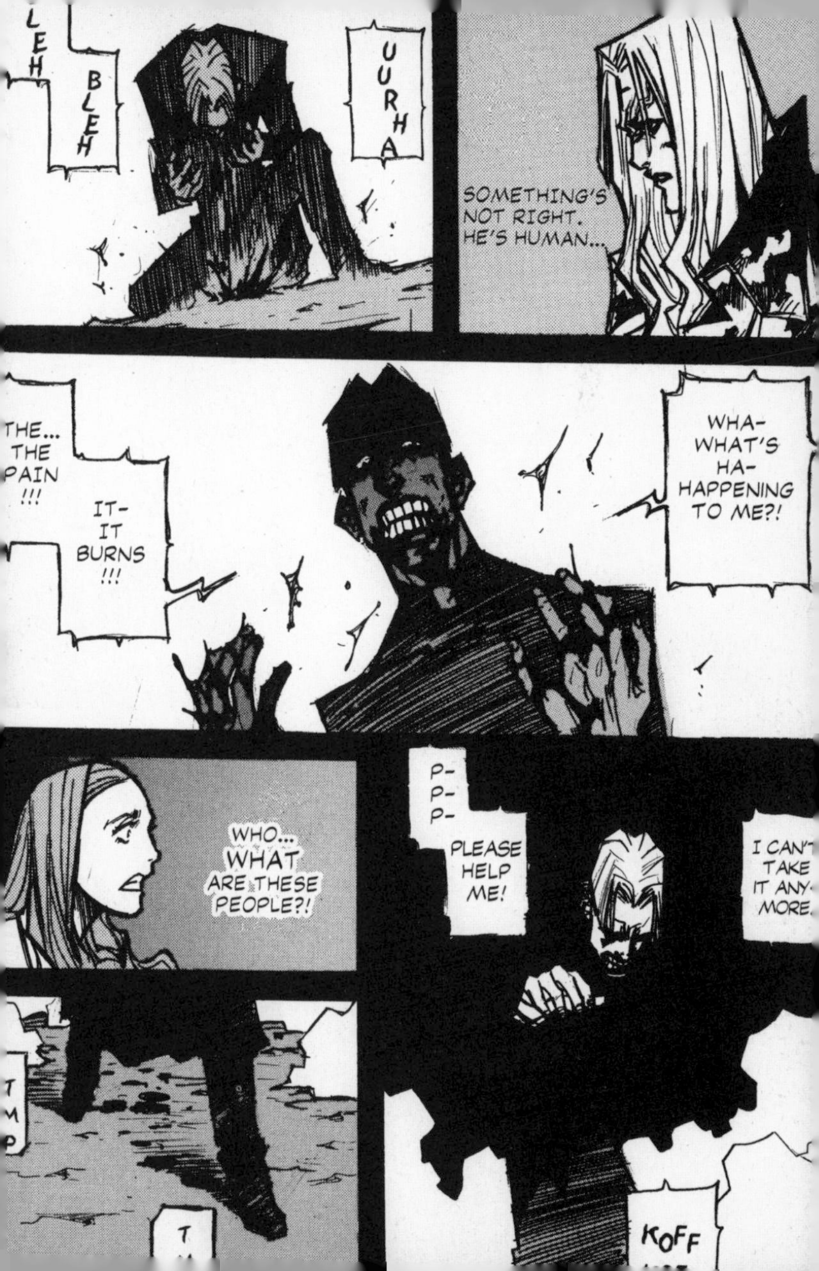
LEH
BLEH
UURHA
SOMETHING'S NOT RIGHT. HE'S HUMAN...
THE... THE PAIN !!!
IT- IT BURNS !!!
WHA- WHAT'S HA- HAPPENING TO ME?!
WHO... WHAT ARE THESE PEOPLE?!
TMP
T
P- P- P-
PLEASE HELP ME!
I CAN'T TAKE IT ANY- MORE.
KOFF

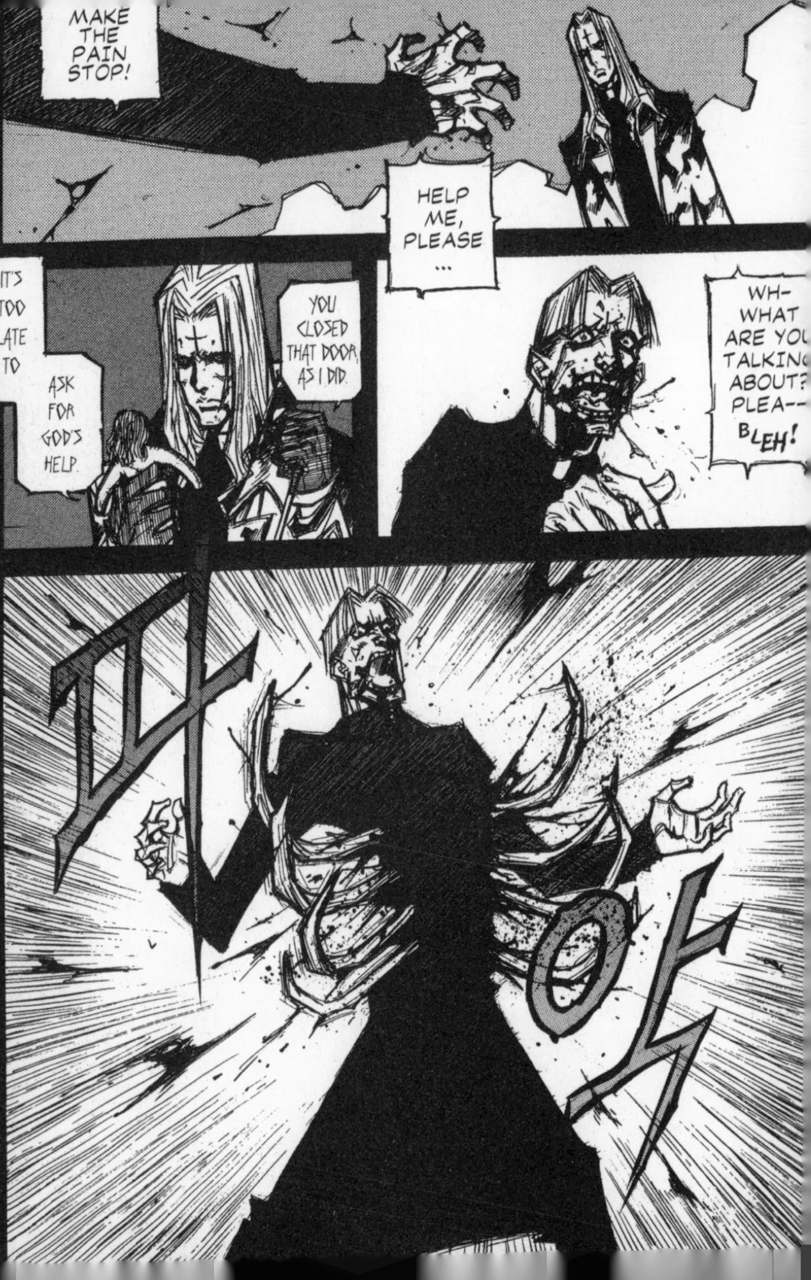
MAKE THE PAIN STOP!
HELP ME, PLEASE ...
IT'S TOO LATE TO
ASK FOR GOD'S HELP.
YOU CLOSED THAT DOOR, AS I DID.
WH- WHAT ARE YOU TALKING ABOUT? PLEA--
BLEH!

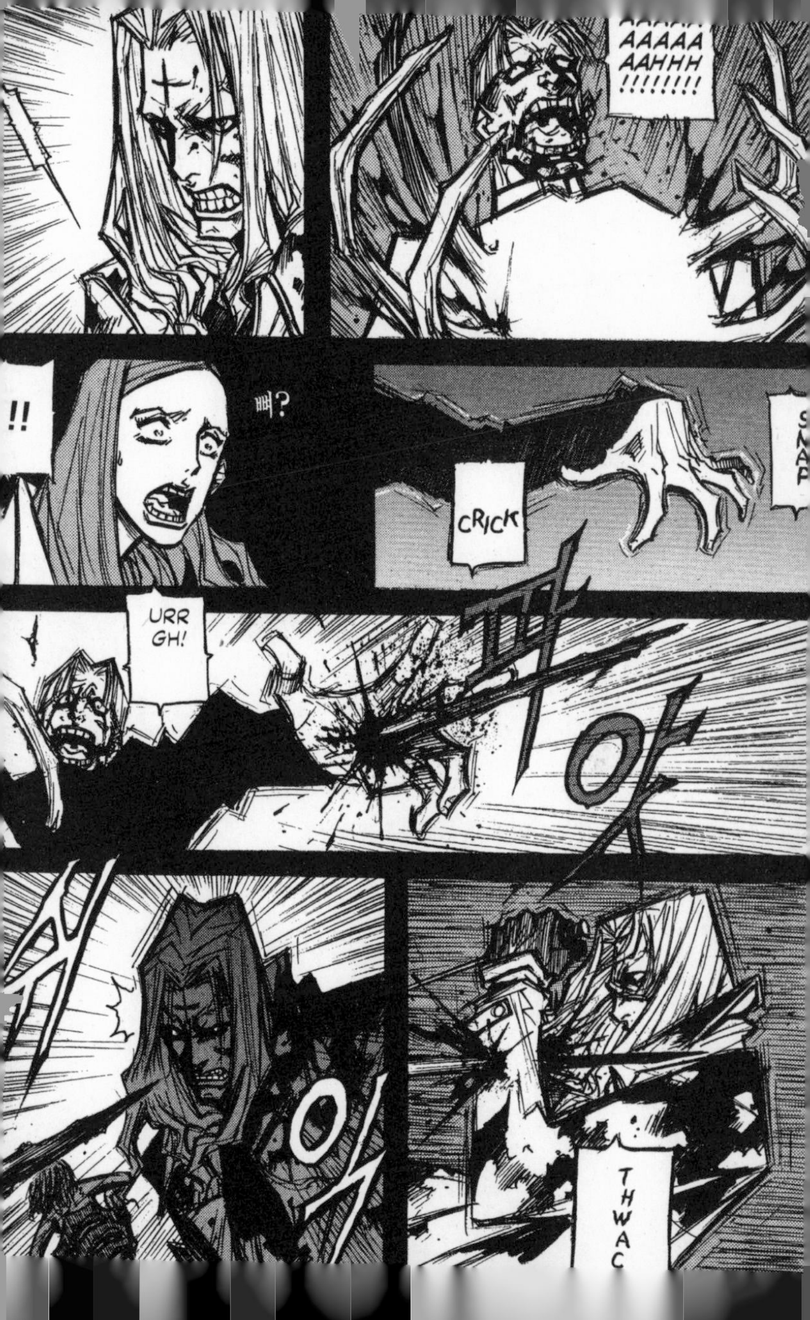
AAAAA
AAHHH
!!!!!!!!
!!
뻐?
CRICK
SNAP
URR
GH!
THWAC

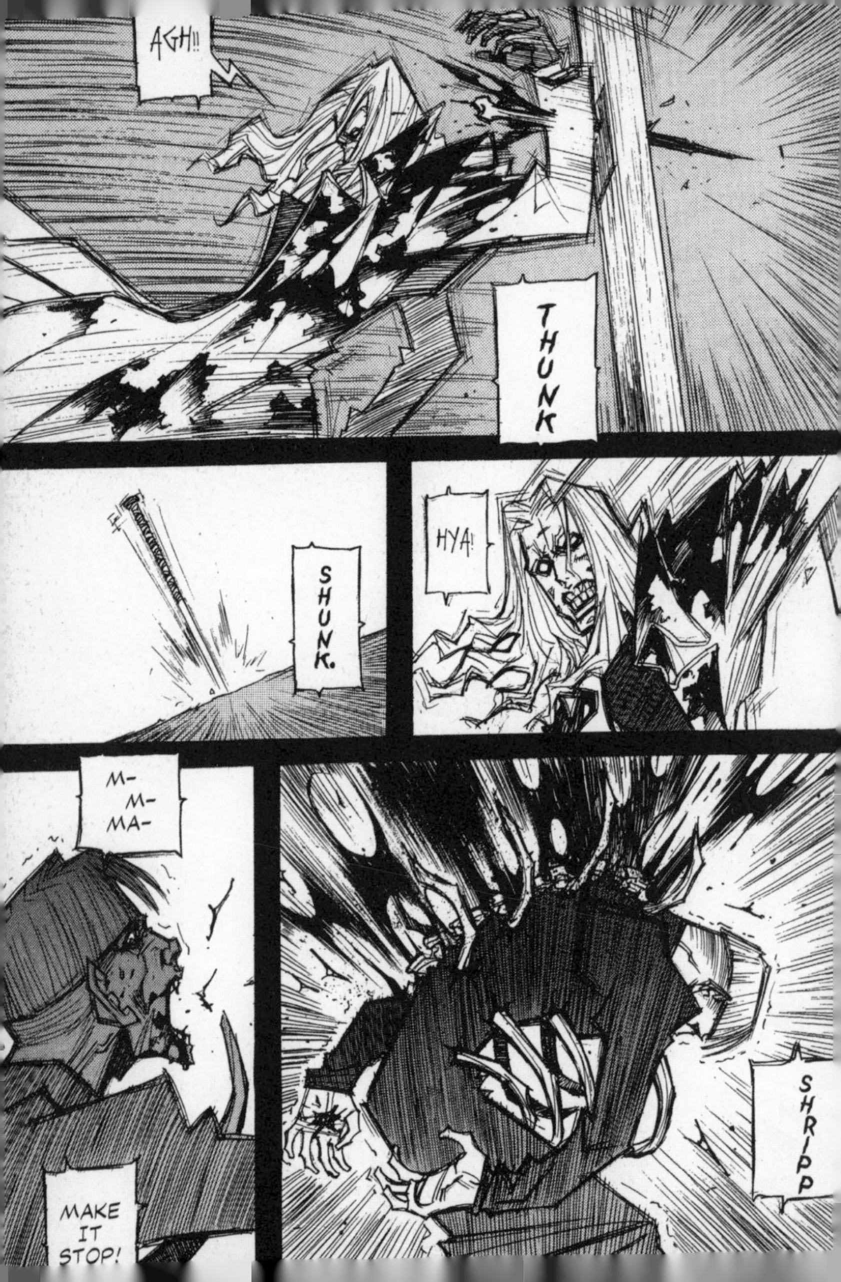
AGH!!
THUNK
SHUNK.
HYA!
M-
M-
MA-
MAKE IT STOP!
SHRIPP

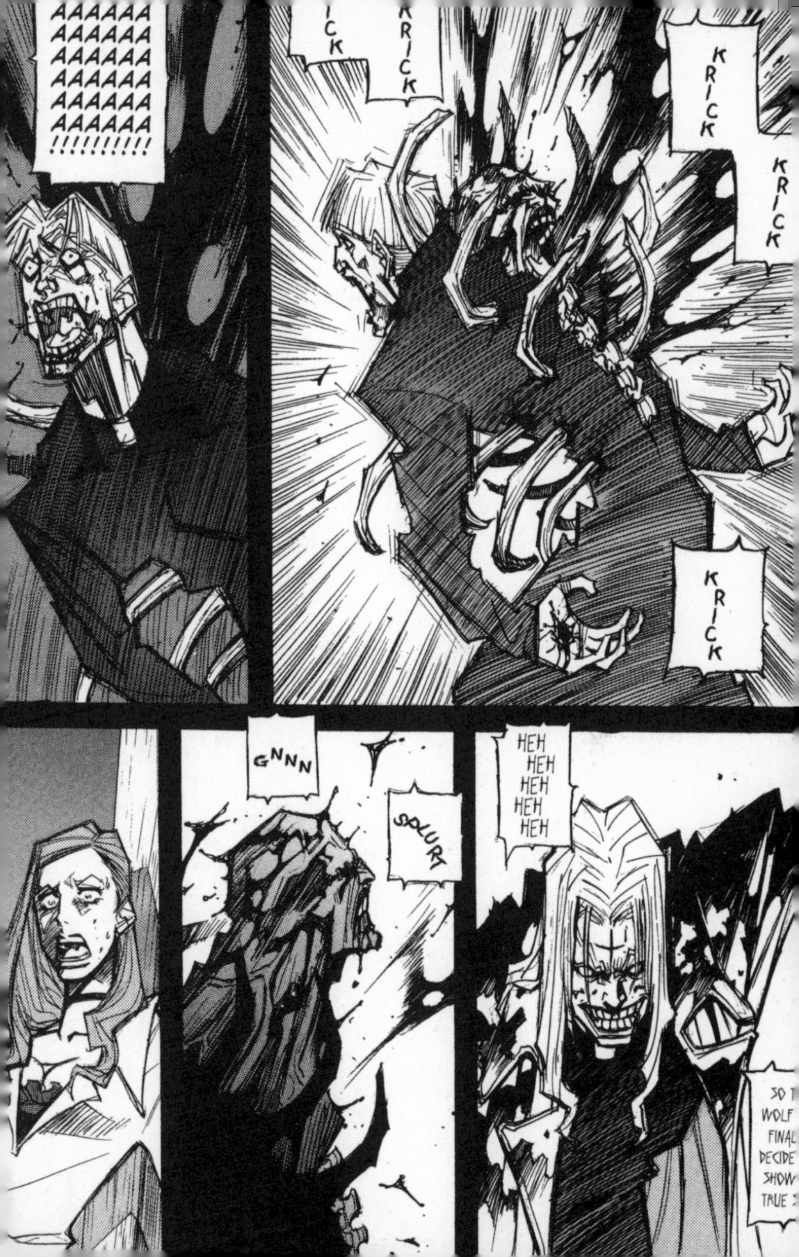
AAAAAAAAAAAAAAAAAAAAAAAAAAAAAAAAAAAA!!!!!!!!!!
ICK
KRICK
KRICK
KRICK
KRICK
GNNN
SPLURT
HEH HEH HEH HEH HEH
SO T WOLF FINAL DECIDE SHOW TRUE

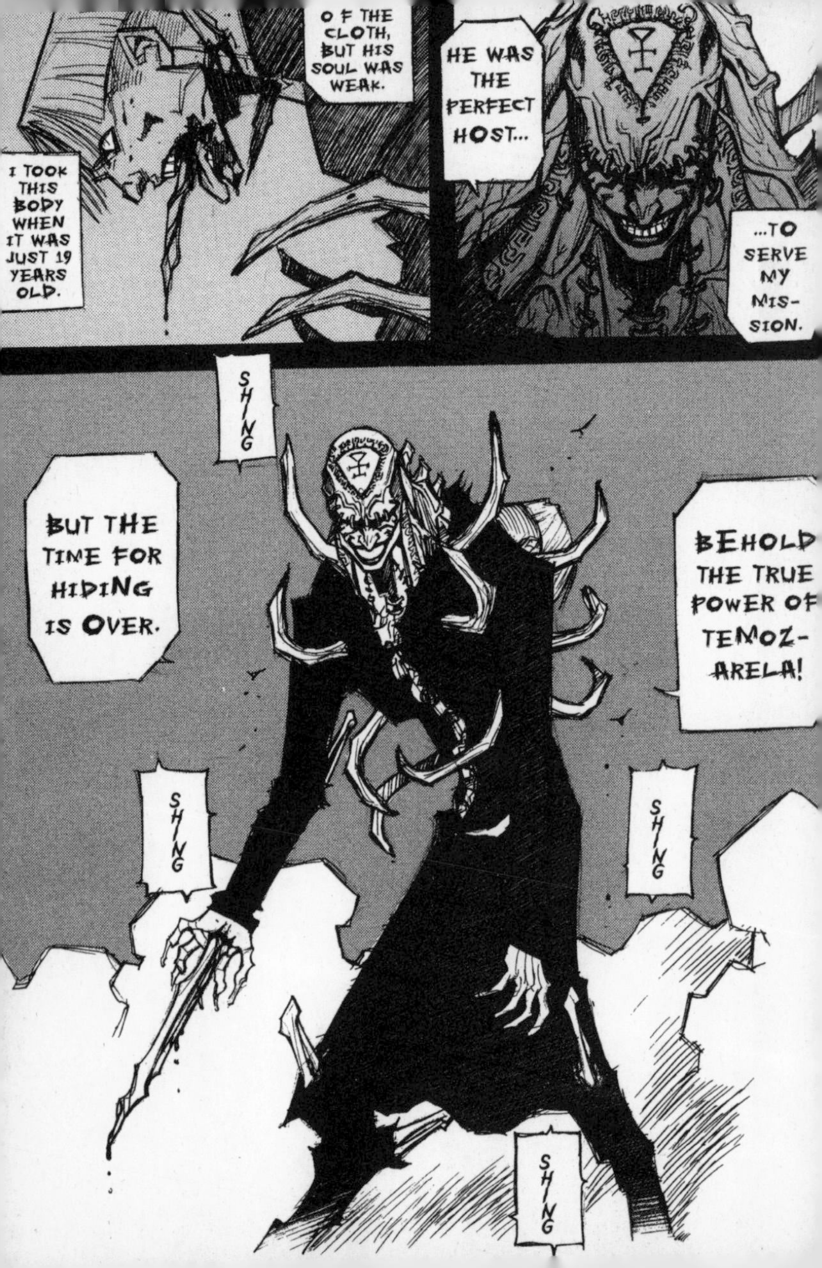
O F THE CLOTH, BUT HIS SOUL WAS WEAK.
I TOOK THIS BODY WHEN IT WAS JUST 19 YEARS OLD.
HE WAS THE PERFECT HOST...
...TO SERVE MY MIS-SION.
SHING
BUT THE TIME FOR HIDING IS OVER.
BEHOLD THE TRUE POWER OF TEMOZ-ARELA!
SHING
SHING
SHING

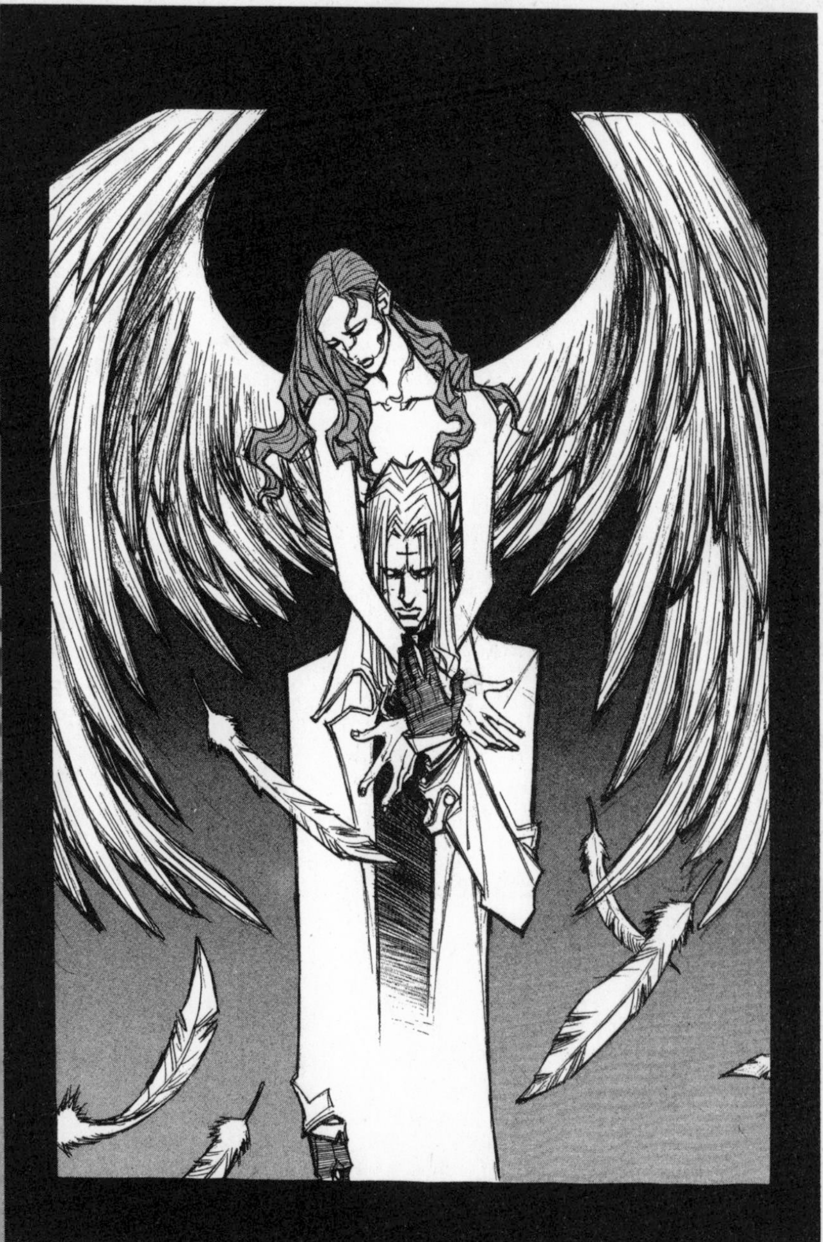

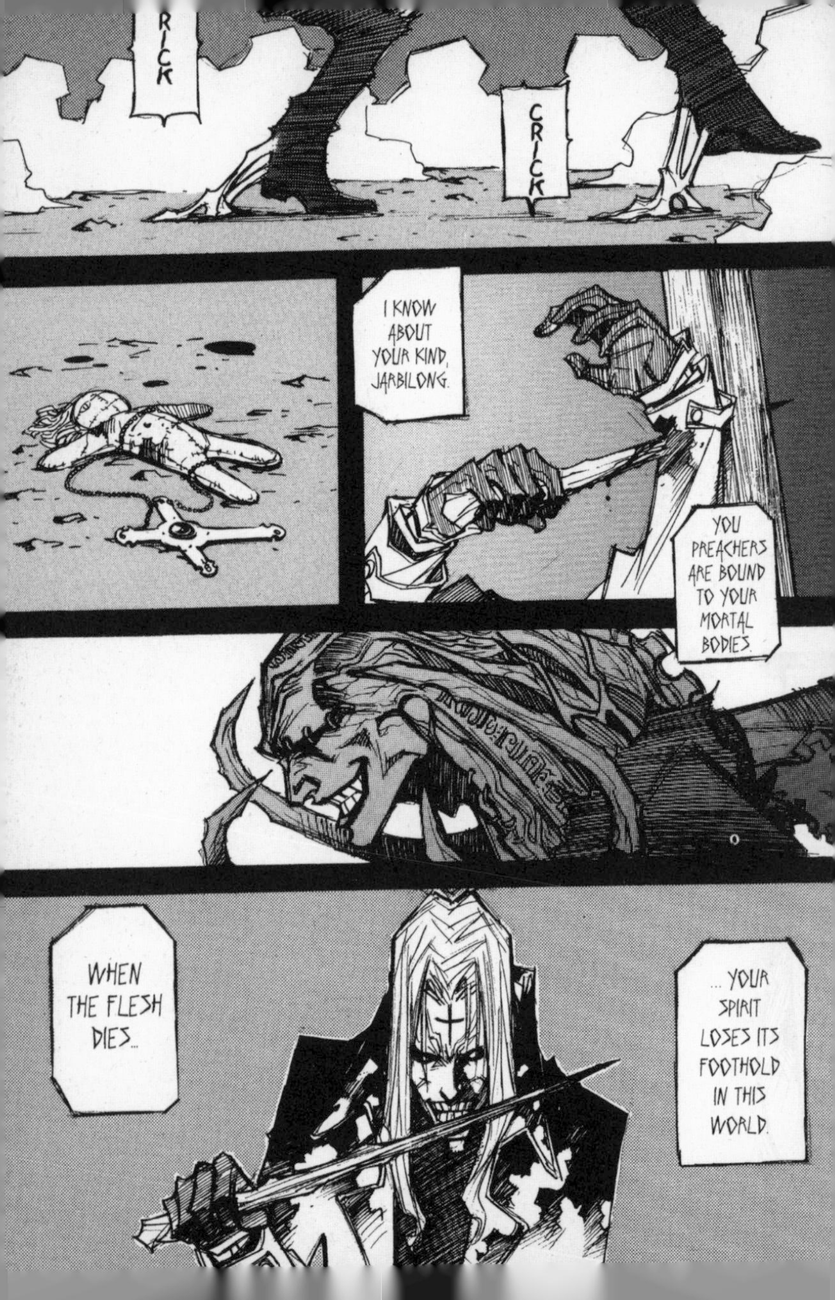
RICK
CRICK
I KNOW ABOUT YOUR KIND, JARBILONG.
YOU PREACHERS ARE BOUND TO YOUR MORTAL BODIES.
WHEN THE FLESH DIES...
...YOUR SPIRIT LOSES ITS FOOTHOLD IN THIS WORLD.

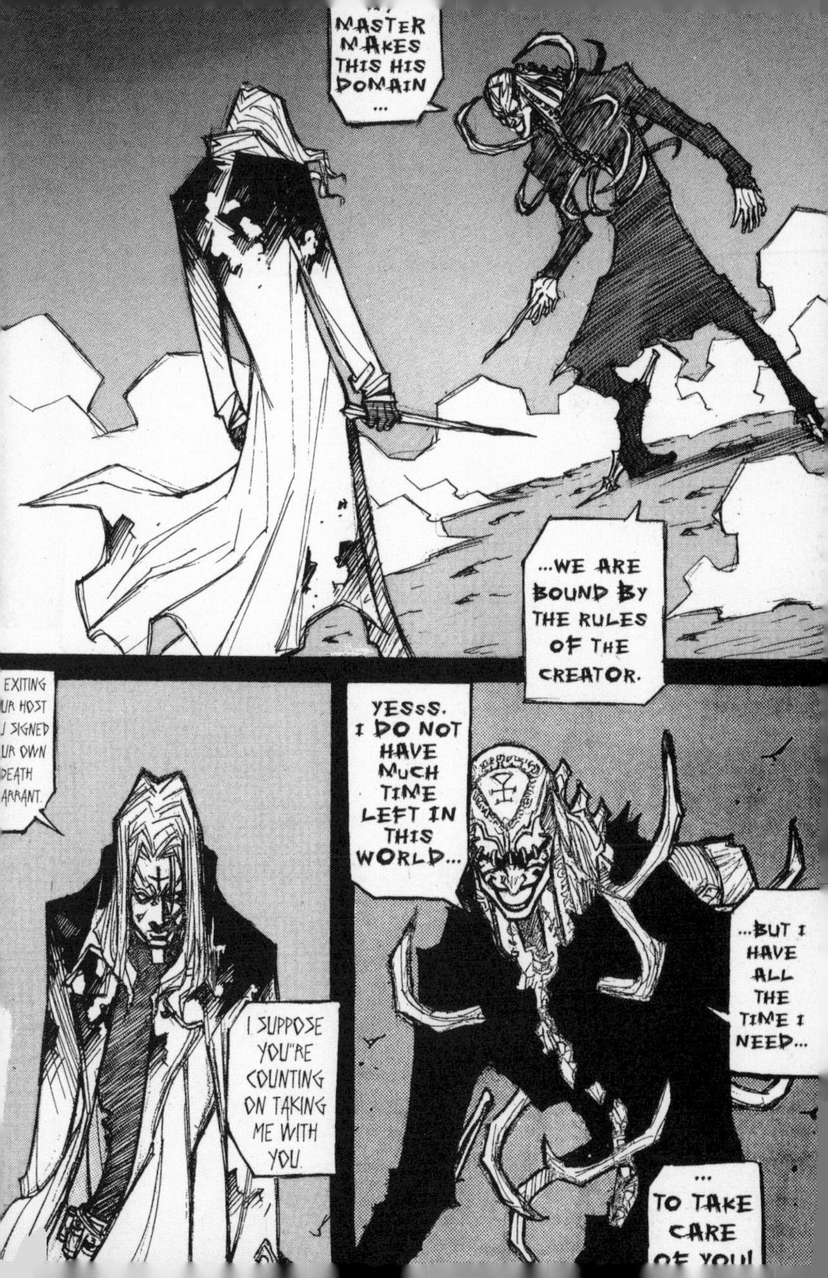
MASTER MAKES THIS HIS DOMAIN ...
...WE ARE BOUND BY THE RULES OF THE CREATOR.
EXITING UR HOST J SIGNED UR OWN DEATH ARRANT.
I SUPPOSE YOU'RE COUNTING ON TAKING ME WITH YOU.
YESSS. I DO NOT HAVE MUCH TIME LEFT IN THIS WORLD...
...BUT I HAVE ALL THE TIME I NEED...
... TO TAKE CARE

MY PILGRIMAGE IS FAR FROM OVER, JARBILONG.
YOU'LL JUST HAVE TO GO TO HELL WITHOUT ME!
THE DAYS OF HEAVEN AND HELL ARE NO MORE!
LORD TEMOZ-ARELA WILL TRANSFORM ALL INTO HIS OWN DOMAIN!
LONG LIVE LORD TEMOZ-ARELA!
GRAAHH

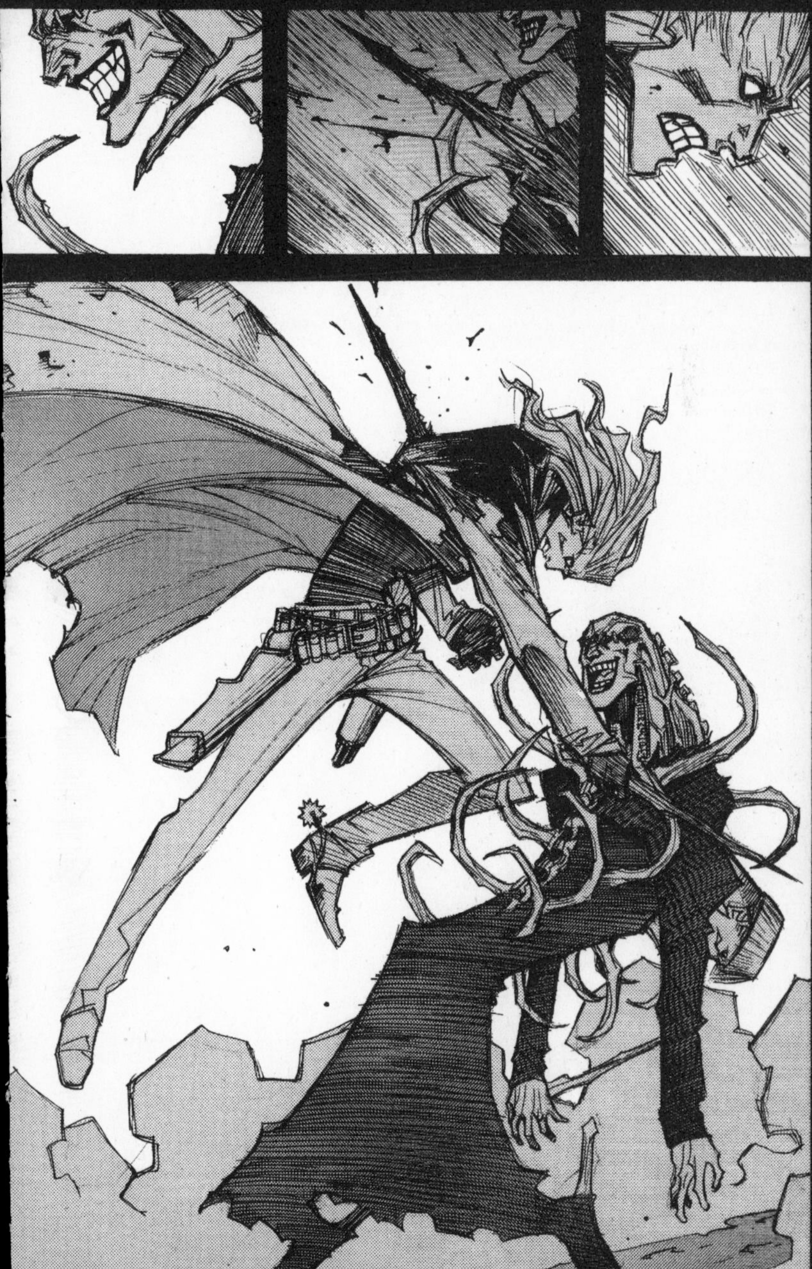

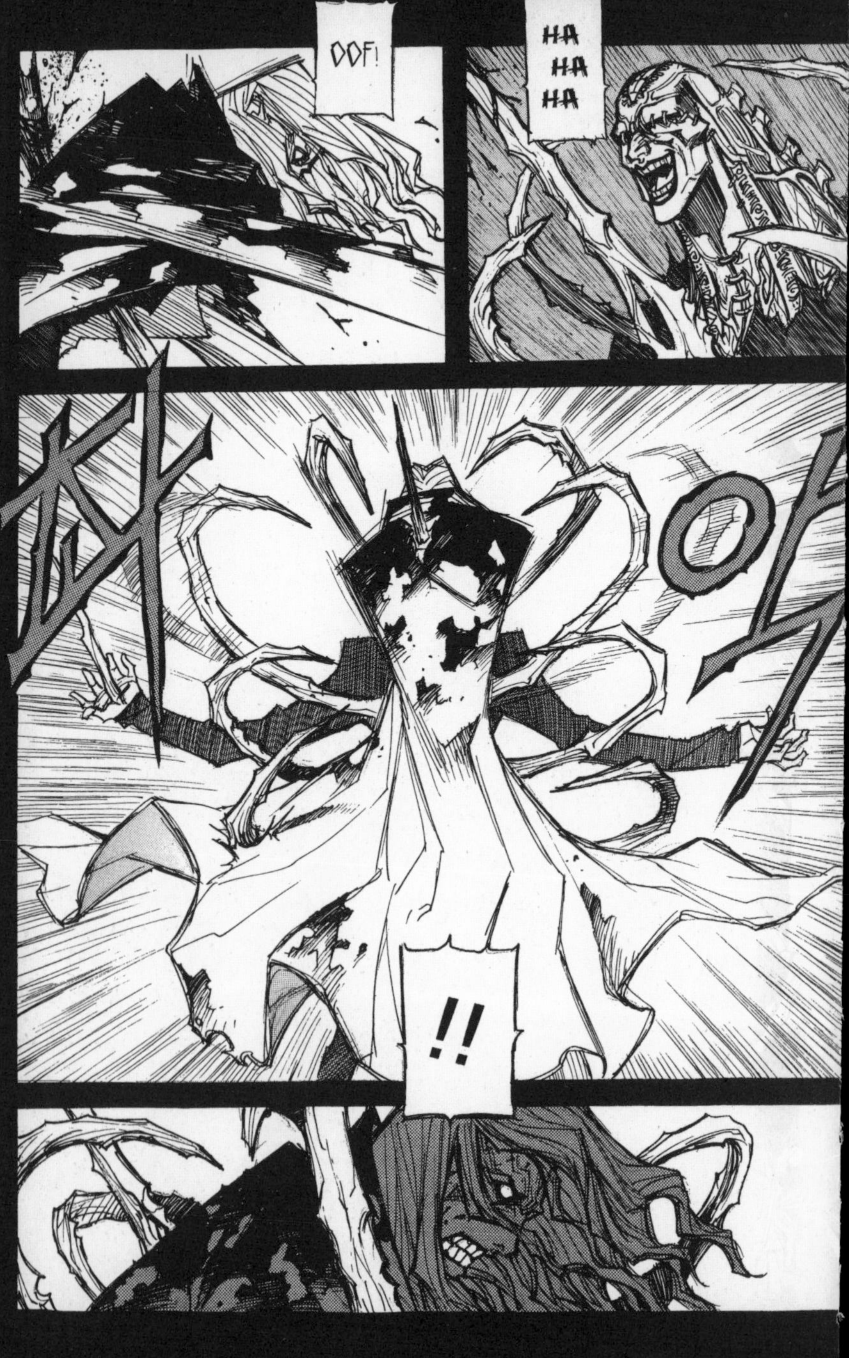
OOF!
HA HA HA
!!

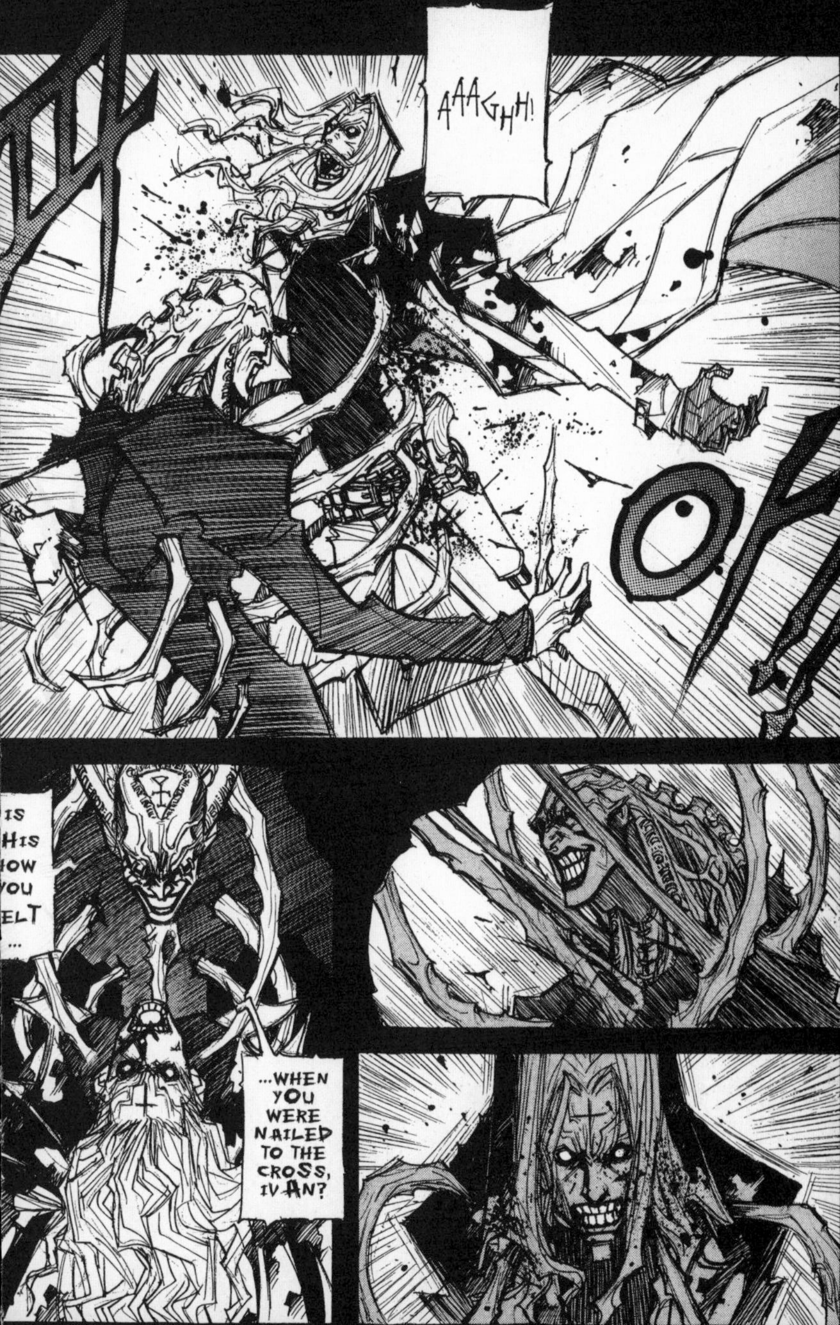
AAAGHH!
IS HIS HOW YOU ELT ...
...WHEN YOU WERE NAILED TO THE CROSS, IVAN?

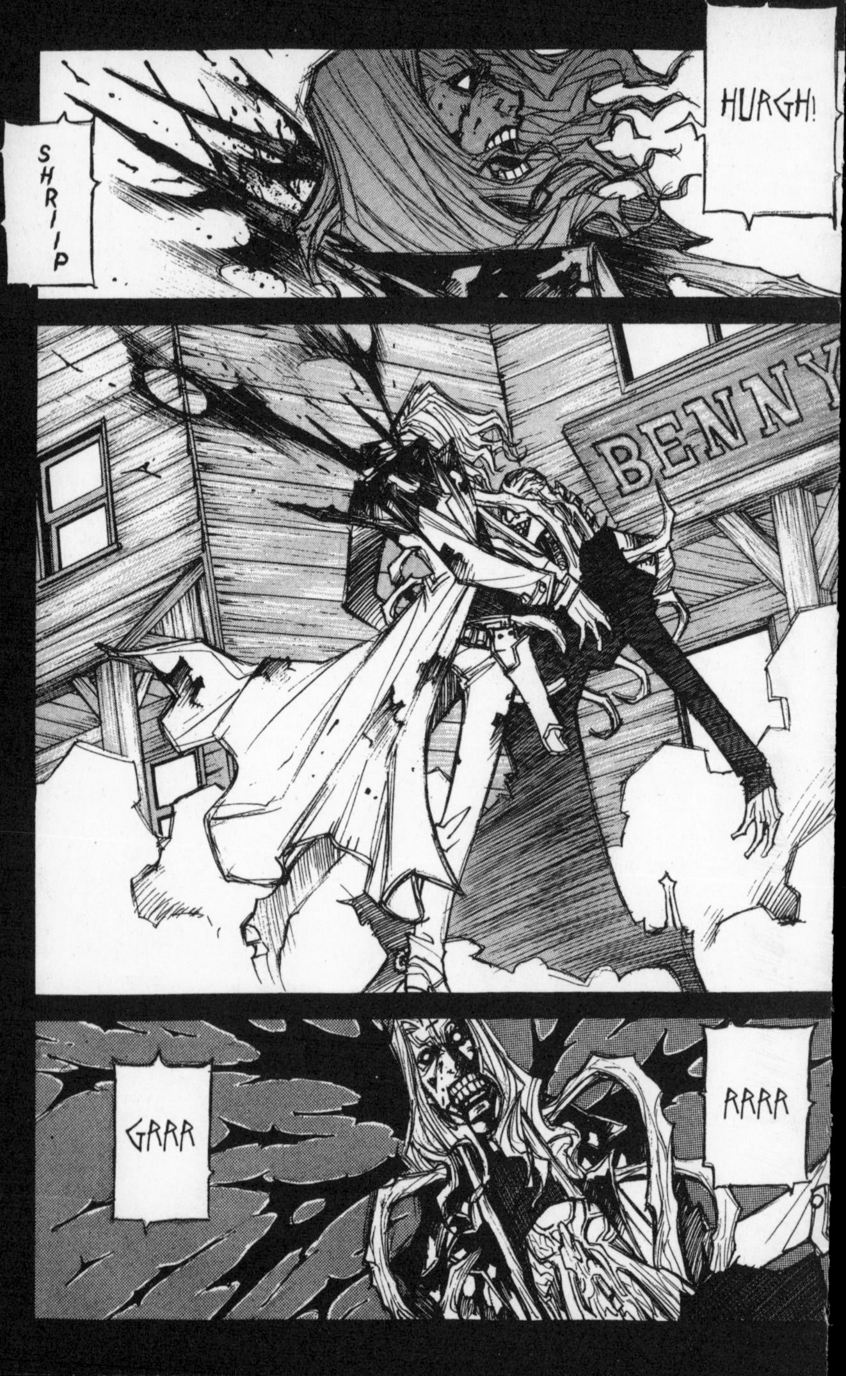
SHRIIP
HURGH!
BENNY
GRRR
RRRR

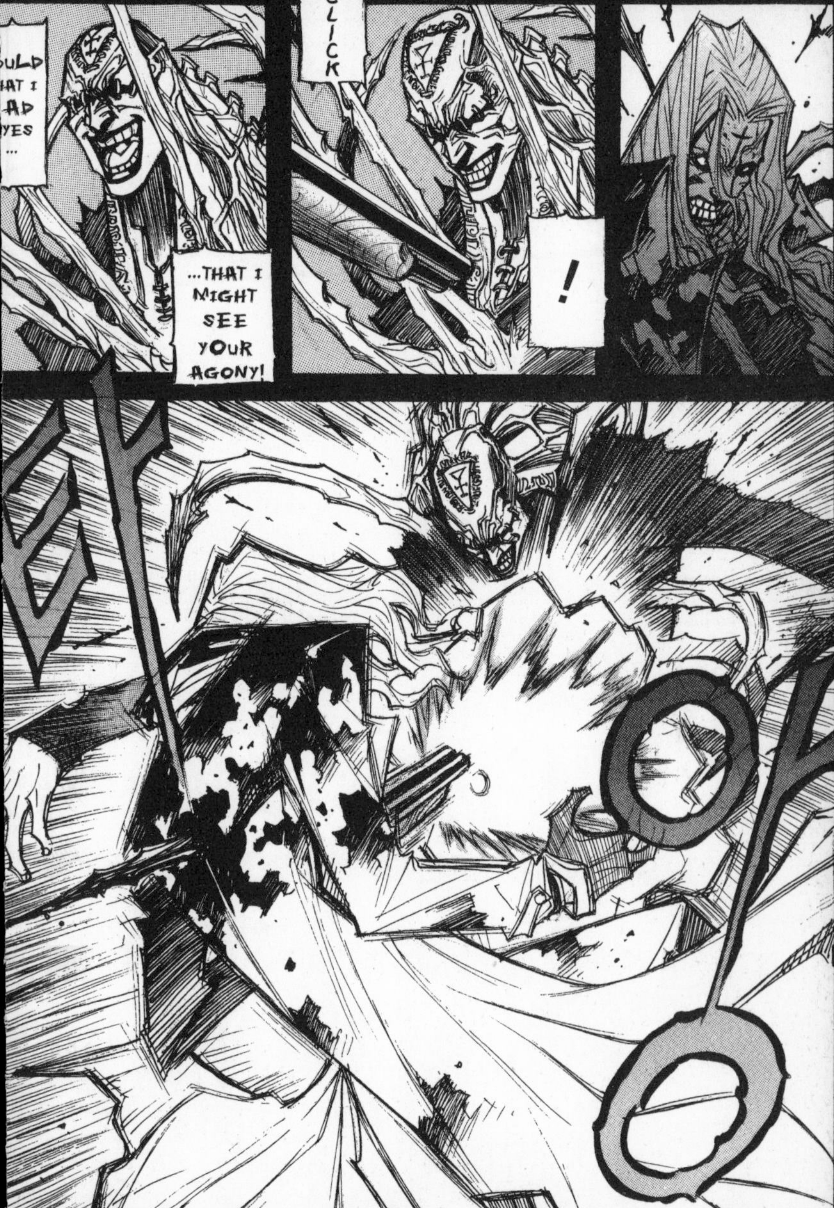
ULD AT I AD YES ...
...THAT I MIGHT SEE YOUR AGONY!
CLICK
!

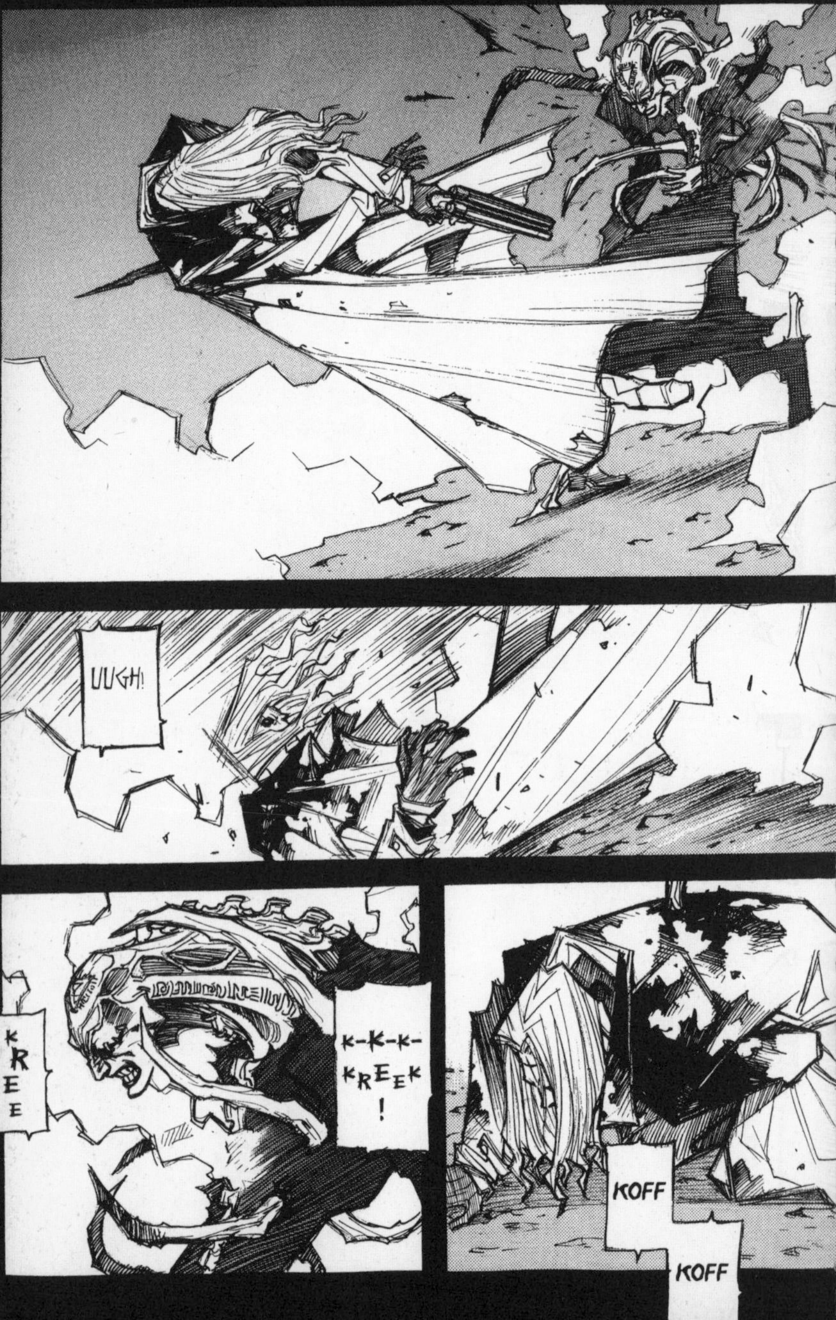
UUGH!
KREE
K-K-K-KREEK!
KOFF
KOFF

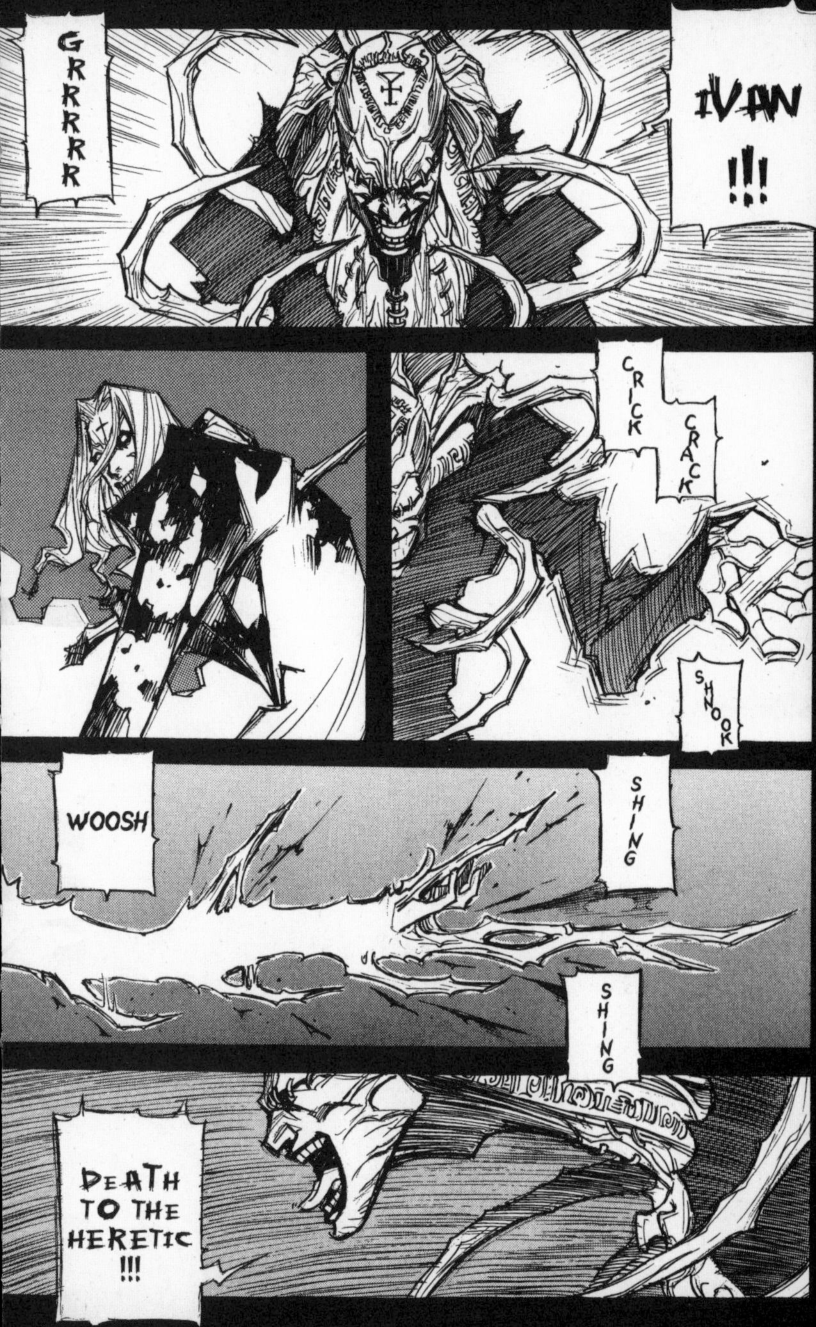
GRRRRR
IVAN !!!
CRICK
CRACK
SHNOOK
WOOSH
SHING
SHING
DEATH TO THE HERETIC !!!

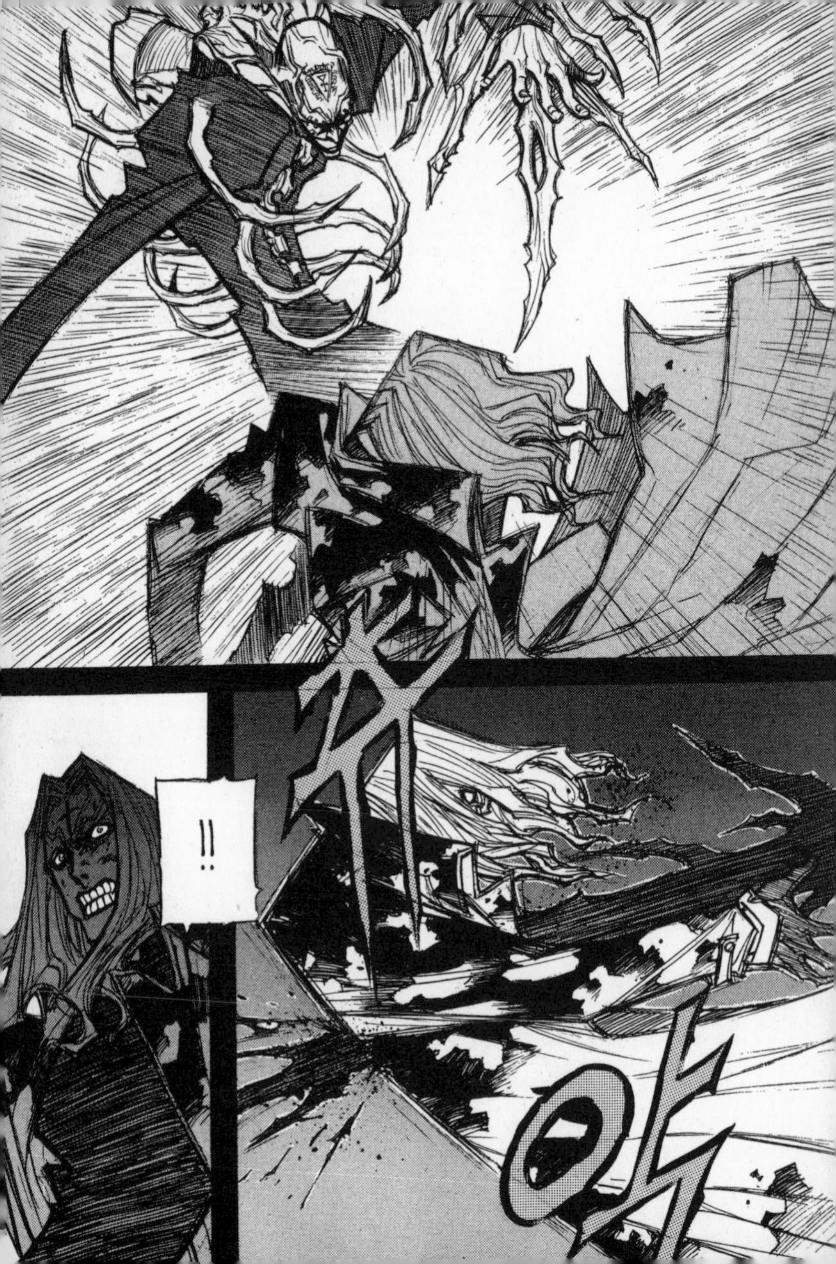
!!

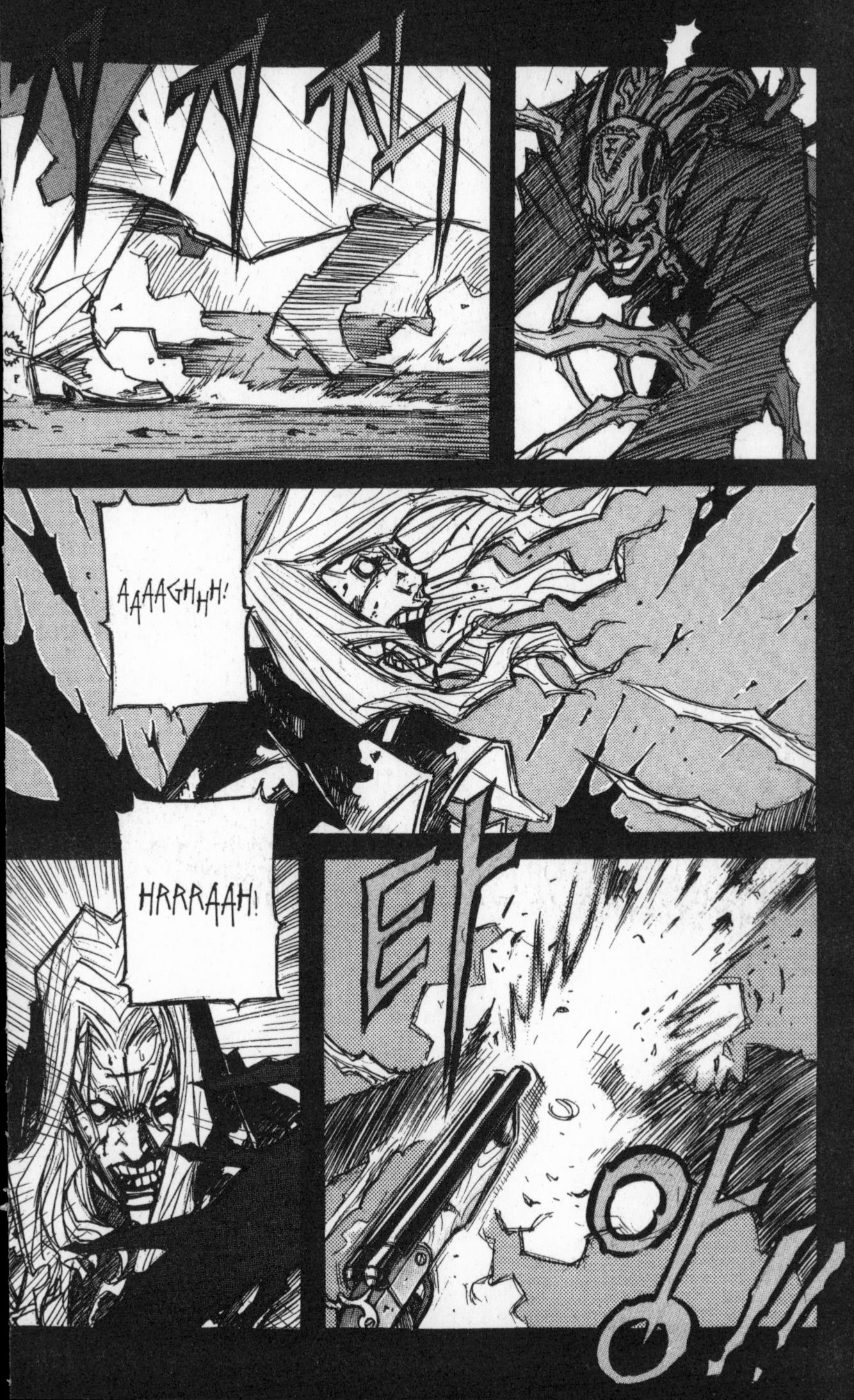
AAAAGHHH!
HRRRAAH!

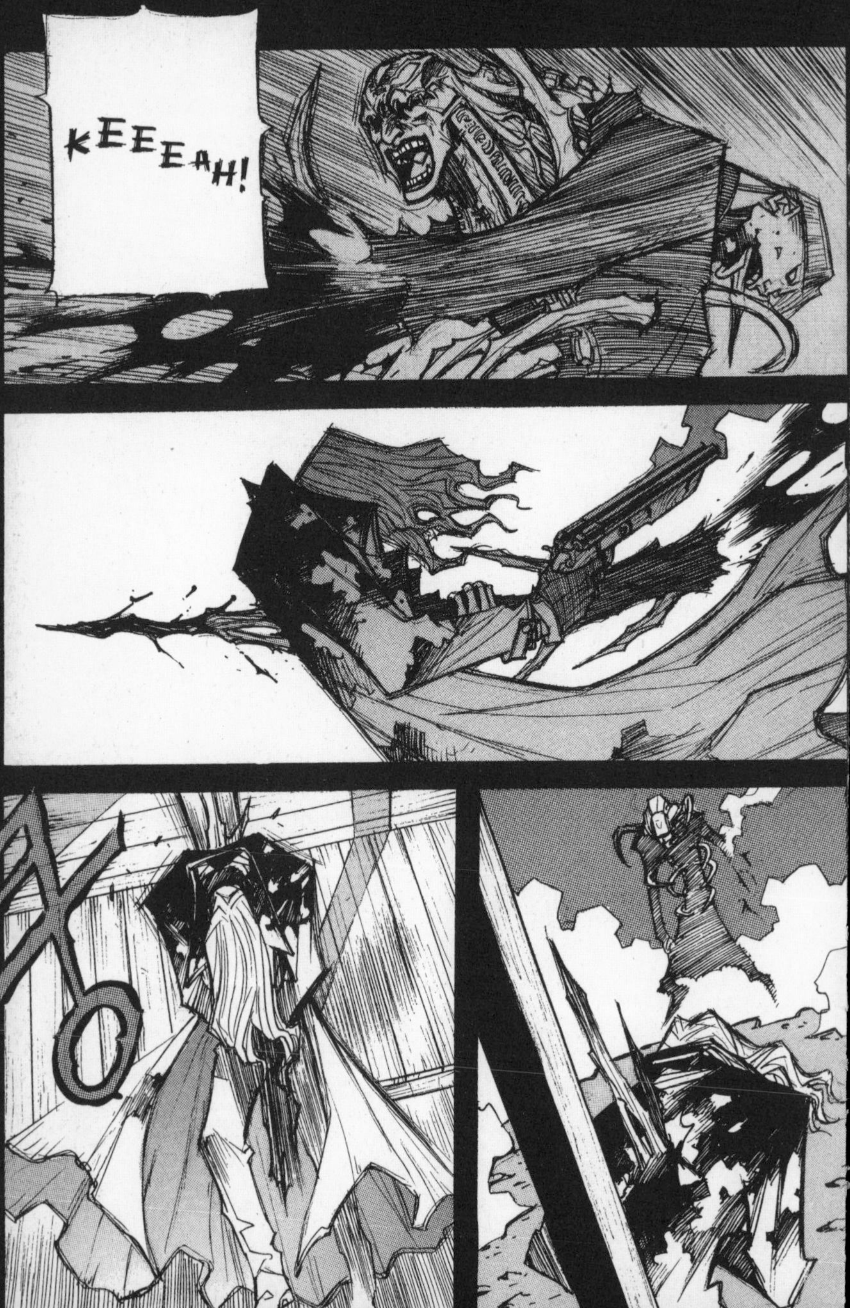
KEEEEAH!

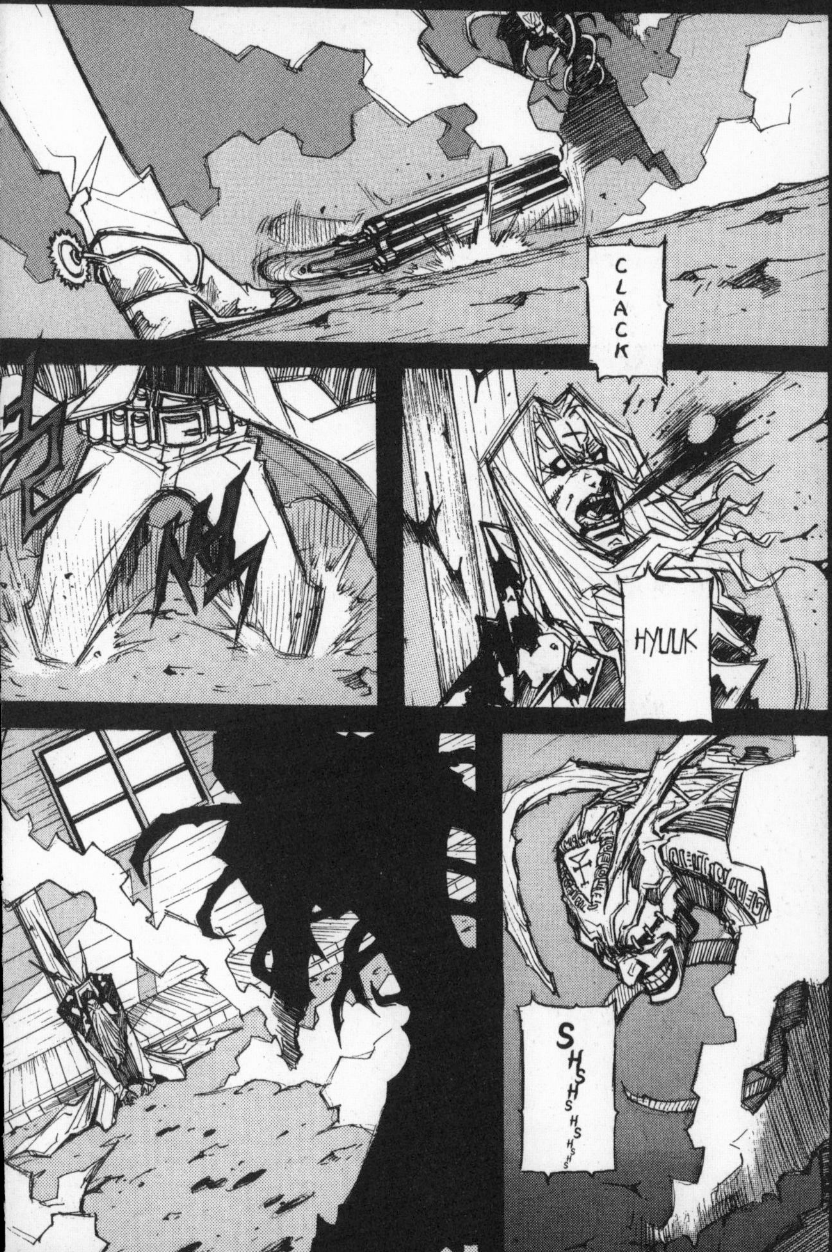
CLACK
HYUUK
SHSHSHSHSHS

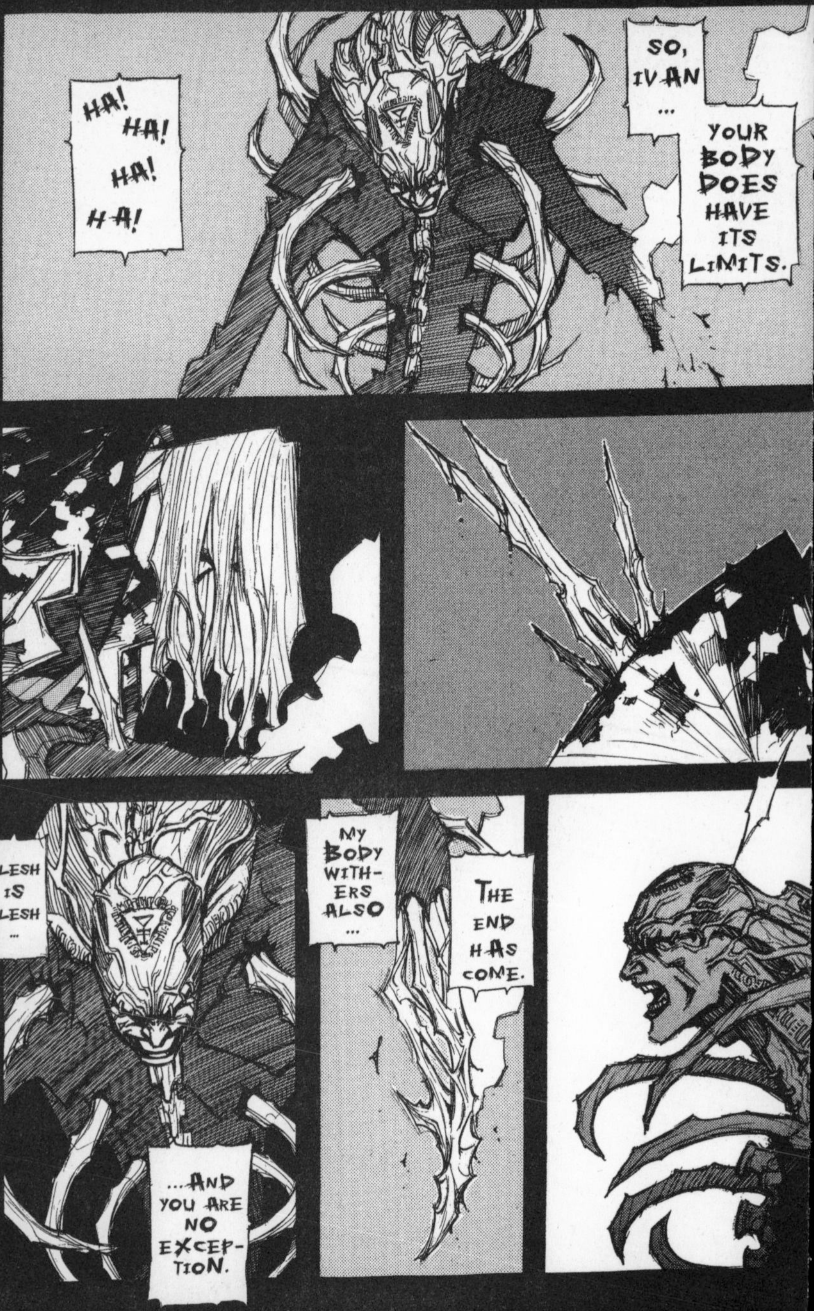
HA! HA! HA! HA!
SO, IVAN ...
YOUR BODY DOES HAVE ITS LIMITS.
FLESH IS FLESH ...
...AND YOU ARE NO EXCEPTION.
MY BODY WITHERS ALSO ...
THE END HAS COME.

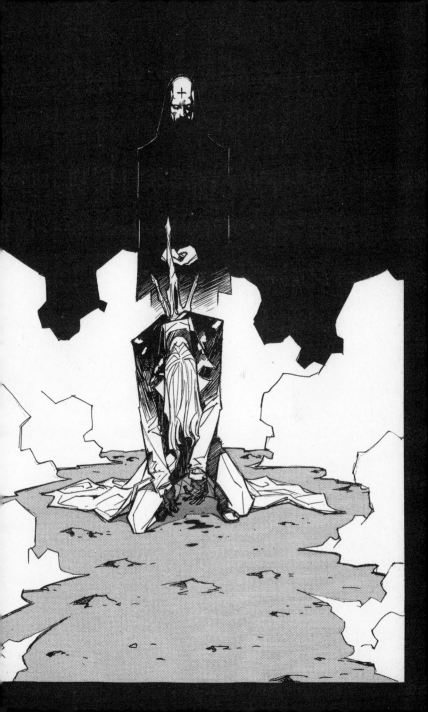

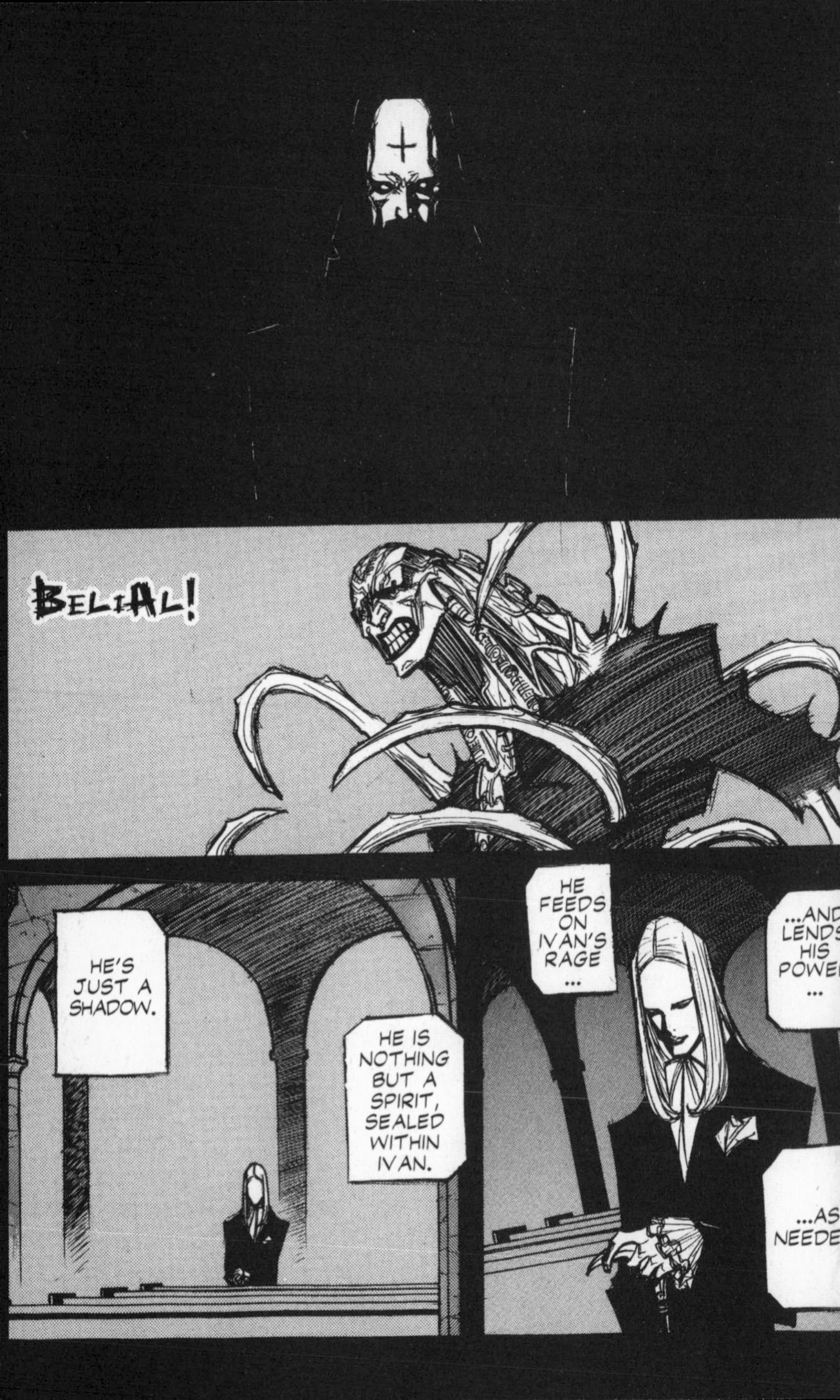
BELIAL!
HE'S JUST A SHADOW.
HE IS NOTHING BUT A SPIRIT, SEALED WITHIN IVAN.
HE FEEDS ON IVAN'S RAGE ...
...AND LENDS HIS POWE ...
...AS NEEDE

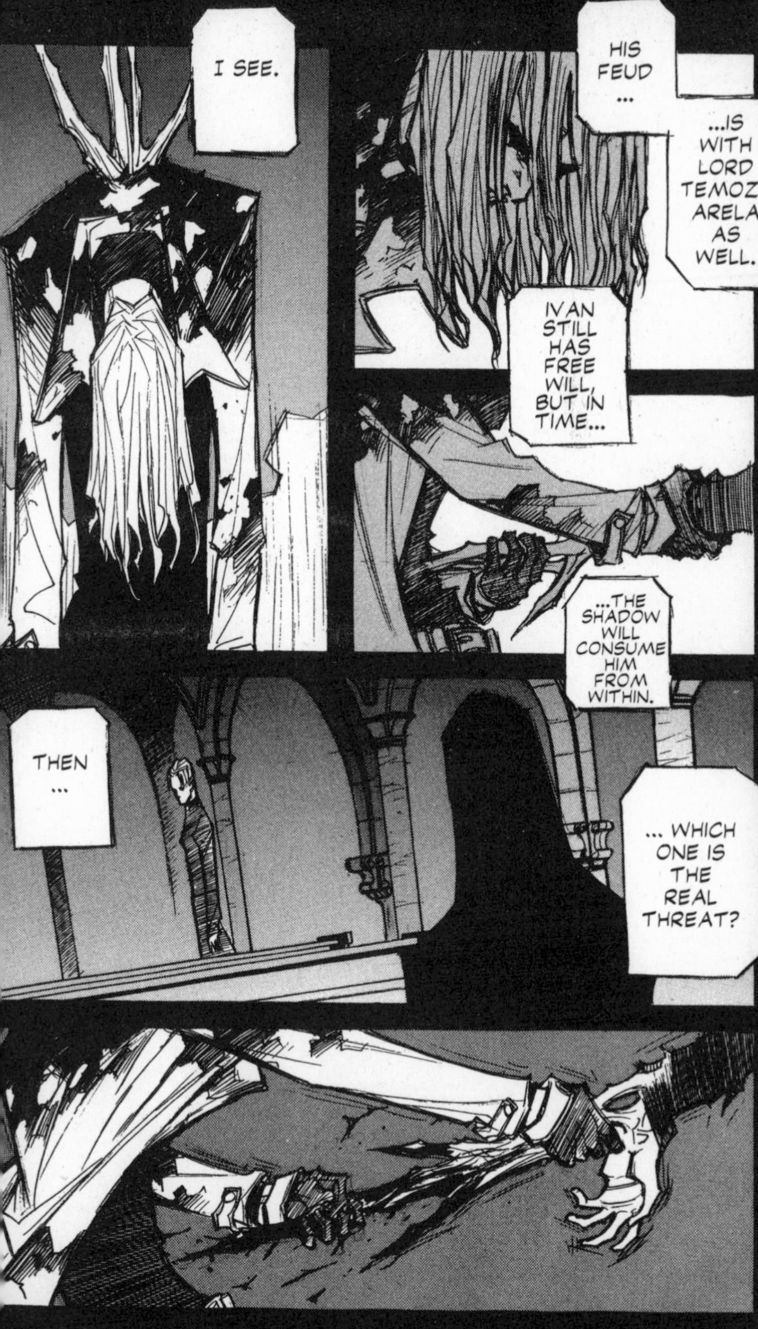
I SEE.
HIS FEUD ...
...IS WITH LORD TEMOZ-ARELA AS WELL.
IVAN STILL HAS FREE WILL, BUT IN TIME...
...THE SHADOW WILL CONSUME HIM FROM WITHIN.
THEN ...
... WHICH ONE IS THE REAL THREAT?

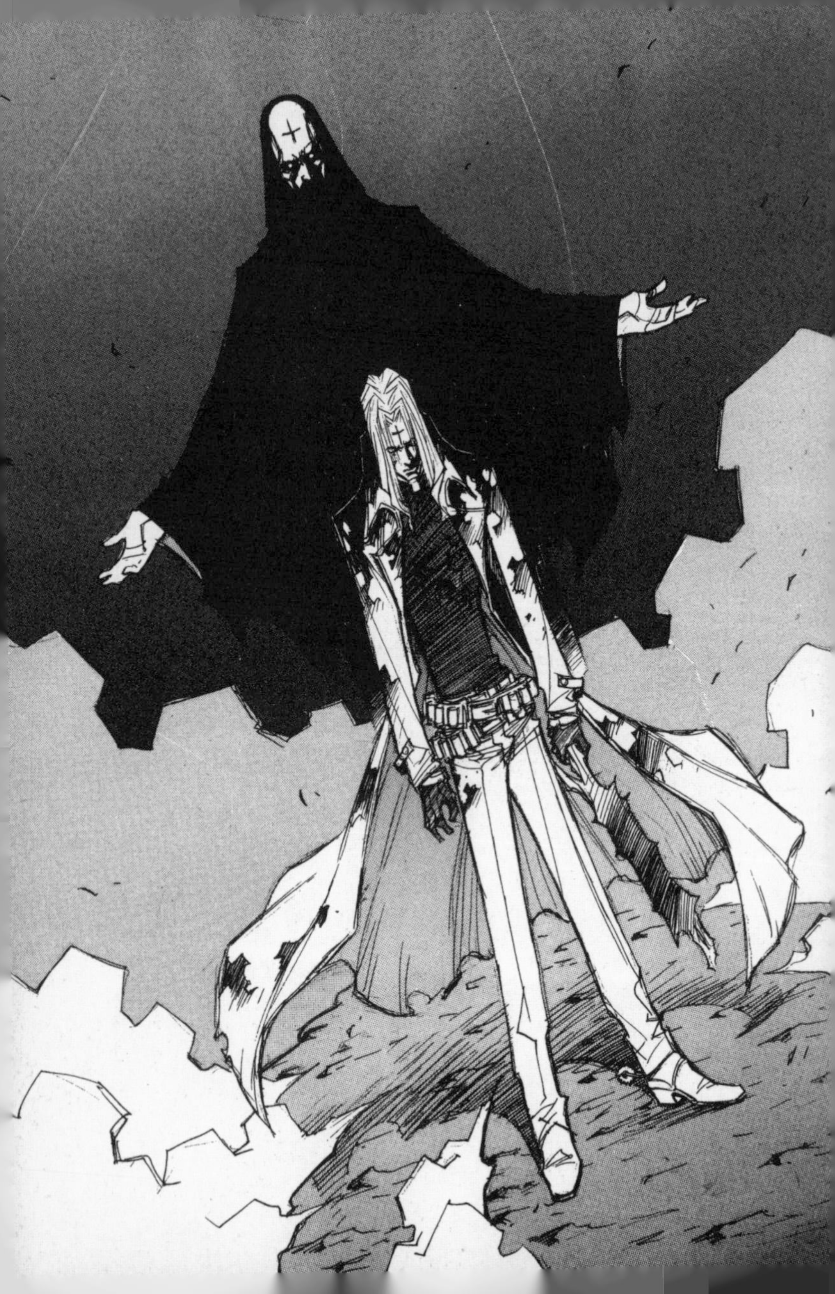

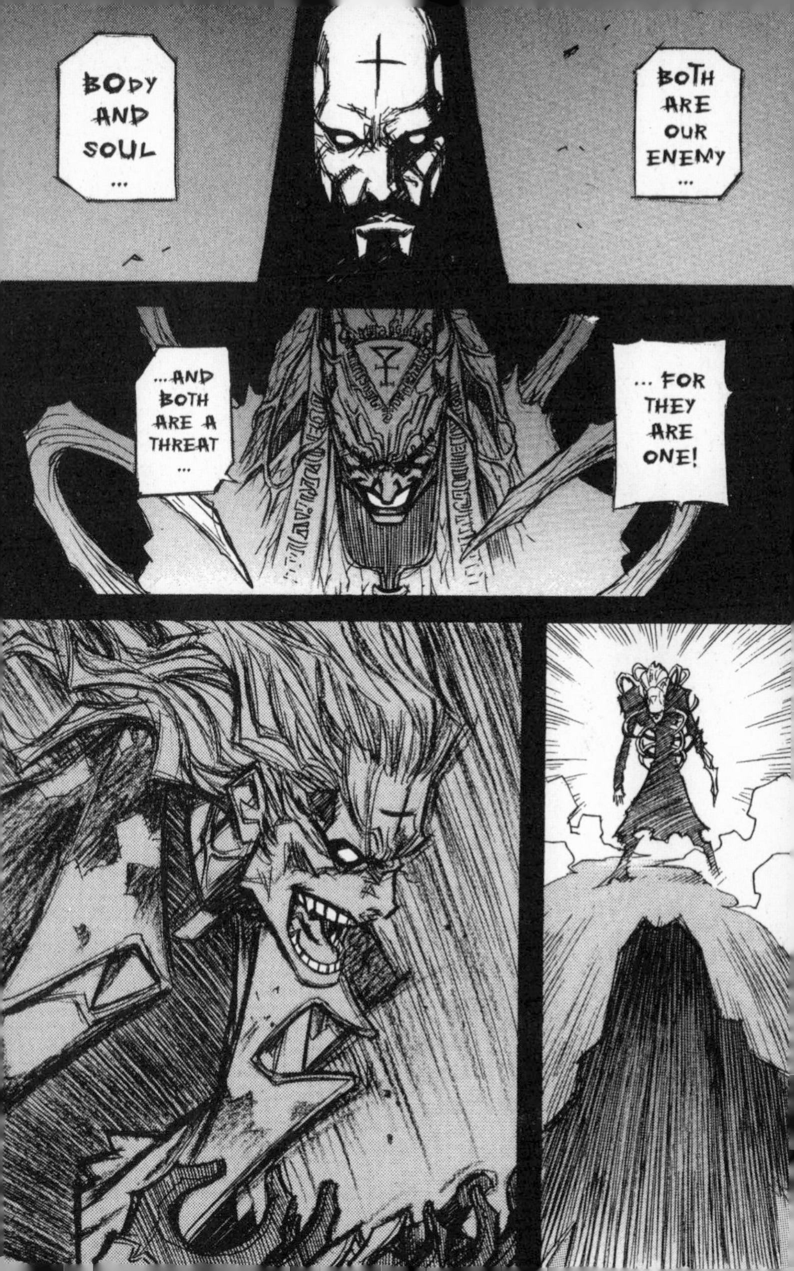
BODY AND SOUL ...
BOTH ARE OUR ENEMY ...
...AND BOTH ARE A THREAT ...
... FOR THEY ARE ONE!

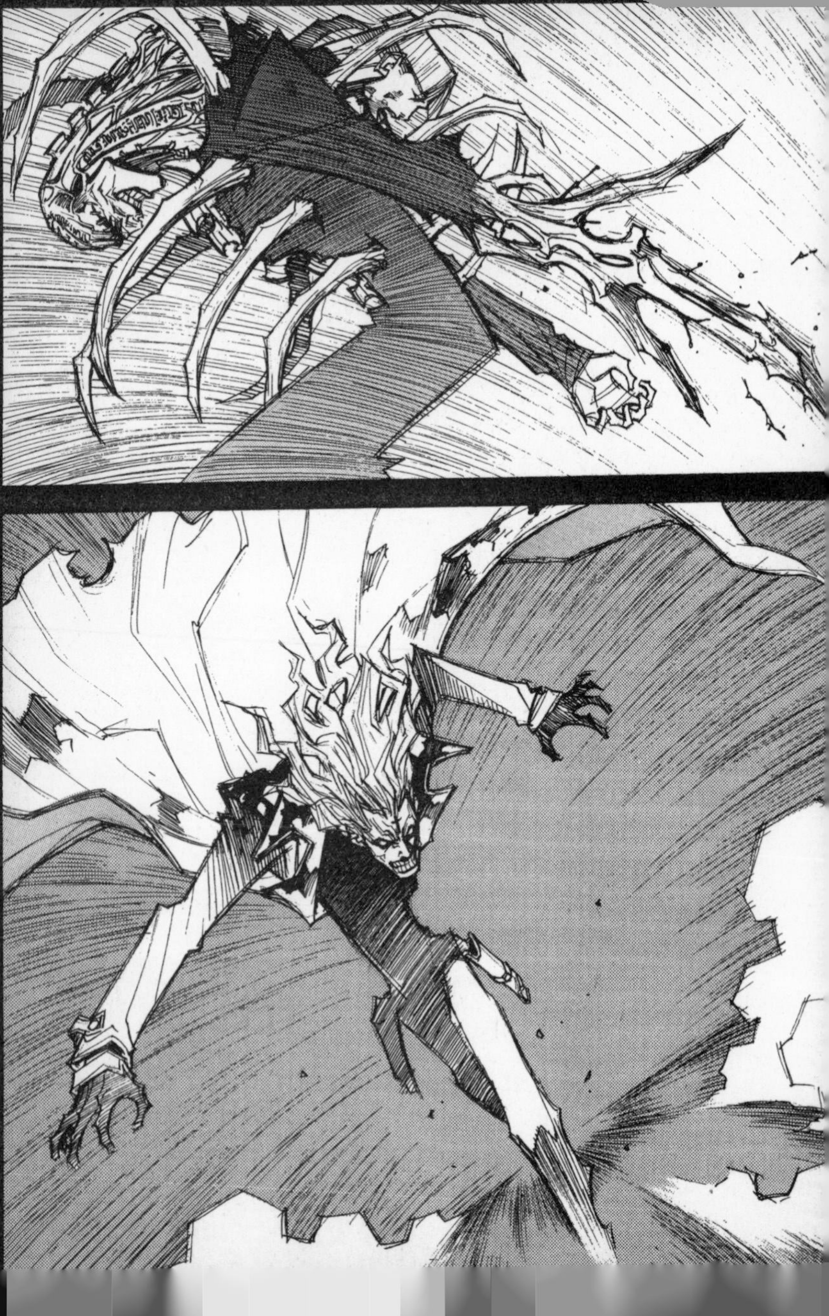

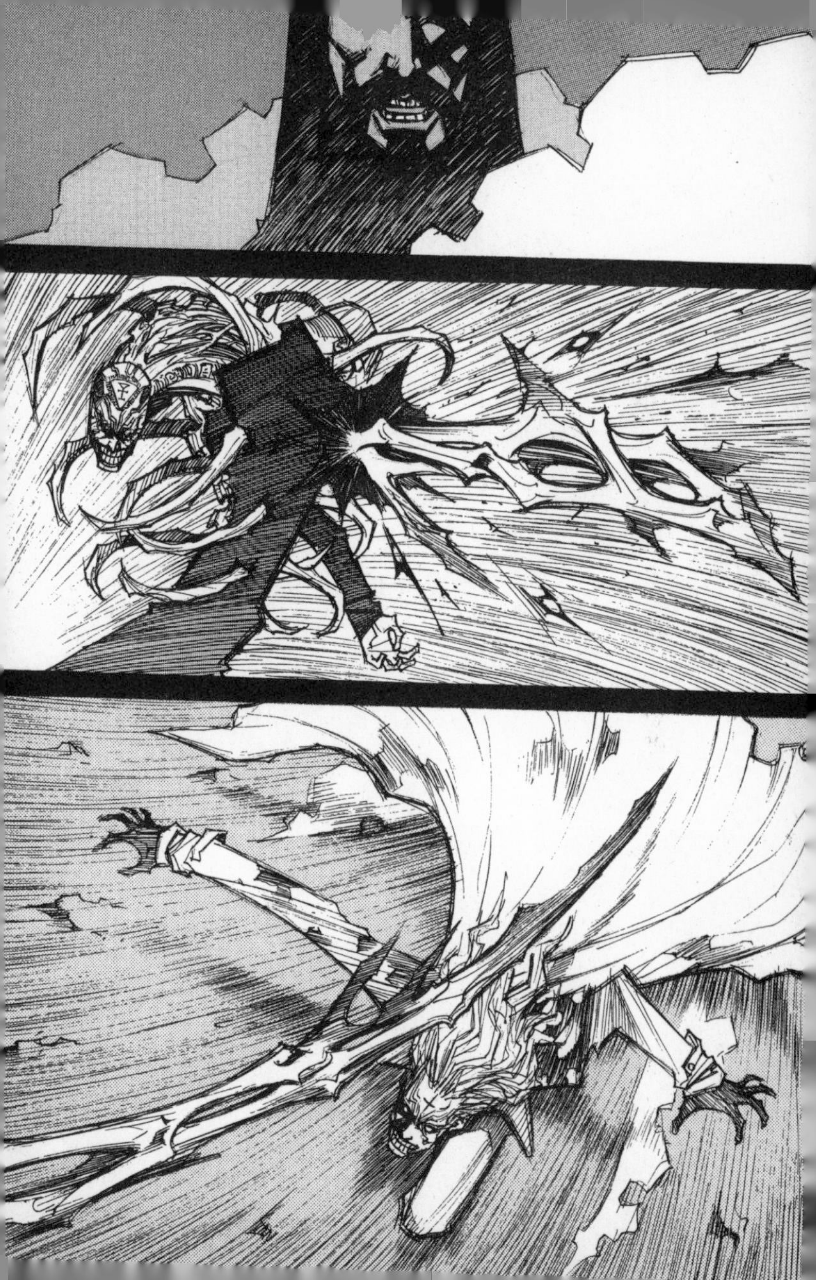

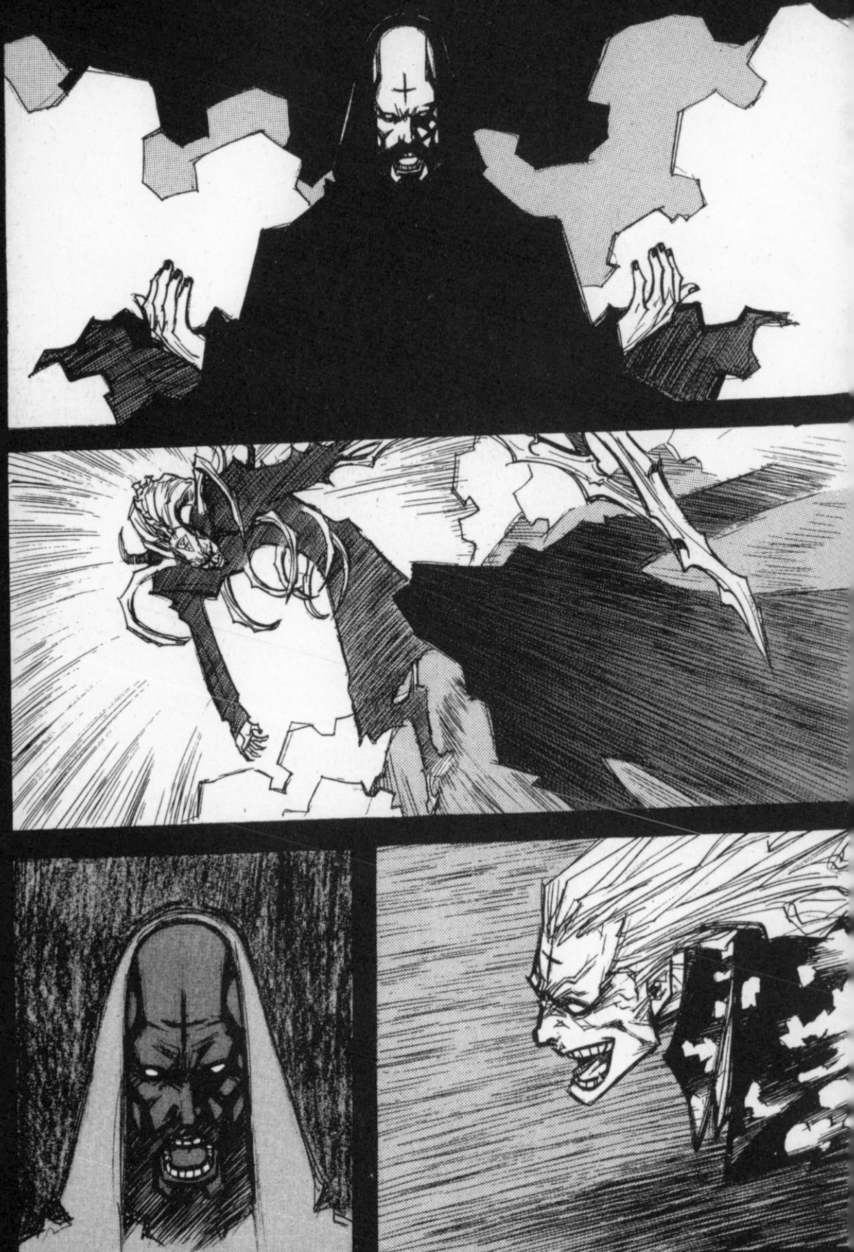

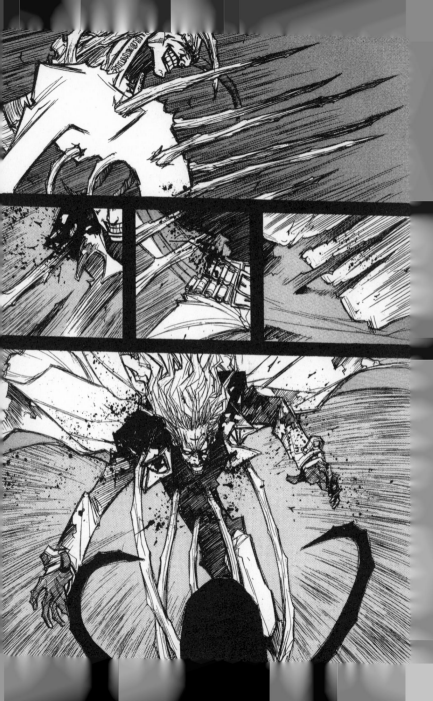

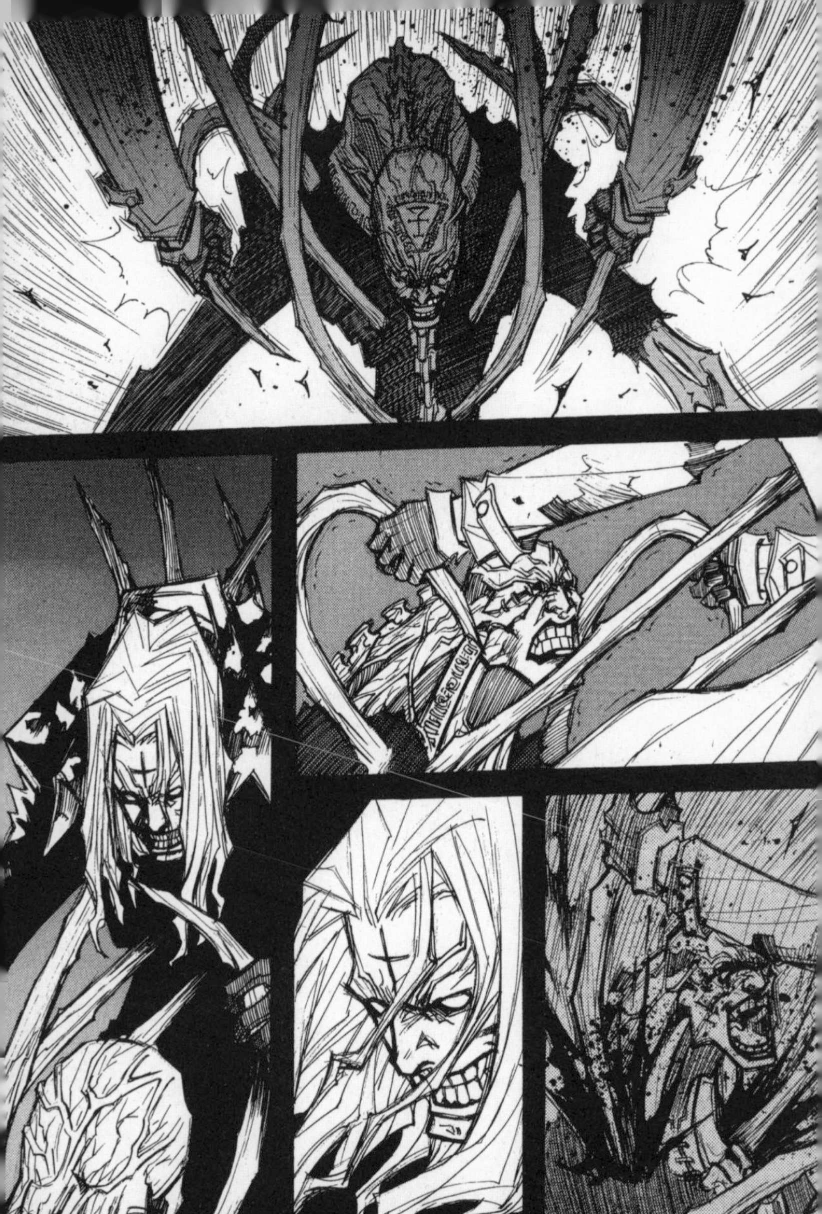

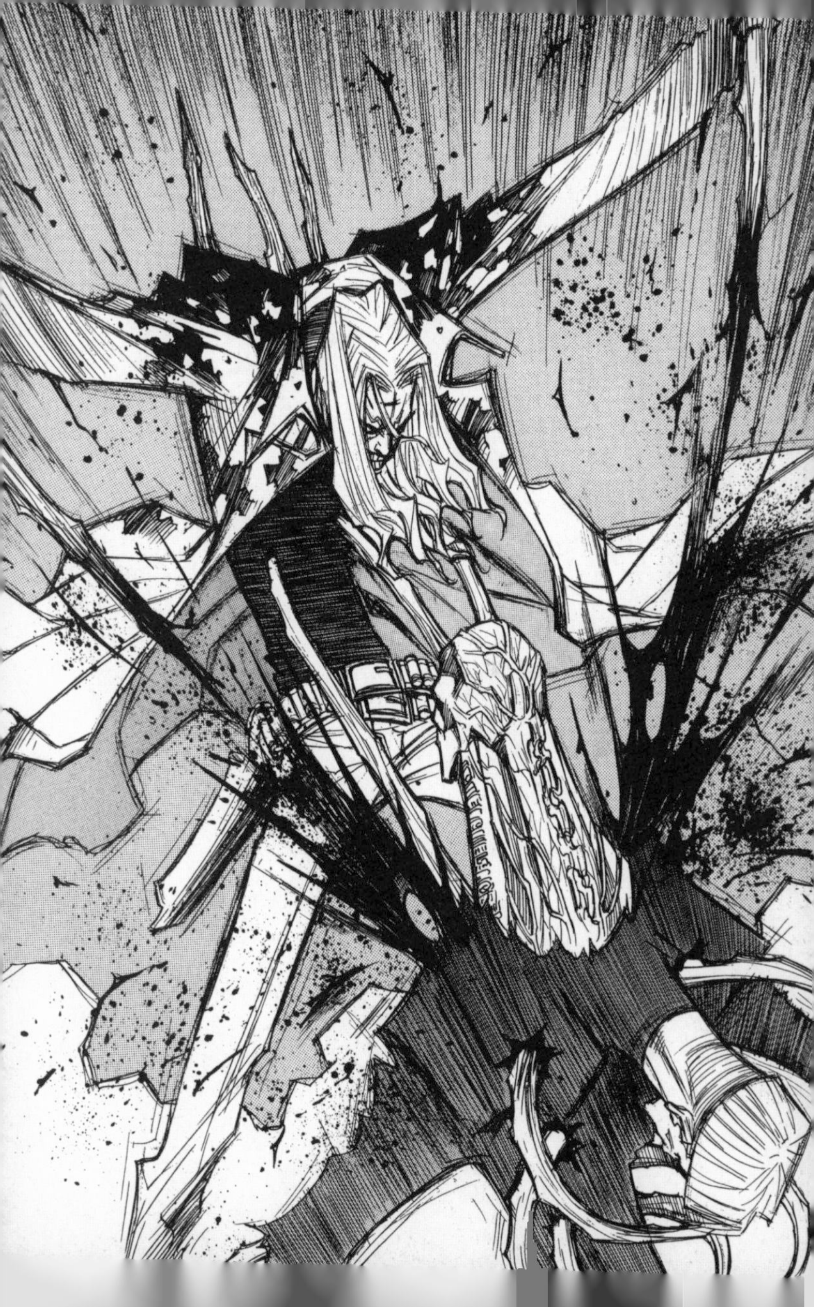

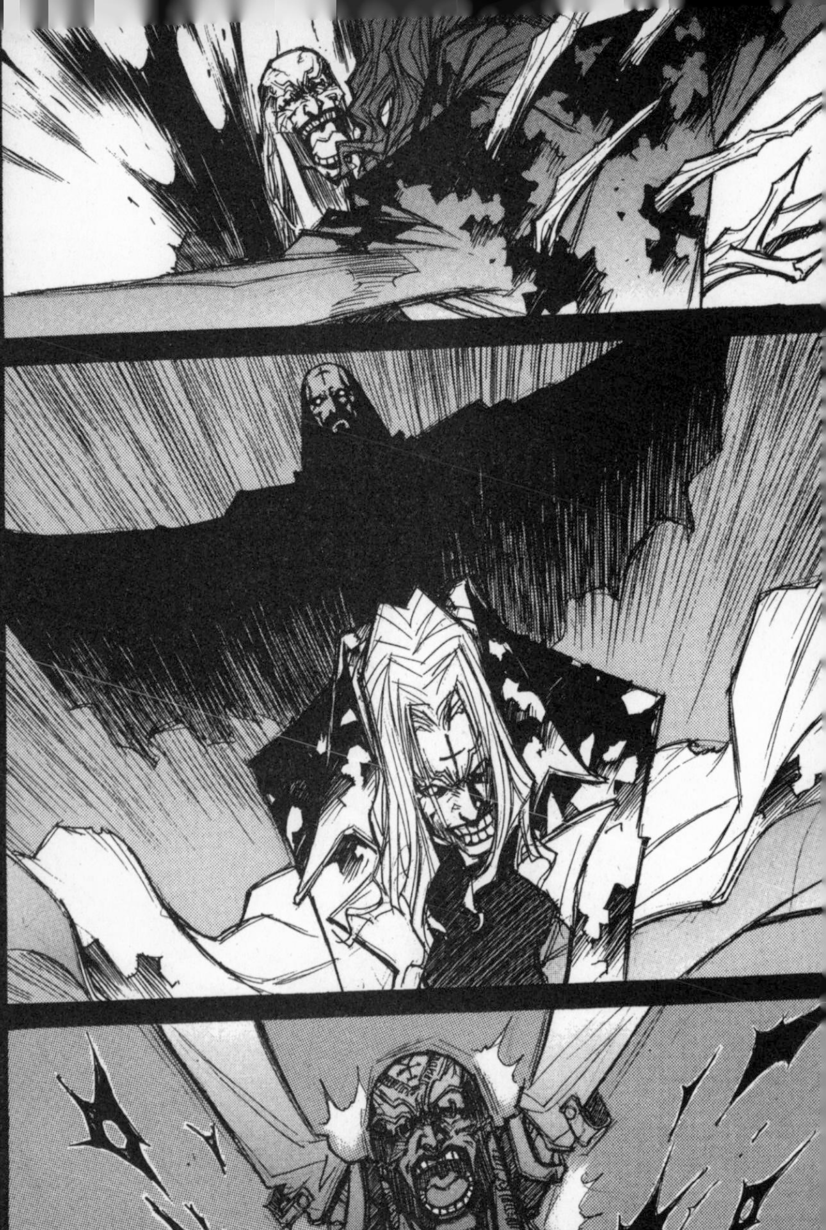

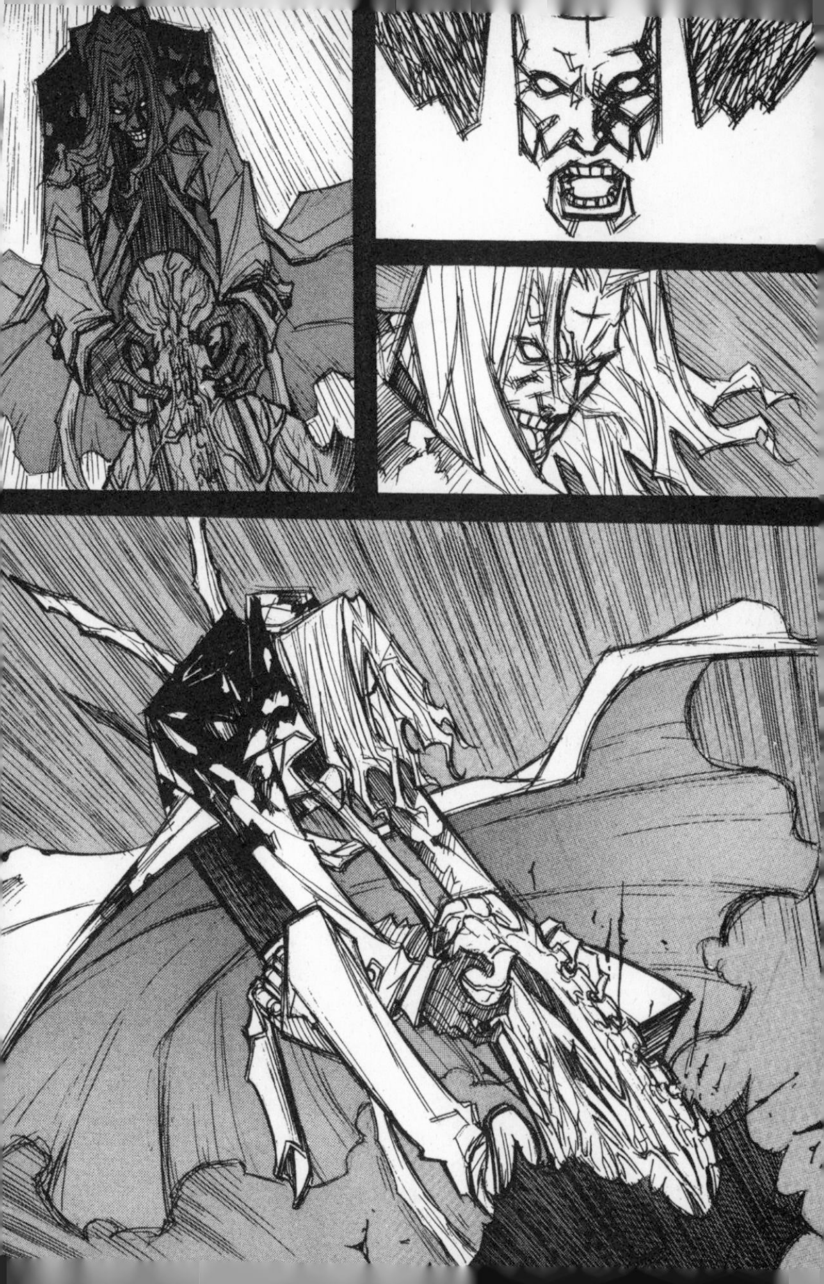

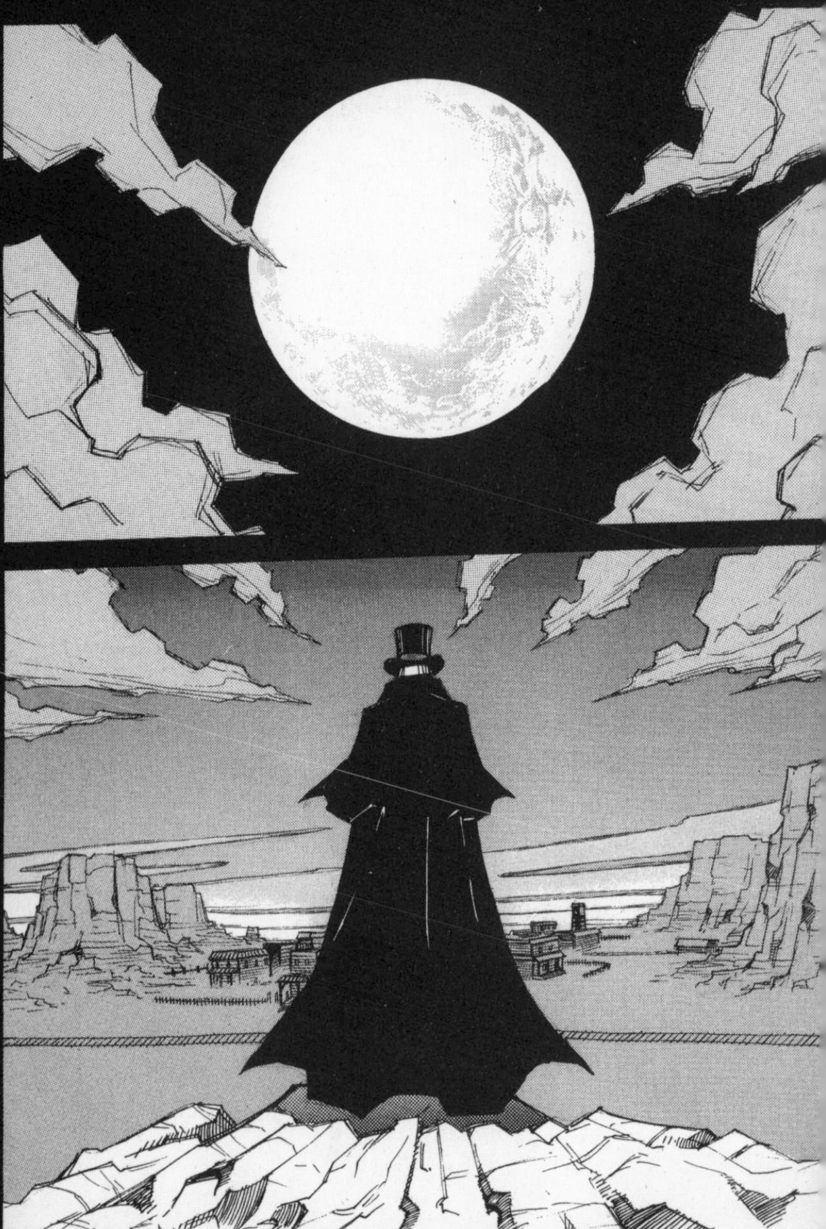

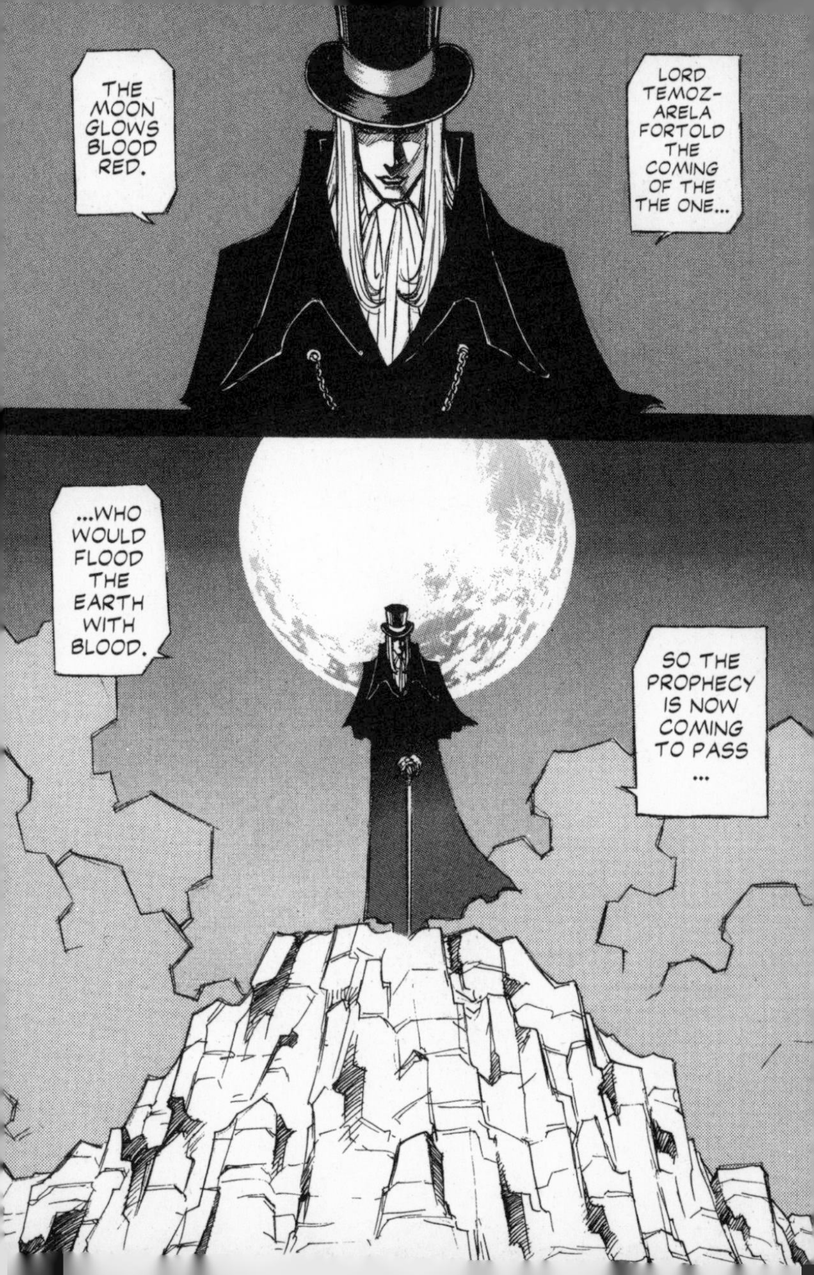
THE MOON GLOWS BLOOD RED.
LORD TEMOZ-ARELA FORTOLD THE COMING OF THE THE ONE...
...WHO WOULD FLOOD THE EARTH WITH BLOOD.
SO THE PROPHECY IS NOW COMING TO PASS ...

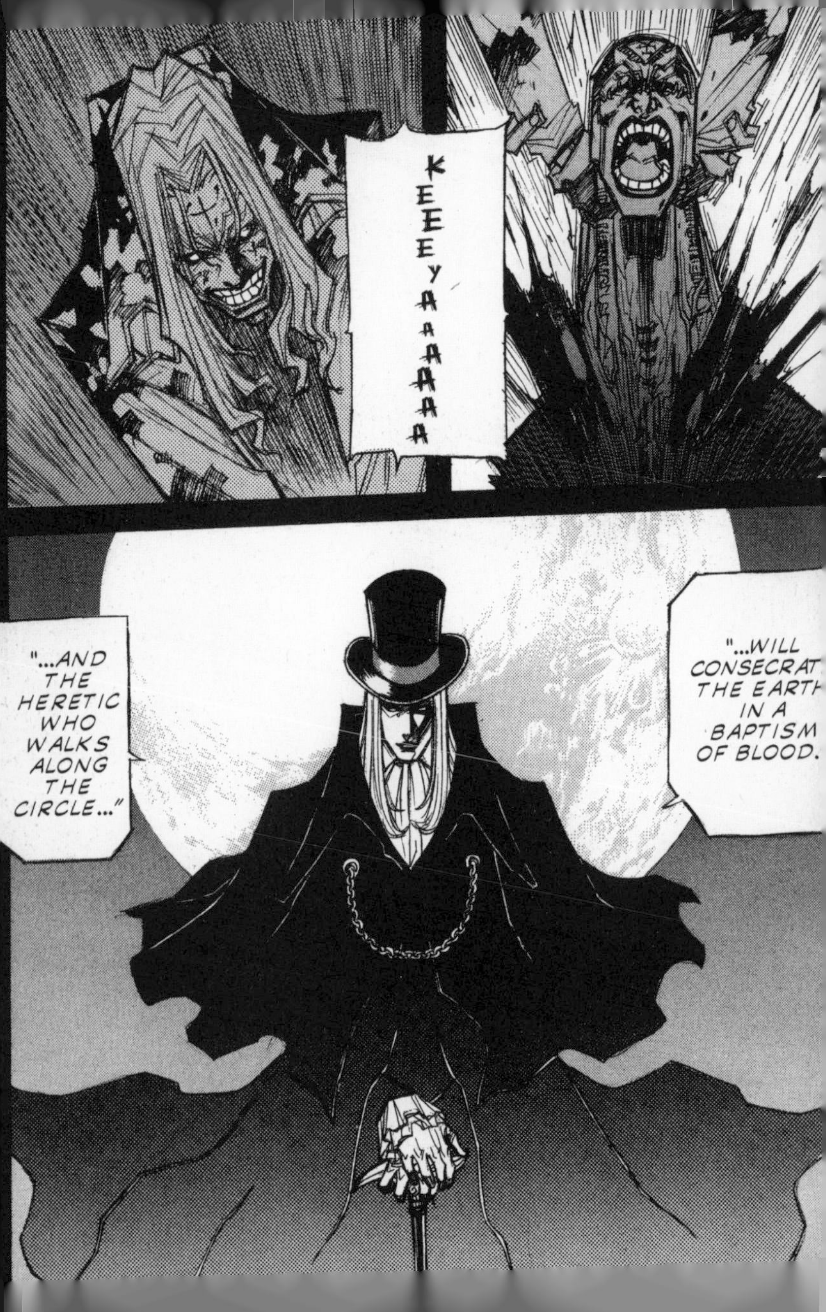
KEEEyAAAAAA
"...AND THE HERETIC WHO WALKS ALONG THE CIRCLE..."
"...WILL CONSECRAT THE EARTH IN A BAPTISM OF BLOOD."

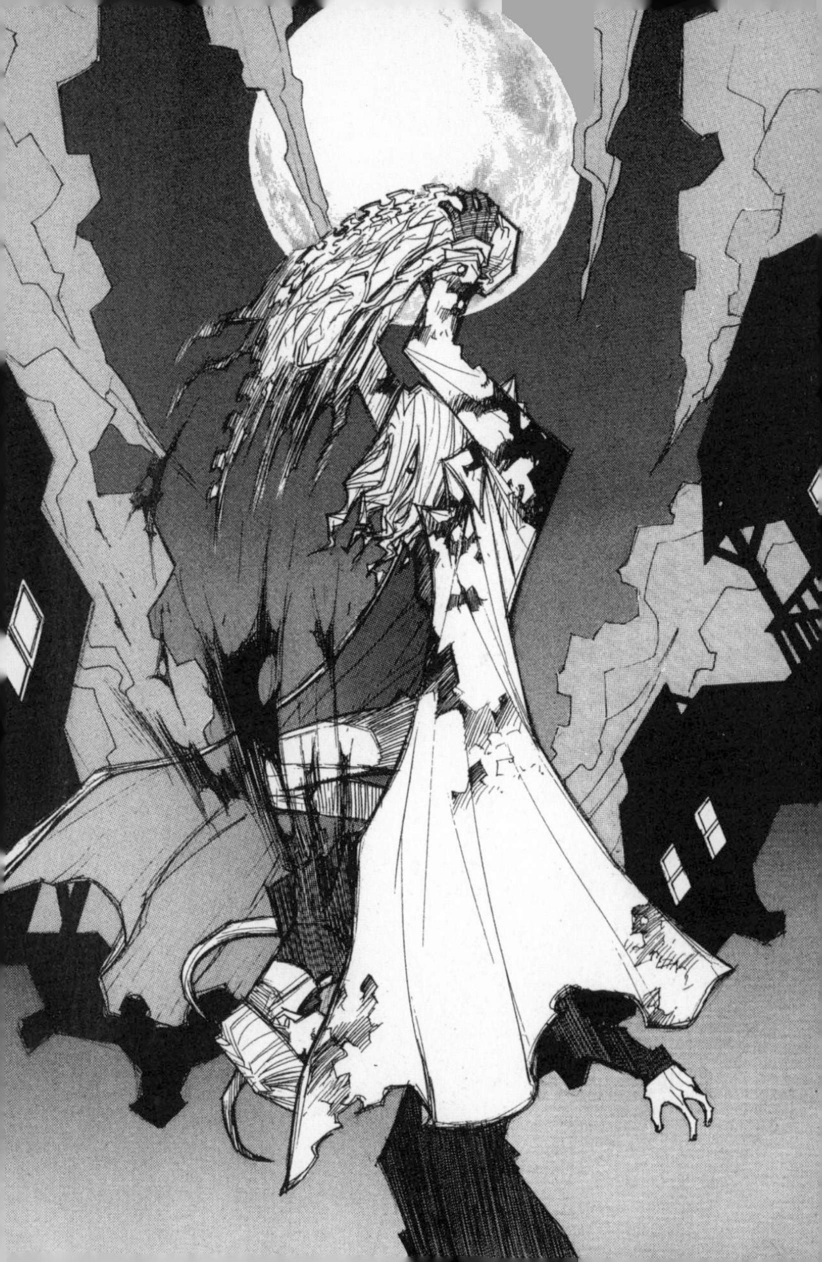

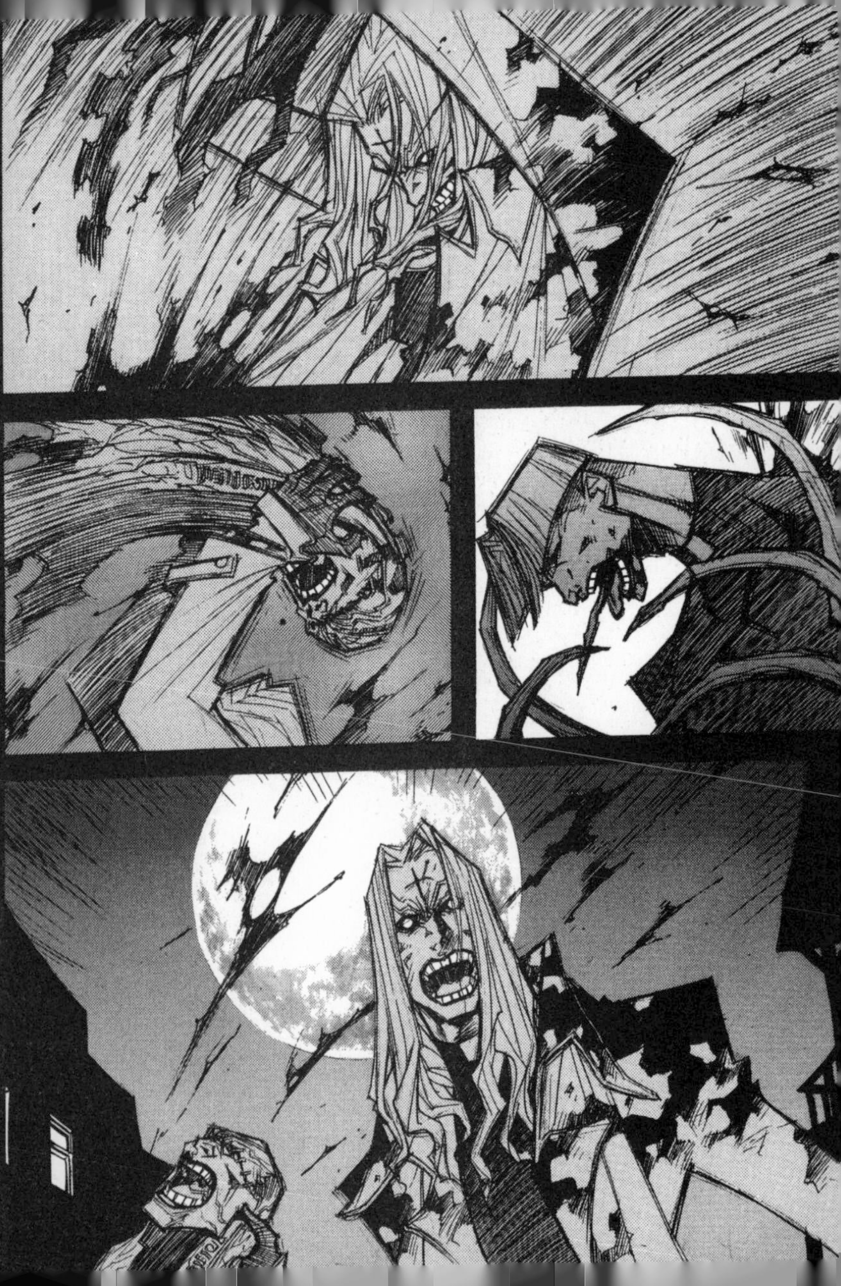

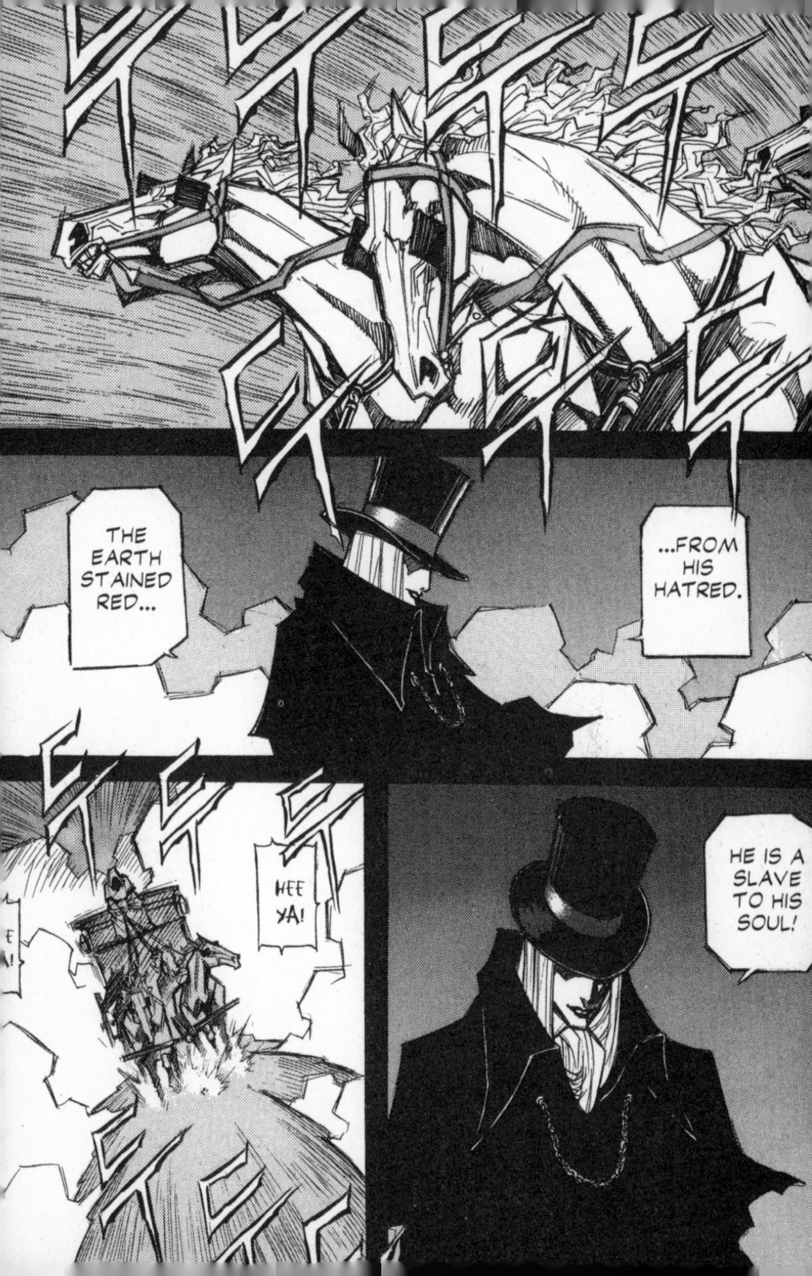
THE EARTH STAINED RED...
...FROM HIS HATRED.
HEE YA!
HE IS A SLAVE TO HIS SOUL!

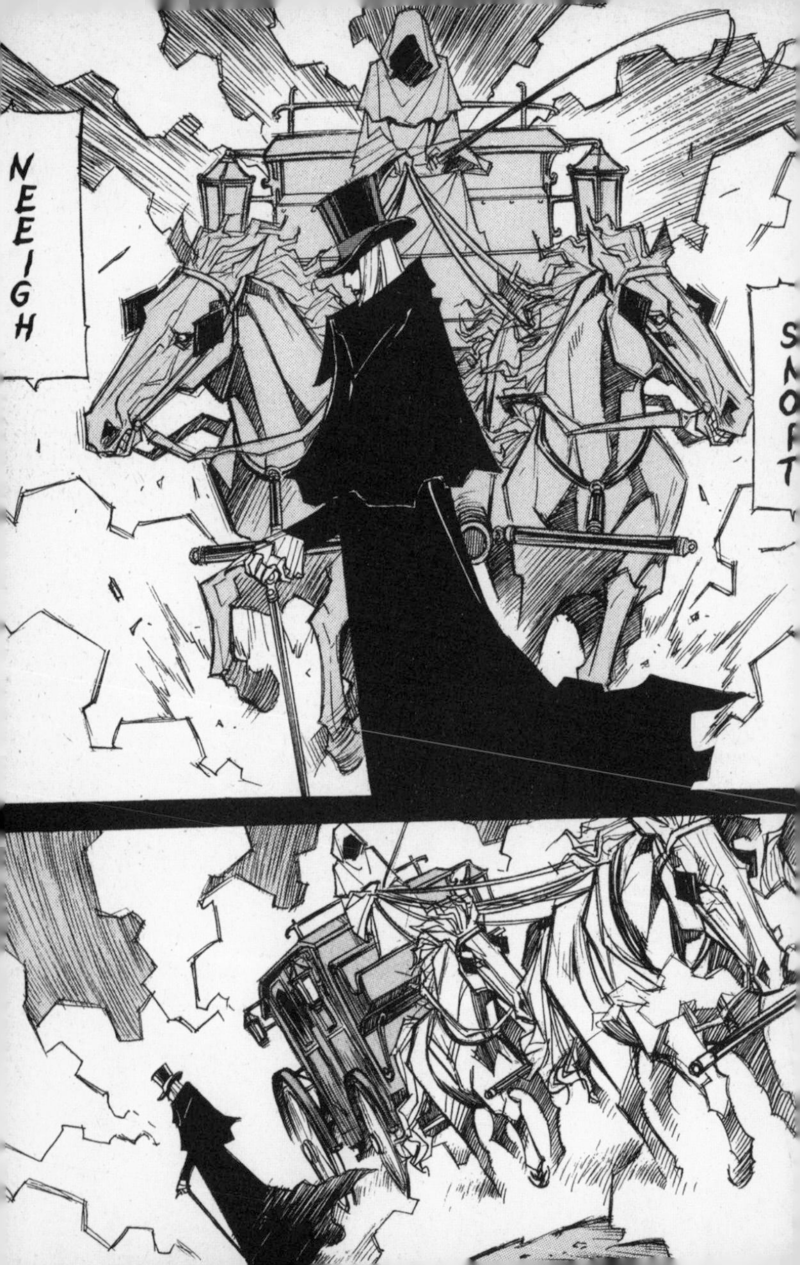
NEEIGH
SNORT

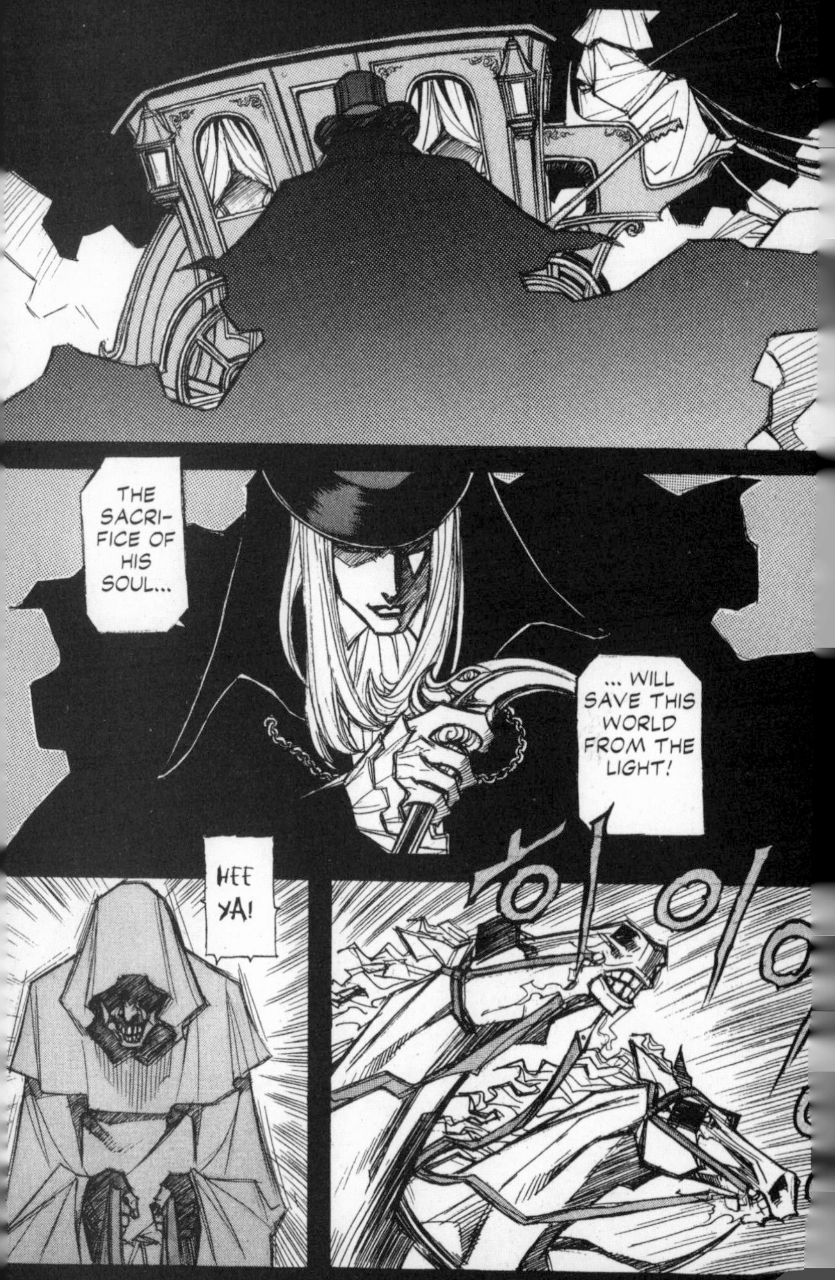
THE SACRIFICE OF HIS SOUL...
... WILL SAVE THIS WORLD FROM THE LIGHT!
HEE YA!

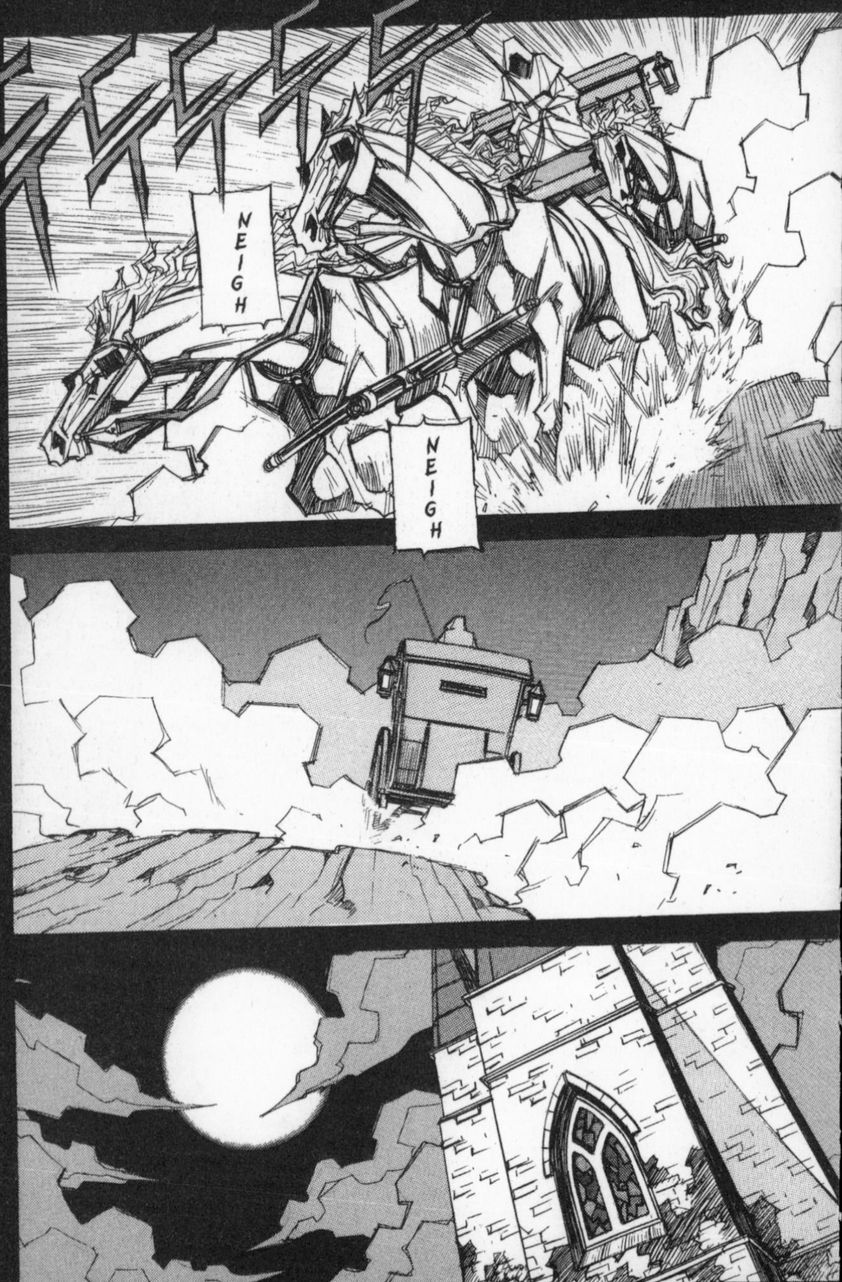
NEIGH
NEIGH

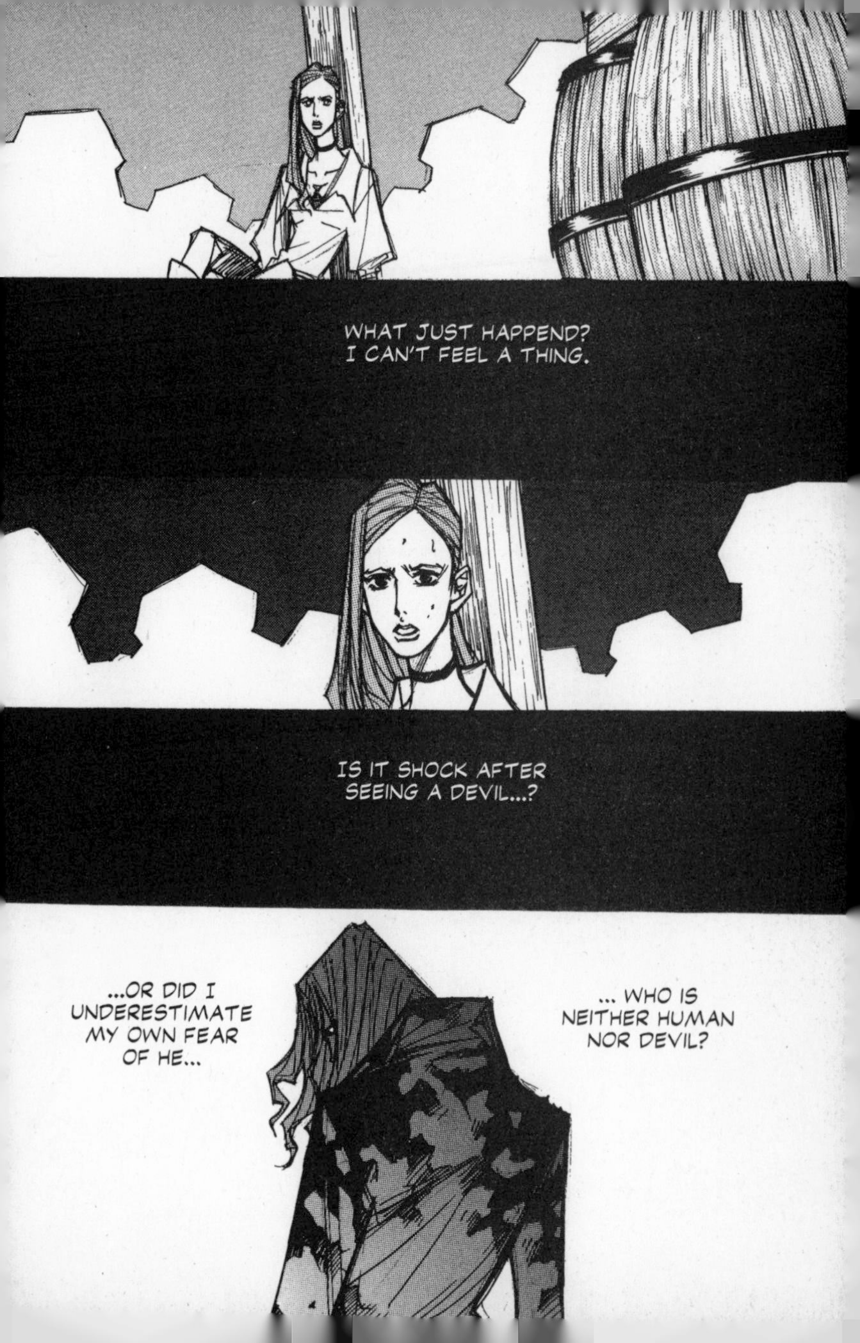
WHAT JUST HAPPEND? I CAN'T FEEL A THING.
IS IT SHOCK AFTER SEEING A DEVIL...?
...OR DID I UNDERESTIMATE MY OWN FEAR OF HE...
... WHO IS NEITHER HUMAN NOR DEVIL?

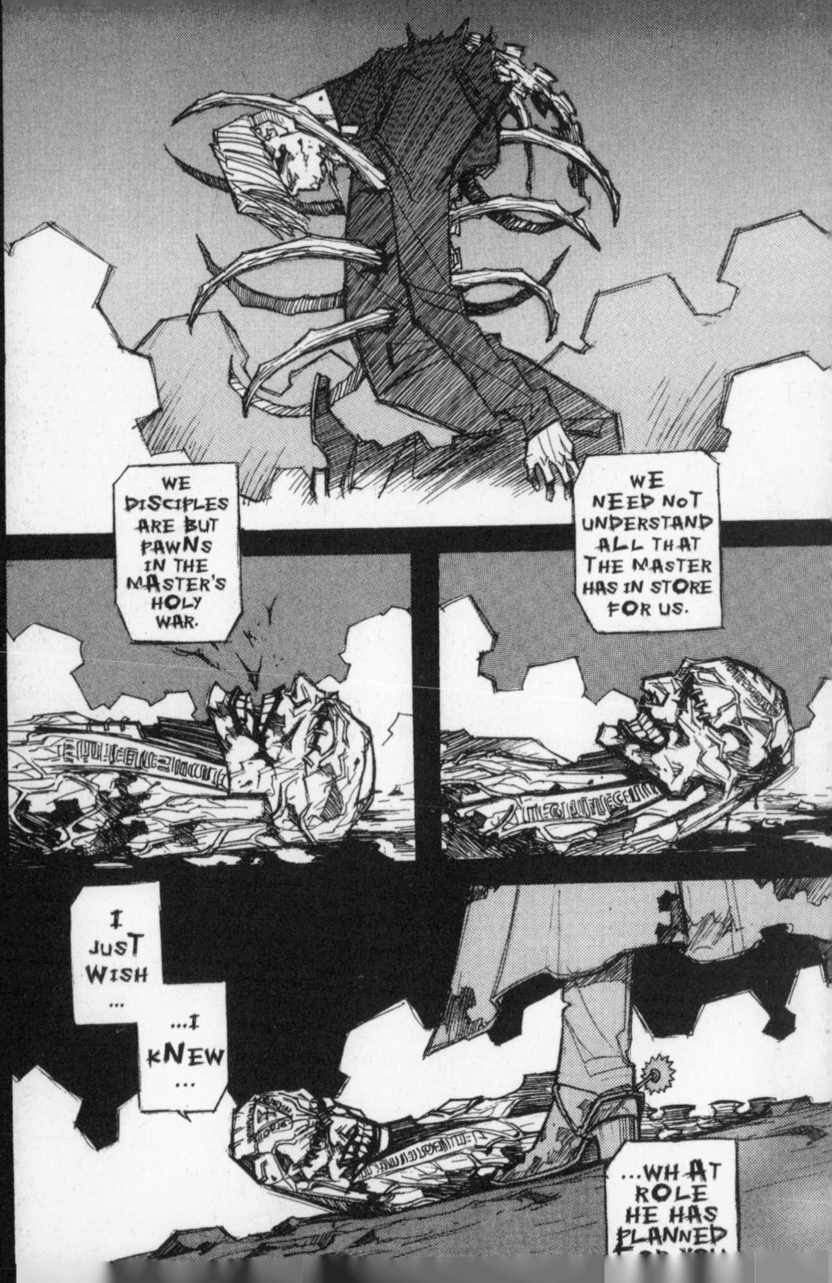
WE DISCIPLES ARE BUT PAWNS IN THE MASTER'S HOLY WAR.
WE NEED NOT UNDERSTAND ALL THAT THE MASTER HAS IN STORE FOR US.
I JUST WISH ...
...I KNEW ...
...WHAT ROLE HE HAS PLANNED

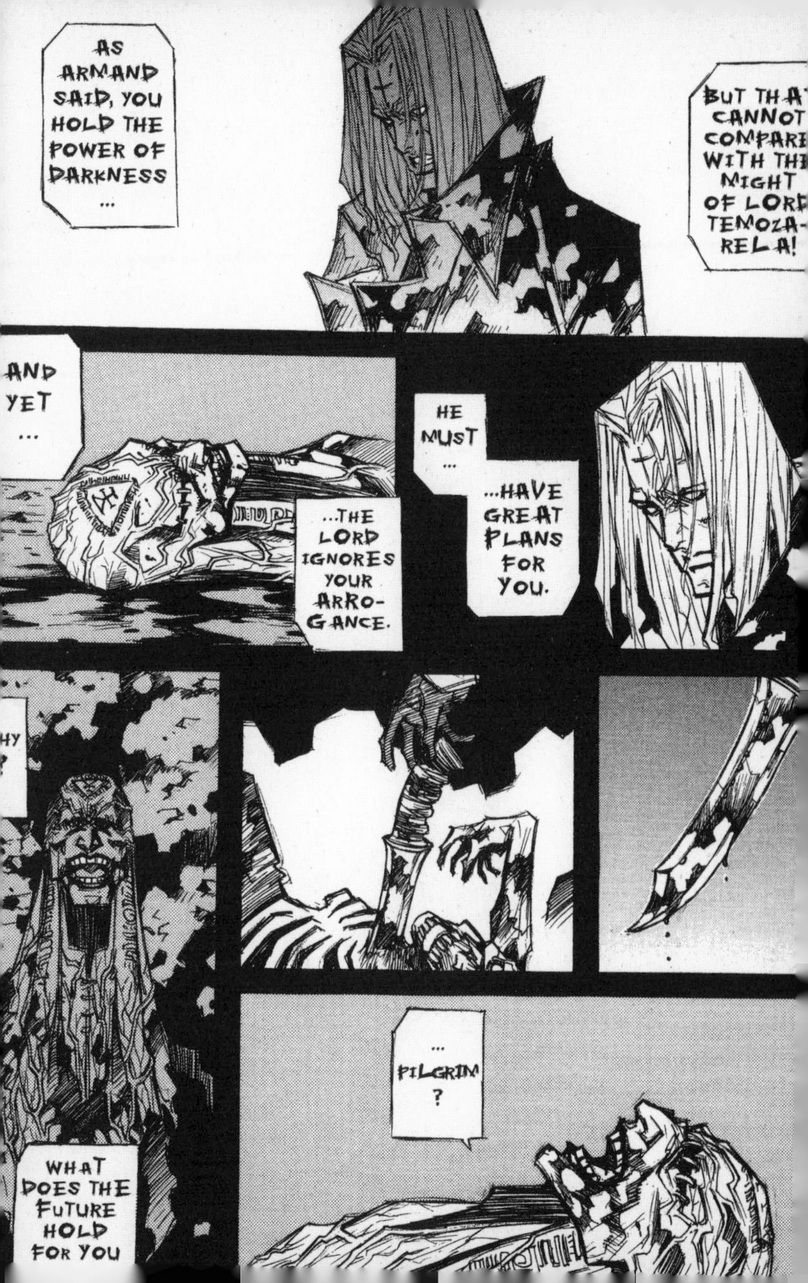
AS ARMAND SAID, YOU HOLD THE POWER OF DARKNESS ...
BUT THAT CANNOT COMPARE WITH THE MIGHT OF LORD TEMOZA-RELA!
AND YET ...
...THE LORD IGNORES YOUR ARRO-GANCE.
HE MUST ...
...HAVE GREAT PLANS FOR YOU.
WHAT DOES THE FUTURE HOLD FOR YOU
... PILGRIM ?

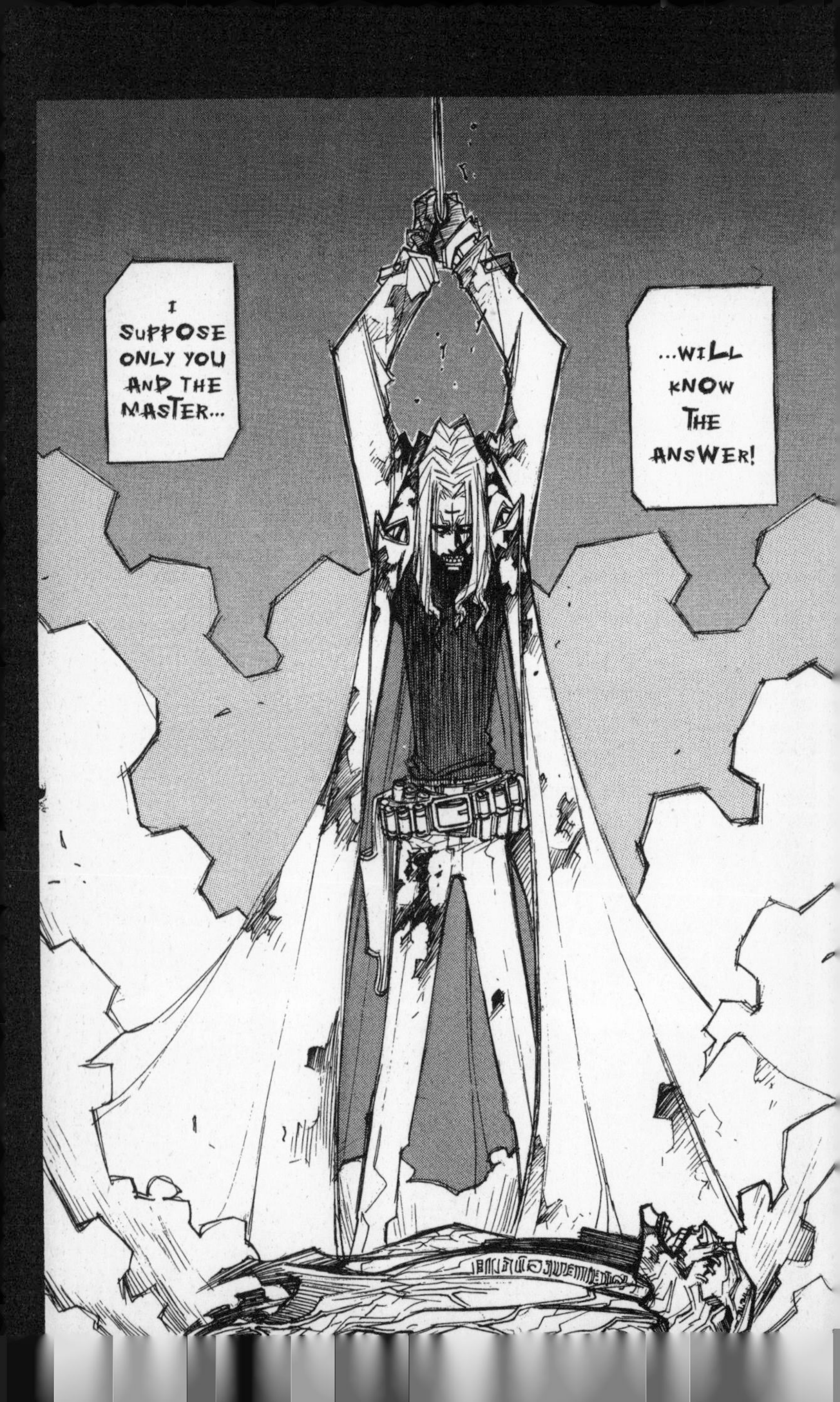
I SUPPOSE ONLY YOU AND THE MASTER...
...WILL KNOW THE ANSWER!

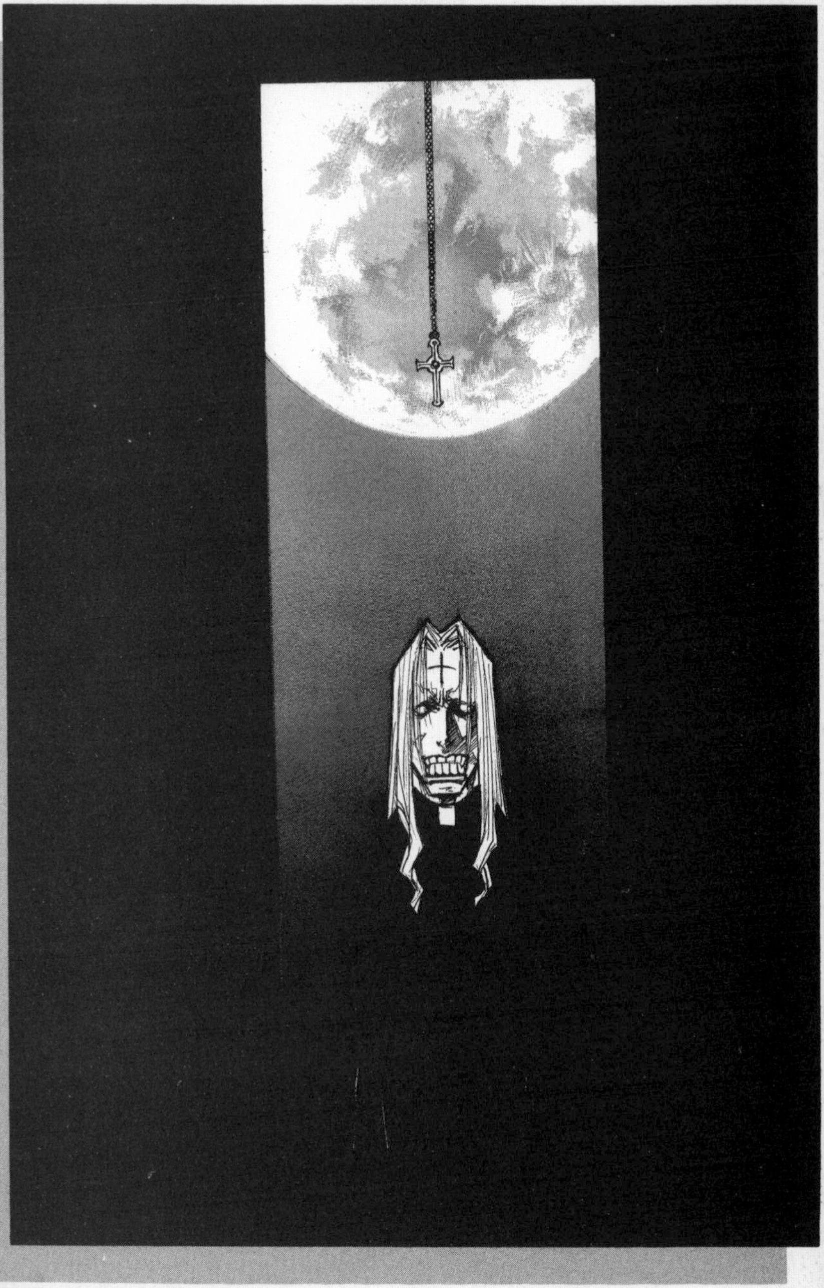

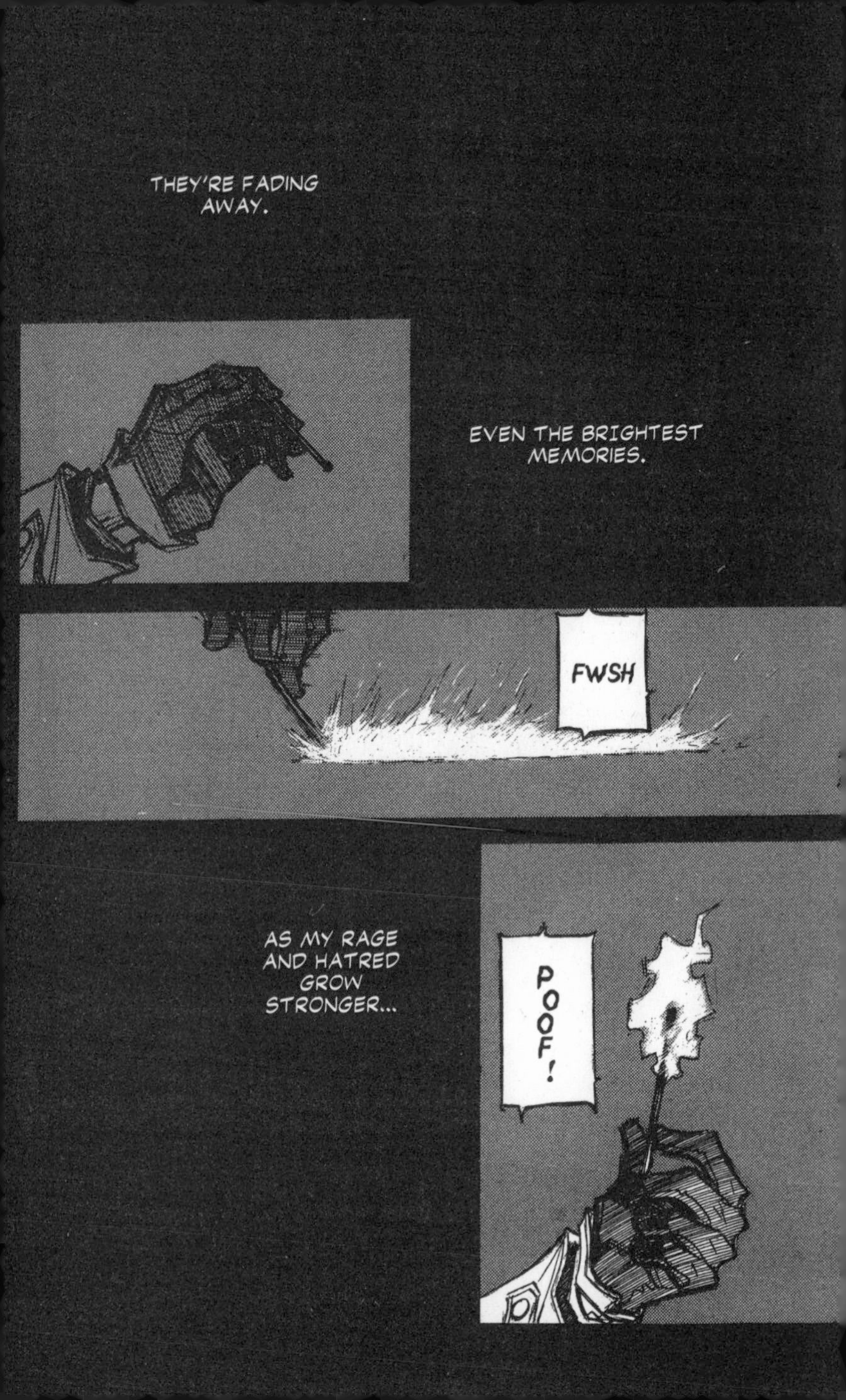
THEY'RE FADING AWAY.
EVEN THE BRIGHTEST MEMORIES.
FWSH
AS MY RAGE AND HATRED GROW STRONGER...
POOF!

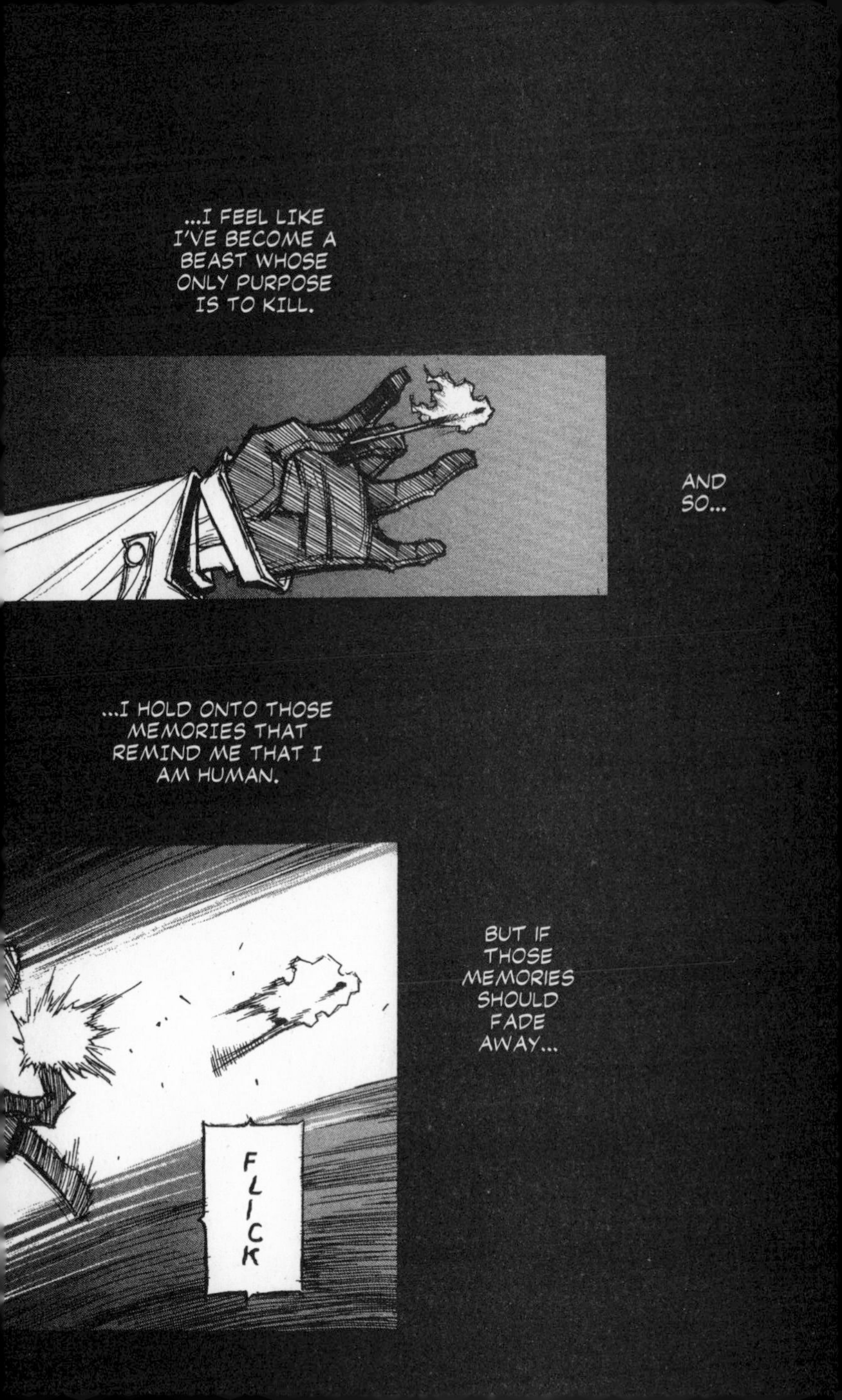
...I FEEL LIKE I'VE BECOME A BEAST WHOSE ONLY PURPOSE IS TO KILL.
AND SO...
...I HOLD ONTO THOSE MEMORIES THAT REMIND ME THAT I AM HUMAN.
FLICK
BUT IF THOSE MEMORIES SHOULD FADE AWAY...

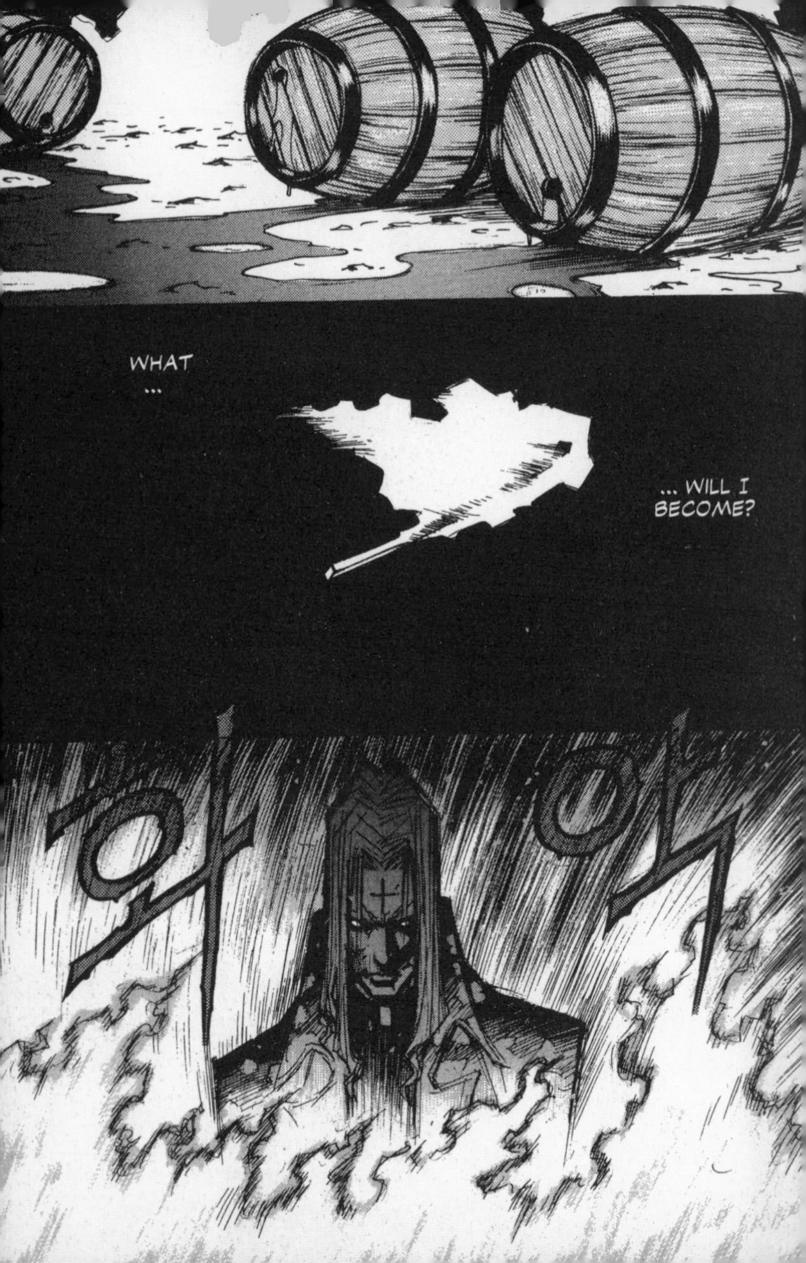
WHAT
...
... WILL I
BECOME?

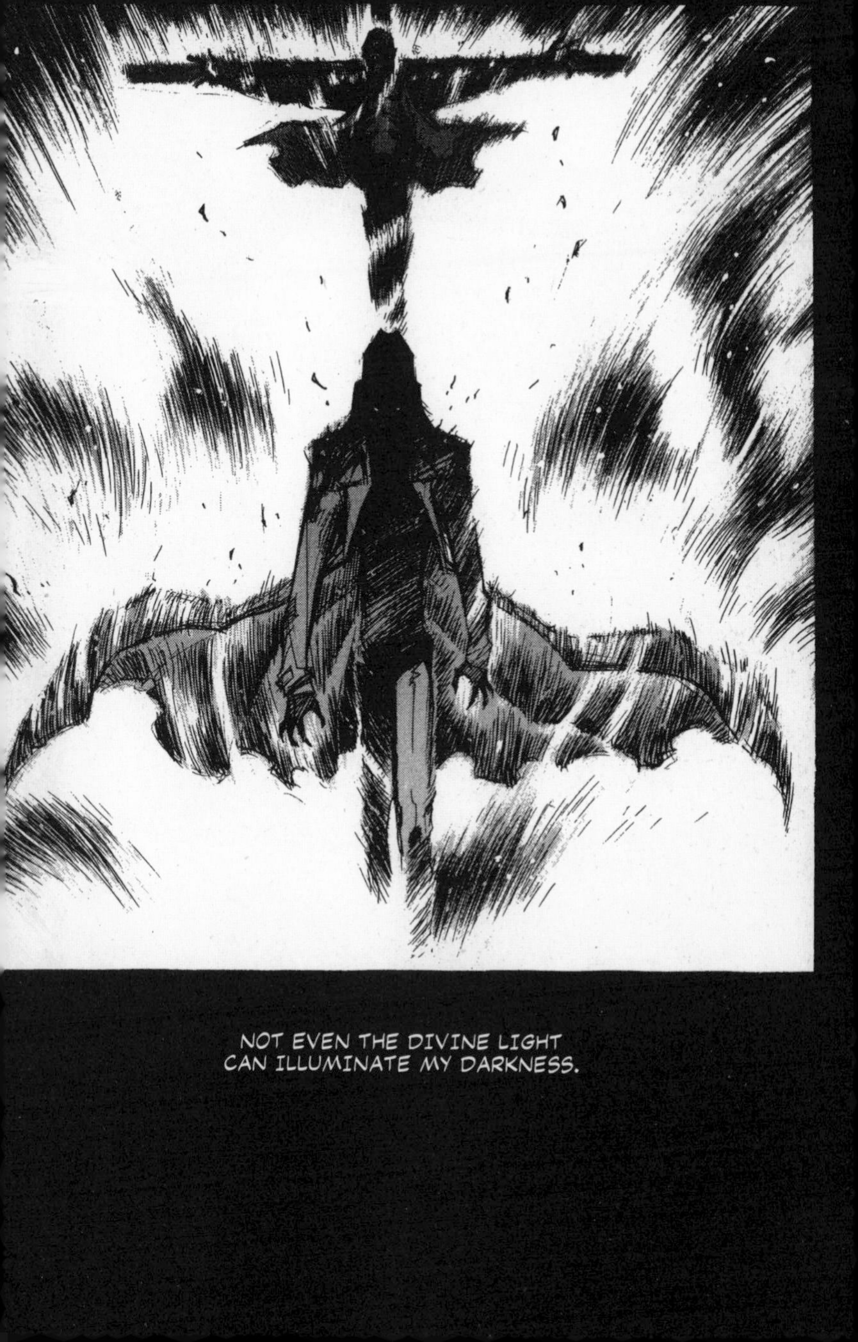

NOT EVEN THE DIVINE LIGHT
CAN ILLUMINATE MY DARKNESS.

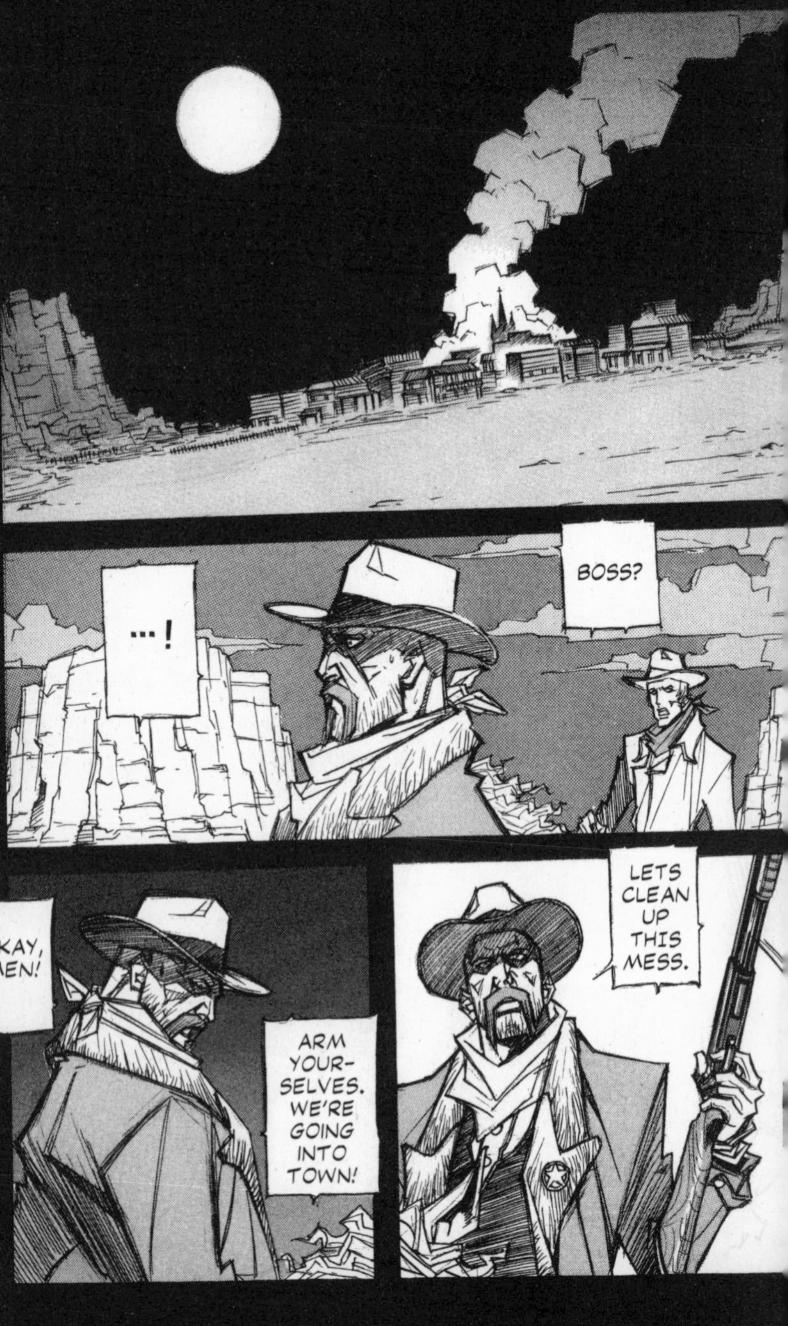

...!
BOSS?
OKAY, MEN!
ARM YOUR-SELVES. WE'RE GOING INTO TOWN!
LETS CLEAN UP THIS MESS.

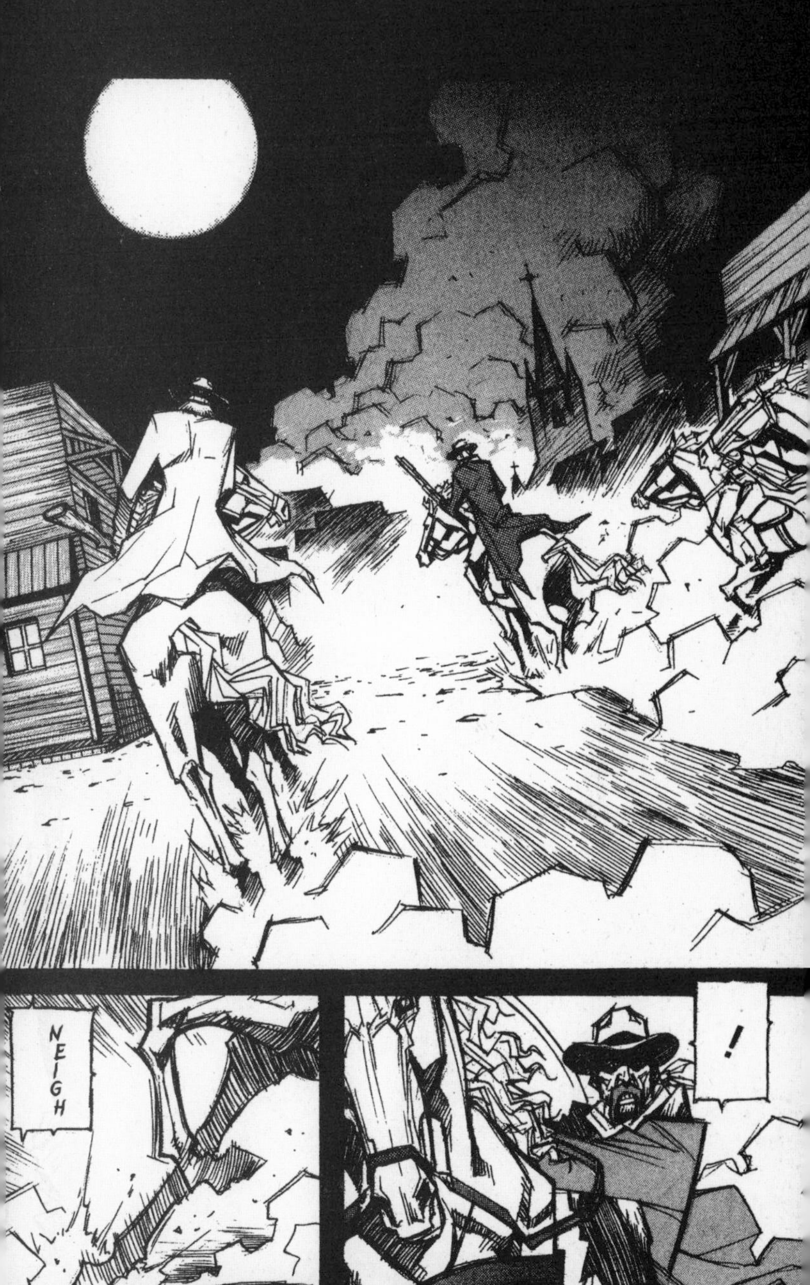
NEIGH
!

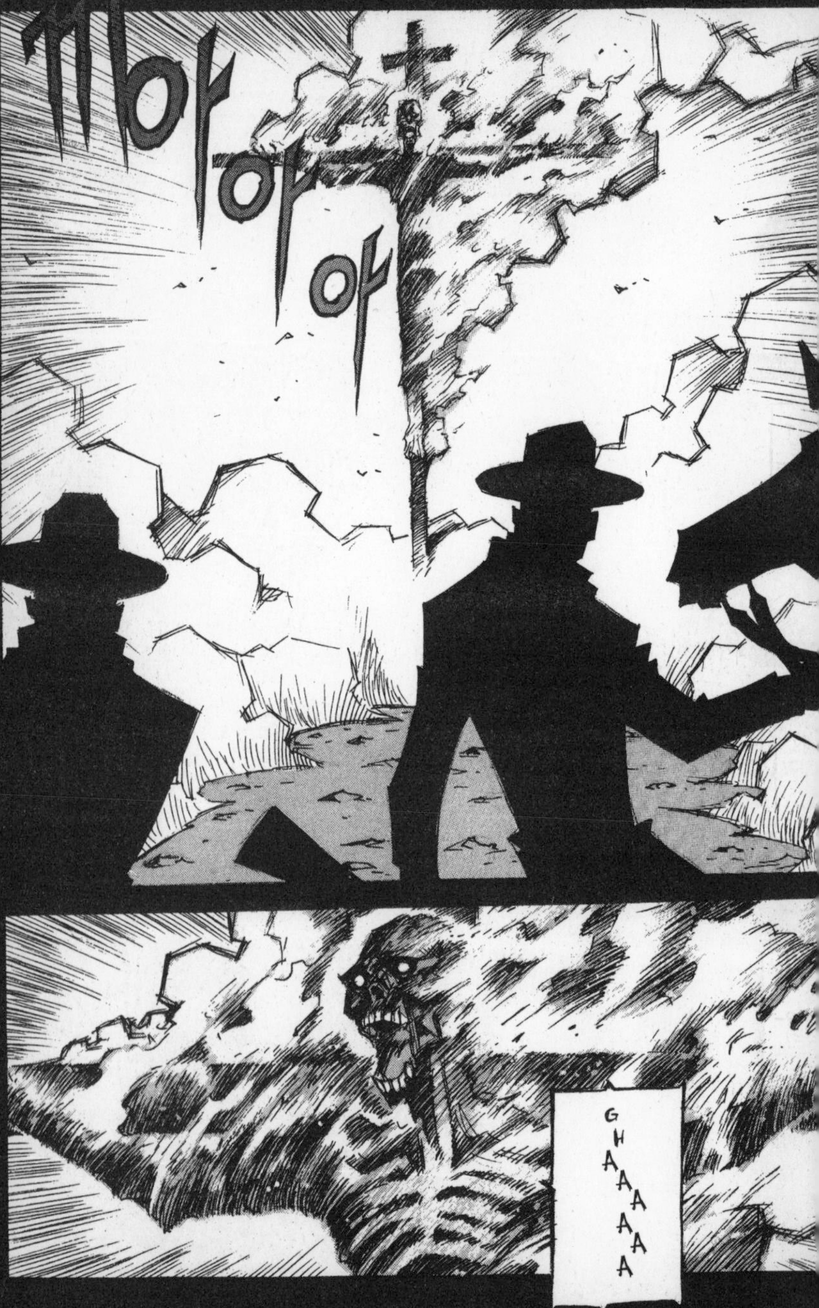
끼아아아
GHAAAAA

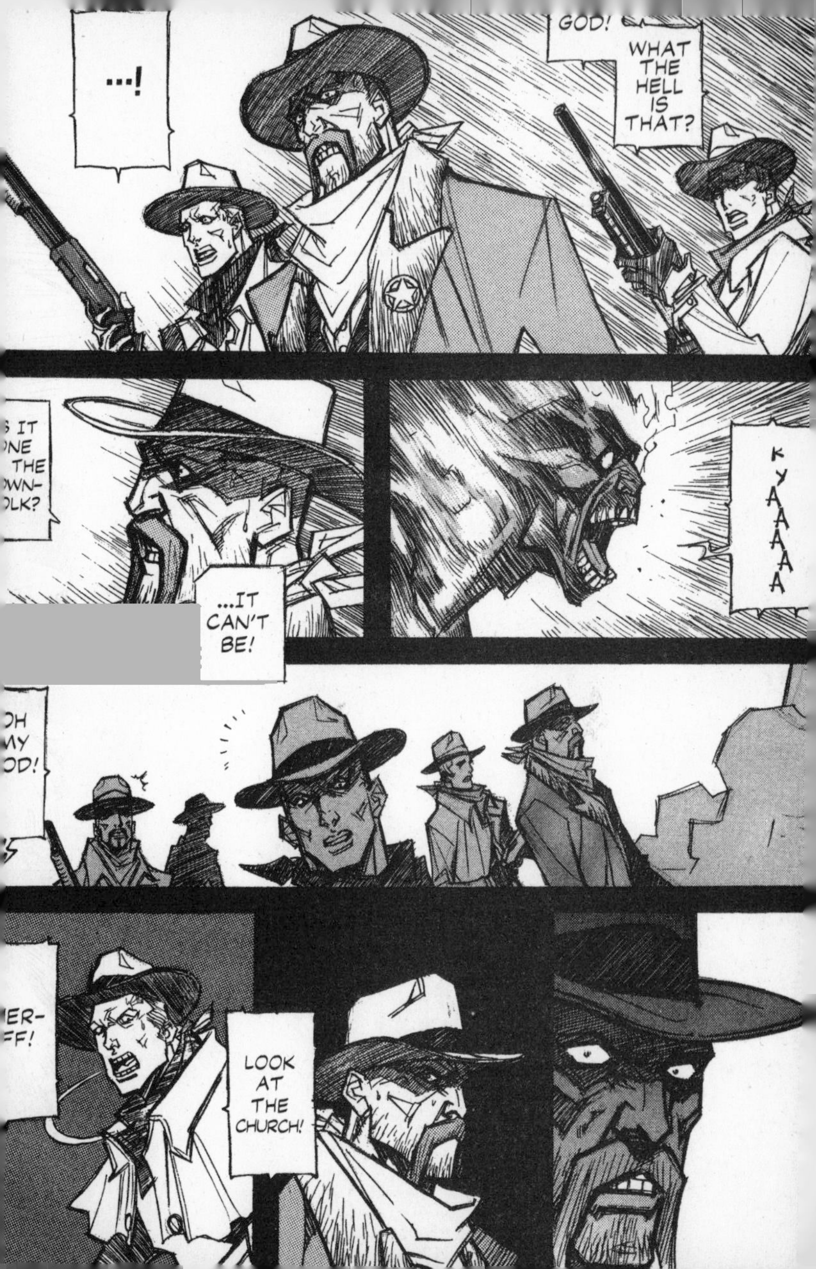

...!
GOD!
WHAT THE HELL IS THAT?
S IT NE THE WN- LK?
...IT CAN'T BE!
KYAAAAA
OH MY OD!
ER- FF!
LOOK AT THE CHURCH!

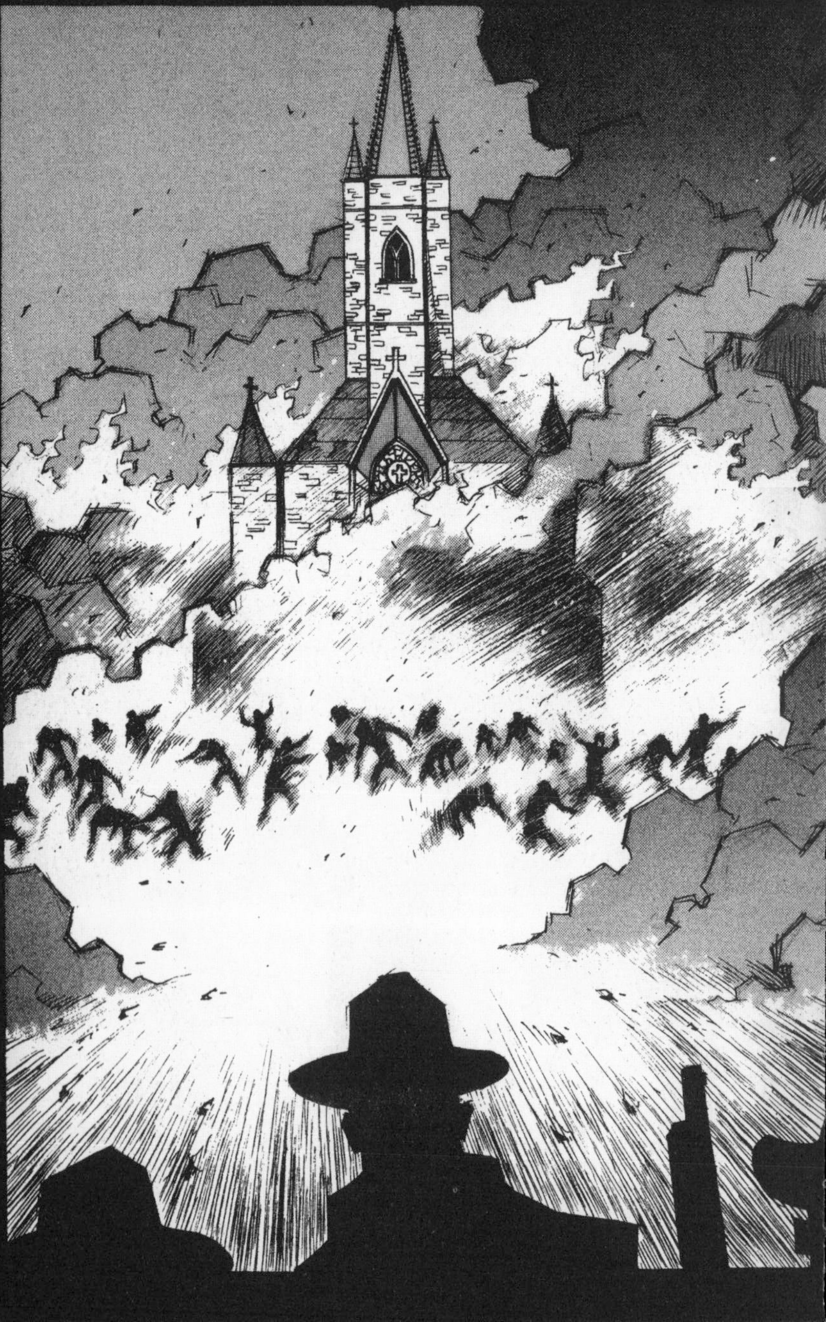

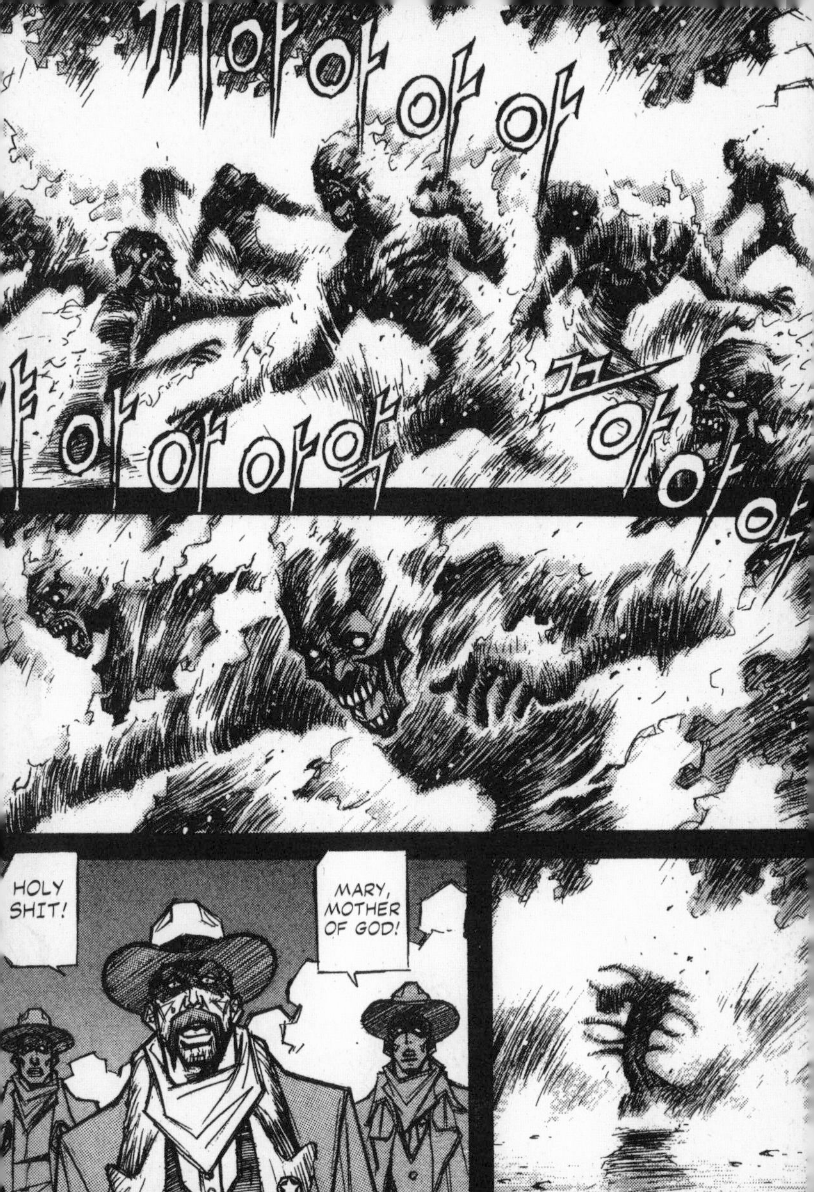

끼아아아아아
아아아아악
끄아아아악
HOLY SHIT!
MARY, MOTHER OF GOD!

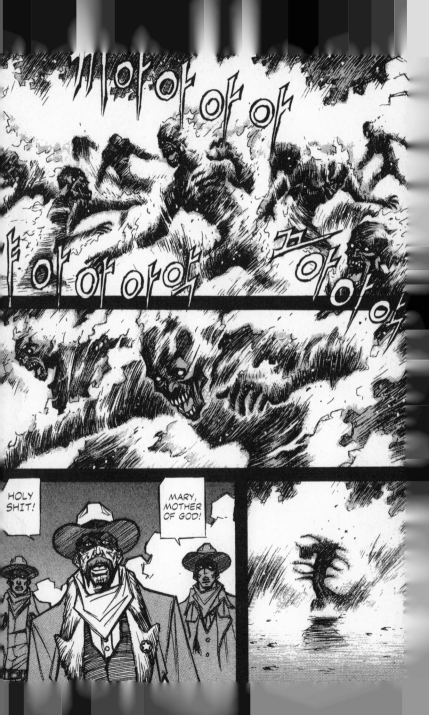

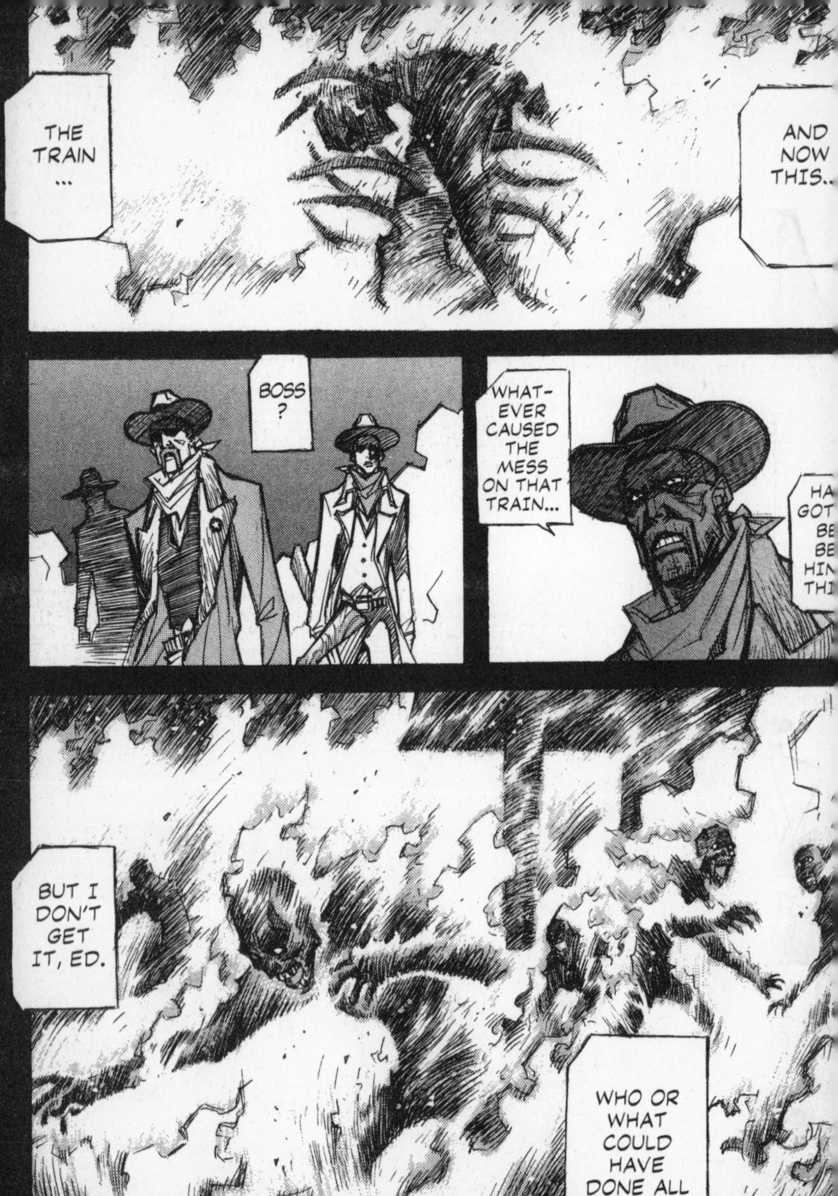
THE TRAIN ...
AND NOW THIS...
BOSS?
WHAT-EVER CAUSED THE MESS ON THAT TRAIN...
HA GOT BE BE HIN THI
BUT I DON'T GET IT, ED.
WHO OR WHAT COULD HAVE DONE ALL THIS?

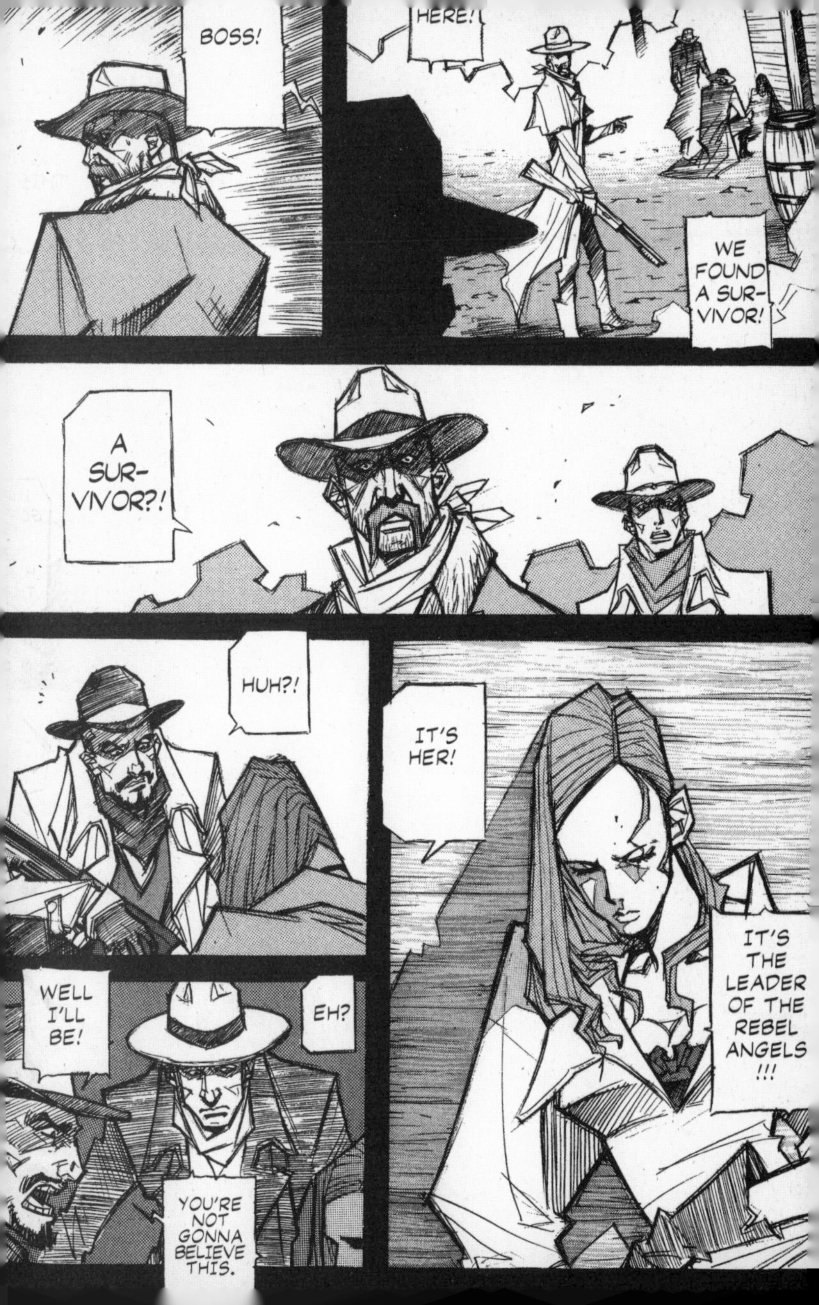
BOSS!
HERE!
WE FOUND A SUR-VIVOR!
A SUR-VIVOR?!
HUH?!
WELL I'LL BE!
EH?
YOU'RE NOT GONNA BELIEVE THIS.
IT'S HER!
IT'S THE LEADER OF THE REBEL ANGELS!!!

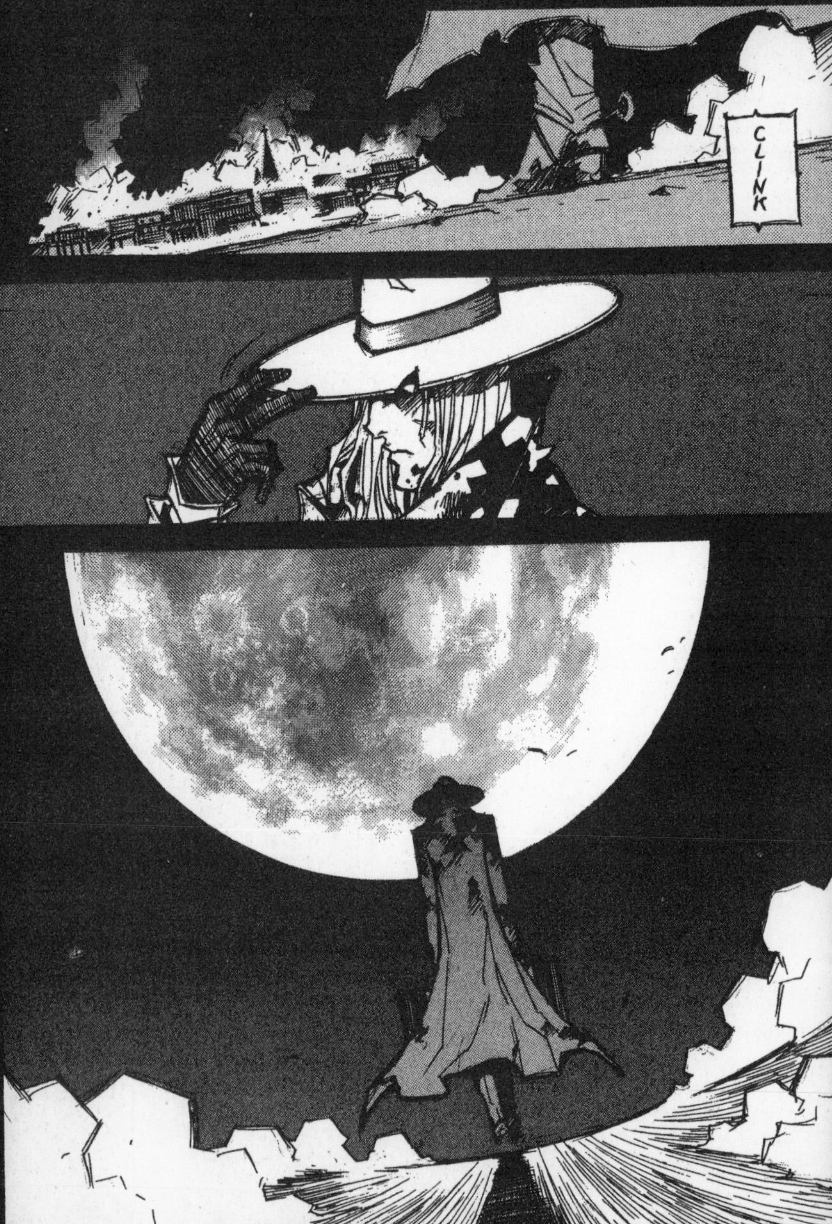
CLINK

IVAN ISAACS WILL RETURN IN PRIEST VOLUME 3: REQUIEM FOR THE DAMNED IN WHICH LIZZIE BECOMES THE VICTIM OF A WITCH HUNT AND THE STORY OF IVAN ISAACS IS PLACED IN HISTORICAL PERSPECTIVE.

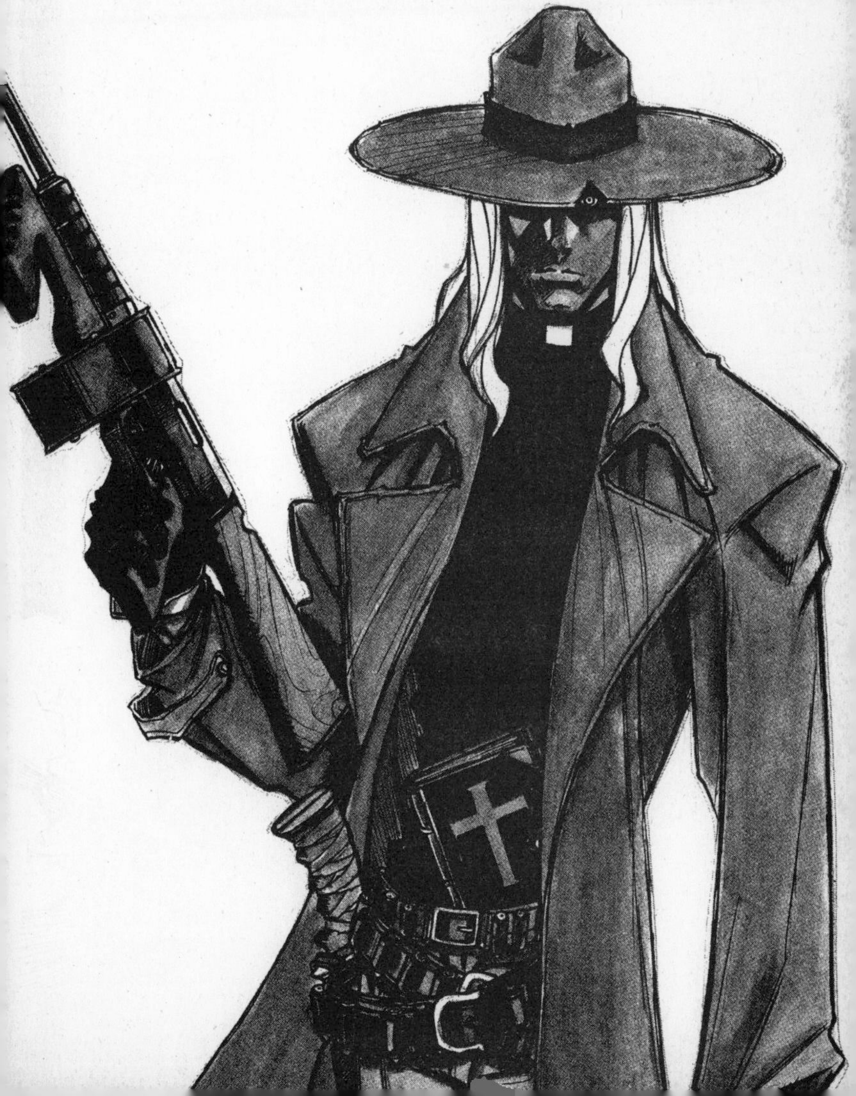

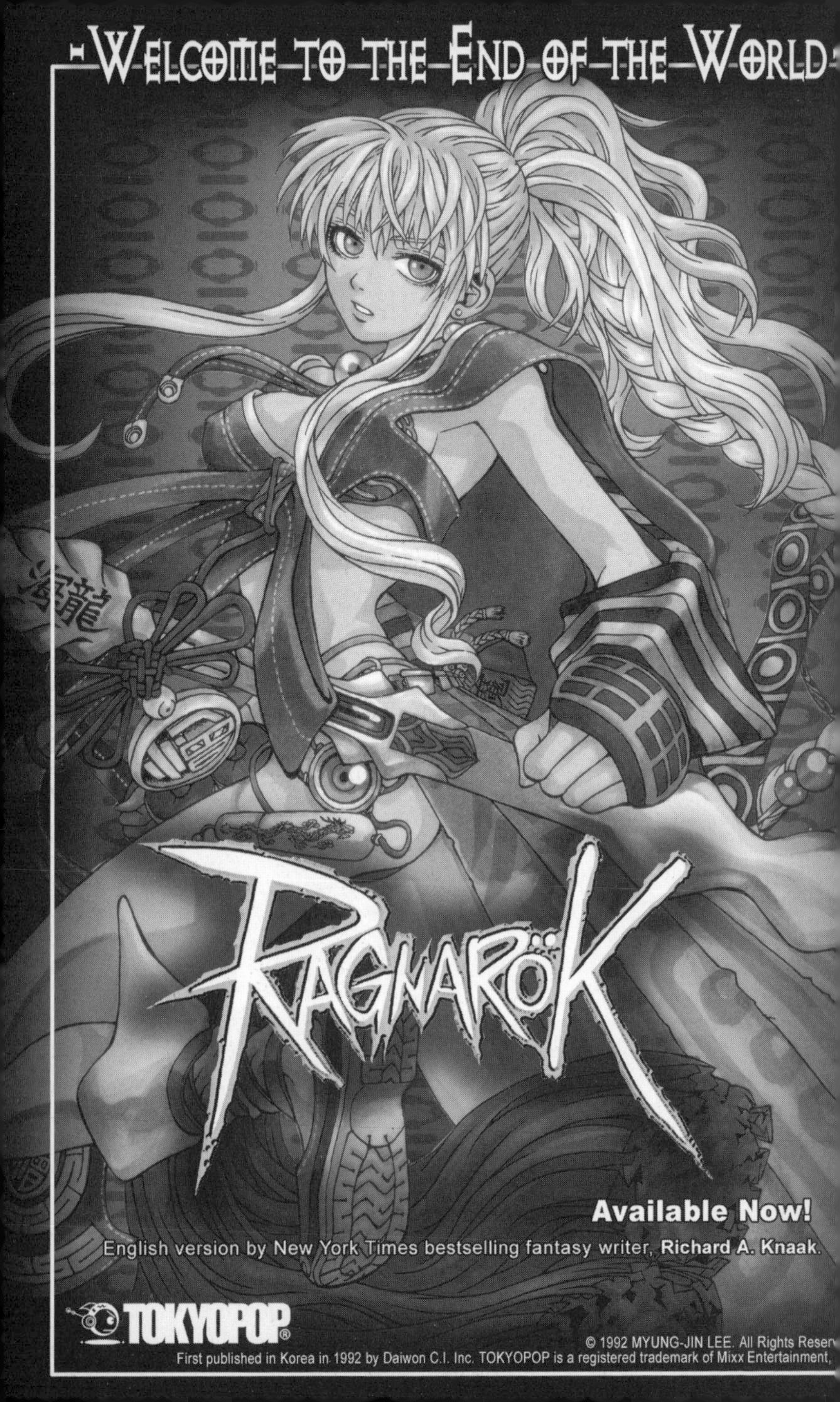
WELCOME TO THE END OF THE WORLD
RAGNARÖK
Available Now!
English version by New York Times bestselling fantasy writer, Richard A. Knaak.
TOKYOPOP®
© 1992 MYUNG-JIN LEE. All Rights Reser
First published in Korea in 1992 by Daiwon C.I. Inc. TOKYOPOP is a registered trademark of Mixx Entertainment,